Building Blockchain Apps

Building Blockchain Apps

Michael Juntao Yuan

♠ Addison-Wesley

Boston • Columbus • New York • San Francisco • Amsterdam • Cape Town
Dubai • London • Madrid • Milan • Munich • Paris • Montreal • Toronto • Delhi • Mexico City
São Paulo • Sydney • Hong Kong • Seoul • Singapore • Taipei • Tokyo

For information about buying this title in bulk quantities, or for special sales opportunities (which may include electronic versions; custom cover designs; and content particular to your business, training goals, marketing focus, or branding interests), please contact our corporate sales department at corpsales@pearsoned.com or (800) 382-3419.

For government sales inquiries, please contact governmentsales@pearsoned.com.

For questions about sales outside the U.S., please contact intlcs@pearson.com.

Visit us on the Web: informit.com/aw

Library of Congress Control Number: 2019950977

Copyright © 2020 Pearson Education, Inc.

Cover illustration by dencg/Shutterstock

ISBN-13: 978-0-13-517232-2
ISBN-10: 0-13-517232-2

1 2019

To Tony and Ju

Contents

Foreword

When I recently reconnected with Dr. Michael Yuan, he had just completed successfully fundraising for his blockchain project CyberMiles ($CMT), which later spun off a technology company called Second State. Dr. Yuan was staying at the forefront of blockchain technology and financing. I thought back to the way he had first described the core technical underpinnings of Blockchain for CMT, in a remarkable technical white paper, and how it had resonated with my own middleware architecture experience and understanding at the time. He was speaking a language I understood. Remarkably, the vision he had first laid out is being realized in Second State and applied to the enterprise blockchain markets.

Dr. Yuan was an avid proponent of open source decentralization in the early 2000s, which is how we got to first meet. Open source software had gone from pariah status in late 1999 ("a cancer") to the very bedrock of the Internet. By 2008 "open source money," as the Bitcoin concept was first called by its semi-anonymous authors, became public. What is remarkable about Bitcoin is that no one "owns it," including any corporation or nation-state. It exists as an open source program on the Internet. Cryptocurrencies are the first killer app of open source ledgers as Internet-centric digital stores of value. It bears repeating that Bitcoin is so special in a way because it is not owned or operated by a single entity but in a sense is a decentralized property of the Internet. It is an open source program. The software implementation is under MIT Licenses (open source), which invites anyone with enough power to come, hash it out, and secure the network. As a result, the operators tend to cluster around cheap sources of power around the world because of the peculiar mathematics (the nuances of Bitcoin) required to secure the network. And it has come to pass that stores of value emerged *ex-nihilo* as open source crypto ledgers, the first killer app of the technology.

The introduction of Ethereum and the concept of smart contracts have revolutionized the crypto financing landscape. Remarkable capital formation dynamics appeared, again ex-nihilism, in the ERC20 realm. The ICO phenomenon has established behind the shadow of a doubt that crypto asset capital markets have the capacity to revolutionize financing in general. It is marking a generational shift. The financial applications of cryptocurrencies are in their infancy; they are only ten years old, and the limits of this Internet money are more psychological than technical.

However, it is perhaps the more philosophical applications of DLTs (Decentralized Ledger Technology) that show even more promise in the future. Take, for example, the notions of (sovereign) identity and medical data attached to said identity. Today we can envision an Internet-centric (meaning decentralized) ID repository of properly secured and private biometric data. Let's not forget that DLTs are distributed Internet-centric secured databases. For all you know, the DLT you are storing data with lives in generic cell phones with cheap algos. Instead of relying on a government to issue and validate identity, we now have within technical reach the notion of "internet Identity" in many onboarding applications. A video conference with trusted parties is enough to establish identity with a high level of trust. Many startups propose to offer this implementation of identity. To this identity one can attach medical data. This medical data, again philosophically, ultimately belongs to the individual. Technically speaking, distributed ledger technologies allow this to exist and, as a society, to reach for "earth-wide, Internet-centric" data constructs. The open source future is bright.

As a historical note, advances in society are usually accompanied or even enabled by advances in ledger technology. Accounting, for all its boring reputation, seems to be essential to mankind's progress. For example, in post-Revolution France, Napoleon used centralized ledgers, maintained centrally by a nation-state, written on paper, for the purpose of raising an army. IBM, the iconic American corporation, was born out of the late nineteenth century nationwide census in the United States. Punch cards were developed to tally the people across the vast continent. The counting problem led an engineering feat and the birth of Big Blue. The generations to come will use DLT in a variety of ways we cannot foresee today.

But back to the present and Dr. Yuan. Michael and his focus on tooling for the smart contract ecosystem are insightful, informed, and timely. In this book, he quickly takes you down the ETH development path. Dapps are used here as concrete examples. The developer can quickly get to programming productivity, which is essential in this fast-moving ecosystem. This book is technical and covers many high-level aspects, including tokenomics. It is aimed at the practitioner and will take you through the steps to install your development environment and start BUIDLing a dapp. Go beyond the financial apps of DLTs and tap the vast potential smart contracts have to offer for the next generation of killer apps. The state of tools and indeed virtual machines in the DLT domain is rapidly evolving, and this book offers a comprehensive development introduction for the professional developer. HODL and BUIDL: The future is bright.

—*Dr. Marc Fleury, founder of Two Prime, founder and ex-CEO of JBoss, ex-SVP of Red Hat*

Acknowledgments

The guest contributors, Tim McCallum, Ash SeungHwan Han, and Victor Fang, added significantly to this book. Timothy McCallum is a software engineer based in Australia. He is an open source contributor to many of the software projects discussed in this book. Ash SeungHwan Han is an entrepreneur based in Seoul, Korea. He provides crucial insights to the operations of crypto funds and exchanges in the developer ecosystem. Dr. Victor Fang is an entrepreneur based in Silicon Valley, California. His company, AnChain.ai, is a world leader in blockchain security.

Early in the development of this book, Jim Yang and Jae Kwon of the Cosmos project provided critical feedback on the overall structure and content. Their early support, advice, and suggestions were invaluable.

The Second State and CyberMiles teams produced much of the open source software and code examples used in the book. In no particular order, I would like to acknowledge Shishuo Wang, Zhi Long, Maggie Wang, Weibing Chen, Luba Tang, Hung-Ying Tai, Meng-Han Lee, Shen-Ta Hsieh, Yi Huang, Dai-Yang Wu, Rao Fu, Vivian Hu, and Lucas Lu.

Finally, I would like to thank executive editor Greg Doench for believing in the book early on and supporting it through the difficult times.

As always, responsibility for any errors in the work is my own.

About the Author

Dr. Michael Juntao Yuan is the CEO of Second State, Inc., a VC-funded startup that builds and commercializes blockchain infrastructure software. He is also a cofounder of the CyberMiles Foundation, which focuses on building a decentralized e-commerce ecosystem on the CyberMiles public blockchain. Dr. Yuan is an investor affiliated with SIG China Ventures and is the principal investigator of multiple research awards from the National Institutes of Health. He received a PhD in astrophysics from the University of Texas at Austin.

Register Your Product

Register your copy of *Building Blockchain Apps* on the InformIT site for convenient access to updates and/or corrections as they become available. To start the registration process, go to informit.com/register and log in or create an account. Enter the product ISBN (9780135172322) and click Submit. Look on the Registered Products tab for an Access Bonus Content link next to this product, and follow that link to access any available bonus materials. If you would like to be notified of exclusive offers on new editions and updates, please check the box to receive email from us.

The code examples in this book come from various open source code repositories. The book's web site, BuildingBlockchainApps.com, has links to these repositories.

Part I

Introduction

In this first part of the book, I introduce the basic concepts of blockchain technology, such as trustless consensus, cryptocurrencies, and cryptoeconomics. For application developers and business executives, it is crucial to understand these concepts, as they establish a common vocabulary for further discussion. It is necessary for you to learn the essential features and key characteristics of blockchain networks in order to design and develop blockchain applications.

An Introduction to Blockchain

The word *blockchain* started as a computer science term describing an abstract data structure. However, as the technology has become popular and even pervasive, the term has caught the imagination of many. Today, *blockchain* has many meanings to many people.

The Blockchain

For computer scientists, a blockchain is a series of connected data blocks. Each block of data can store any information, but typically it stores a set of *transactions*. The information inside a block is represented by a unique *hash*. Each block's data content contains the hash of the block that precedes itself on the chain (Figure 1.1).

> **Note**
>
> A cryptographic hash is a short representation of a large amount of data. It is extremely easy to compute. But if you only know the hash, it is extremely difficult to figure out the original data that produces this hash.

Why do we want to store data in this blockchain structure? Why can't we just use a database? Well, a key feature of the blockchain is that it is hard to alter any data on the chain.

Imagine that you have a blockchain with 1,000 blocks. Now, someone wants to alter the content in block 10. As the person alters the data, the hash of block 10 also changes. Block 11 contains the hash of block 10, so the content in block 11 also changes, which in turn results in a change in the hash of block 11. This process propagates down the blockchain. So, to make any change in any block, you will end up reconstructing all the blocks that follow it. That is known as a *hard fork*, which creates a new blockchain that is incompatible with the existing one, even as they both use the identical software. In that sense, a blockchain is immutable. It is impossible for someone to "silently" modify the history of a blockchain.

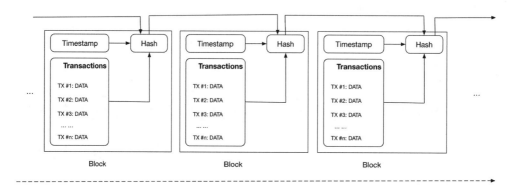

Figure 1.1   A blockchain

As you can see here, the longer the blockchain, the more stable it becomes. When you do transactions on the Bitcoin network, you will often hear that your transaction is securely "confirmed" after six or more blocks (about an hour, as the Bitcoin network creates one block every ten minutes). After six blocks, it is unlikely for an alternative blockchain fork to emerge and gain acceptance by the community. So, it is essentially certain that your transaction has been recorded as part of the permanent history.

While you can store any data in a blockchain, the most common use case of the blockchain is to store transaction records. That makes sense since the historic accuracy and validity of monetary transactions are critical. In practice, blockchains are used as digital ledgers to record transactions.

The Collaborative Ledger

Now, a database can also record (or *journal*) change histories. People have used spreadsheets or databases as transactional ledgers since the invention of the personal computer. The ledger itself is neither complicated nor a significant value-add.

The question remains: why do we need to bother with a new, more computationally intensive data structure like the blockchain? The answer lies in the second key feature of the blockchain: It is easy to organize a collaborative network around the blockchain.

Since each block is added to the chain individually, we can design a network where one or more parties propose the next block, and then all network nodes (i.e., participating computers on the network) can validate the proposed block and reach a consensus on whether it should be appended to the blockchain. If a proposed block is deemed invalid by most network participants, the blockchain can abandon it or even punish its proposers. For more technical details on blockchain consensus, please see Chapter 2.

The rule for validation depends on the specific blockchain. For example, the Bitcoin blockchain miners examine the cryptographic signatures and account balances for each transaction recorded in the block for its validity.

By doing so, the blockchain becomes a collaborative ledger.

Cryptocurrency

The ledger records the movement of some currency. A major innovation is the realization that the blockchain can define its own "currency" to transact. It is called *cryptocurrency* because the validity of such currency is ensured by cryptography used in blockchain networks. For example, each transaction of such currency is digital signed to make sure it is authentic and unique. The cryptocurrency is also known as *crypto tokens* or just *tokens*. I will use these terms interchangeably throughout this book.

The rules for transaction validation allow a blockchain to create its own *monetary policy* that governs its cryptocurrency. For example, the Bitcoin blockchain defines the following rules for the creation and consumption of its cryptocurrency (i.e., Bitcoins):

- New block proposers will receive newly created units of the Bitcoin currency.
- There will be only 21 million Bitcoins in total, and hence the block award decreases over time.
- Each Bitcoin can be divided into a million Satoshies to be used in transactions.
- Bitcoin miners will receive Bitcoins for validating transactions in a new block.

The interesting aspect here is that such monetary policies are codified in the blockchain software for Bitcoin. No one can change a policy without creating a new blockchain (i.e., a hard fork).

The cryptocurrency created by the blockchain has a crucial function. It provides an engineering mechanism, through incentive design (or economics engineering), to accomplish something software engineering cannot accomplish alone: creating trust.

We can build trustless yet collaborative networks using blockchain technology together with cryptocurrency design.

> **Note**
>
> For a long time, the technology community believed that the "enterprise" use of blockchain technology was to build a distributed ledger inside a company or a group of companies that already have trusted relationships. The trusted network validators and nodes made it easy to develop high-performance consensus protocols. Companies like IBM and Microsoft promoted the use of such permissioned or trusted blockchains.
>
> However, after several years of experimentation, it became clear that such "enterprise" use of blockchains in a trusted/single company/centralized environment has limited impact on business practices. The trusted blockchain is just another data management software solution at the disposal of corporate IT departments. Such use of blockchains creates no network effect.

Smart Contracts

When the Bitcoin blockchain miners validate transactions, they are checking only for the most basic accounting rules. For instance, the transaction sender must have sufficient funds in her account and must sign the transaction with her private key. It is easy for Bitcoin miners to verify those transactions and reach consensus.

Now, instead of checking the basic accounting rules, the blockchain miners can run any kind of computer program and then reach consensus on the correctness of the computing results. The consensus results can then be saved to the blockchain for a permanent record. That is the idea behind the smart contract. The consensus mechanism developed for Bitcoin can be used to establish trust for any type of computation.

The Ethereum blockchain is among the first public blockchains to support smart contracts. It features a Turing complete virtual machine, known as the Ethereum Virtual Machine (EVM). The EVM runs on all nodes to validate the correctness of arbitrary computation tasks. Programs written for the EVM are stored in accounts on the blockchain. Any transaction that involves the account will be validated against the program by Ethereum miners before the transaction can be recorded on the blockchain. Smart contracts have become the most important applications for the blockchain.

The truly revolutionary idea behind blockchains is trustworthy computing results generated from uncooperative participants on trustless networks.

A Trustless Network

The original killer application of blockchain technology is the Bitcoin. The Bitcoin was created by and is managed by a completely trustless network. Anyone can get on the Bitcoin network to validate transactions, propose new blocks, and receive Bitcoin awards if the block is accepted by the consensus. Bitcoin network participants do not know each other and do not trust each other. Yet, the system is designed to prevent any of the participants from making malicious changes to the blockchain.

The exact mechanism Bitcoin uses for consensus is called *proof of work* (PoW). We will discuss the technical details of PoW in Chapter 2. For now, just know that there are mechanisms for untrusted network participants to agree on which transactions are valid and should be recorded in the blockchain. Core to the consensus mechanism is the use of cryptocurrencies that incentivize participants to behave according to rules (e.g., not validate invalid transactions). This use of cryptocurrencies as incentives is known as *cryptoeconomics*.

The ability to reach consensus without a central trusted authority is powerful. The greatest Internet companies today are all built on the network effect. Companies like Uber and Airbnb act as central authorities for the networks they built. They make the rules, especially the rules around how money is transacted in the network. They make sure everyone follows the rules and in the process extract great profits. But are they really needed? Can the network function without the company being the rule maker and arbitrator? Why can't the network participants themselves own the network and reap the profits?

However, past efforts to replace Uber and build a coop-style nonprofit transportation network have largely failed. There are a few reasons, listed here:

- Replacing the centralized company with a centralized nonprofit does not solve the trust issue. Many nonprofits are corrupt and mostly enrich their operators. The drivers and riders still have no real "ownership" of the network.

- A centralized nonprofit lacks the means to award early adopters and jump-start the network. Uber, however, can raise venture capital (VC) money and spend heavily on incentives until the network effect is self-sustainable.

A blockchain network with crypto tokens could solve both problems. The network is run by untrusted peers and hence cannot be corrupted. The network can issue tokens to compensate early adopters through a process like an initial coin offering (ICO). Furthermore, by turning network participants (drivers and riders in the Uber example) into token holders, we can establish a monetary network and create loyalty to the network Uber has never been able to build.

New Ways of Collaborating

This untrusted network opens new ways for people to collaborate. For instance, imagine that there is a valuable data set, but no one owns the whole data. Each participant in the network owns a piece of the data set, but they are reluctant to share, as the party that shares the last will benefit the most. In this scenario, the society often cannot make use of this data set.

Note

A concrete real-world case is the medical data held by hospitals—while extremely valuable collectively, no hospital is incentivized to share its own piece of the data.

Now, let's imagine a network where all parties can contribute data. When revenue is generated from the use of such data, the network will distribute the revenue to parties according to pre-agreed upon splits, and each distribution is independently validated by network participants so that there is no chance for cheating.

Such a data collaboration network was possible prior to blockchain technology, but it requires a centralized authority trusted by everyone to determine and distribute the revenue income. The trusted central authority has both incentives and opportunities to cheat, and that has made such trusted networks difficult to establish.

The Fat Protocol

The characteristic of a blockchain network is that it can create value without a central corporation. The value of the network is not in a company's shares but in the network protocol and is reflected as the value of the network tokens. This theory is called the *fat protocol theory*, originally proposed by Joel Monegro from Union Square Ventures. For example, on today's Bitcoin or Ethereum network, no company has reached significant valuation, and yet the networks themselves are worth tens of billions of dollars. Figure 1.2 shows how Internet protocols are "thin" and hence applications capture most of the value, while blockchain protocols are fat and can themselves capture value.

The very existence of modern corporations is because external transaction costs between the corporation and its partners are much higher than the internal transaction costs within the departments.

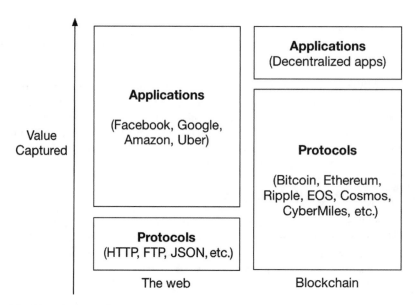

Figure 1.2   The thin versus fat protocols (adapted from https://www.usv.com/blog/fat-protocols)

That is due to the command-and-control structure corporations can impose on their internal departments. However, in today's economy, as communication costs drop, external transaction costs drop to the point where companies are increasingly relying on outsourcing or contracting labor (see the earlier Uber and Airbnb examples).

The trustless blockchain networks will further reduce external transaction costs. Those networks streamline the transactions of not only information but also money. The public blockchain network, together with crypto tokens, enables new business models that could either replace today's corporations or create new opportunities that cannot be solved by corporations.

The rules of collaboration and consensus of a blockchain network are embedded and enforced in the network protocol itself. This is of course different from the human-driven rules in most corporations. The blockchain collaboration rules are algorithmic, automatic, fast, fair, and consistent. To fully take advantage of blockchain networks, we should codify as many collaboration rules as possible into the network protocol.

In Code We Trust

The smart contracts can often closely resemble legal contracts in the real world. For example, the transaction parties might enter an escrow agreement that the fund will be paid out only when certain conditions are met. It is now up to network validators and maintainers to assert whether such conditions are met and how the transaction should be executed when new blocks are appended to the blockchain.

However, unlike legal contracts that are enforced by the centralized government power, the smart contracts can automatically apply collaboration rules on the blockchain. The rules are written in code and checked by trustless participants of the network to prevent corruption or collusion. Because of that, we consider smart contract code the "law" in blockchain networks. The code is executed as written. Even if the code contains bugs or side effects unexpected by its author, it is still trusted as a source of truth and enforced as the law.

Conclusion

In this chapter, I discussed the key concepts of blockchain networks. Through cryptocurrencies, a blockchain network combines software and economics engineering to create trust in a network of uncooperative participants. This could disrupt the greatest Internet companies today, as the network effects are no longer created by large companies at the center of such networks. The network is instead maintained by the software code shared by every participant. In code we trust.

2

Reaching Consensus

The central idea behind blockchain networks is not really the technology—hash algorithms and public key infrastructure (PKI) technologies have existed for many years. As we discussed in the previous chapter, the chief innovation in Bitcoin is a new incentive structure to make sure that although every individual in the network is uncooperative (i.e., decentralized), they will nevertheless collectively behave in a way that maintains the integrity and security of the network. Economic incentives from cryptocurrencies are working in tandem with technological solutions in blockchain networks to solve problems that were previously impossible to address with technology alone.

The most important example of this seamless collaboration between software engineering and economic design is the blockchain's consensus mechanism.

What Is Blockchain Consensus?

Since a public blockchain is a distributed ledger maintained by untrusted participants, it is crucial to reach network-wide consensus on which transactions are valid and should be recorded on the blockchain. Automated consensus is the core idea behind blockchains. How to improve the efficiency of consensus without compromising security is one of the most important challenges facing blockchains today.

To be fair, the human society has long developed ways to reach consensus. For example, all types of voting systems are designed to reach consensus. Enabled by technologies, we now also have informal voting systems such as Facebook likes and Reddit upvotes. However, human voting is too slow and subject to humans' unreliable interpretation of rules. It cannot handle high-speed, high-volume transactions required by a global computing network.

Algorithms can help us reach consensus much faster on the Internet scale. Such examples include Google page ranks, Google Ads auctions, online reputation scores, matching algorithms from Uber to Tinder, and so on. However, such algorithms are typically only appropriately correct. They cannot guarantee the accuracy of individual transactions. The blockchain network goes one step further and provides an automated computational method to definitively validate and record transactions.

While many blockchain projects innovate on the consensus mechanism to be "proof of XYZ," we believe that, fundamentally, there are only two types of consensus—proof of work (PoW) and proof of stake (PoS).

Proof of Work (PoW)

The Bitcoin is a classic example of a PoW consensus blockchain. While it suffers from various technical problems such as low performance, poor scalability, and wasteful electricity use, it has proven secure against highly motivated attacks by individuals, organizations, and even nation-states. It builds a trillion-dollar global network without requiring trust in any of its participants. So far, no one has been able to create a fraudulent transaction in the blockchain—despite the massive financial payoff such hacks could bring. That is a monumental achievement by Bitcoin's creator, Satoshi Nakamoto.

In a PoW system, miners compete to solve a math puzzle for each block. The first one to solve this problem is the first to propose a new block and receive the Bitcoin award associated with the block. The "winner" can include any pending transactions he chooses in the block but cannot include any invalid ones (i.e., all transactions must be properly signed, and their originating accounts must have sufficient funds). If other miners detect that there are invalid transactions in the block, they will propose competing blocks.

The community of miners "votes" by each independently choosing which competing blocks to build the subsequent new blocks upon. Let's say that there is a malicious miner who includes a large unauthorized Bitcoin transaction to herself whenever she wins the math contest to propose a new block. But, no one else will build on her block since other miners are also selfish and have no incentive to break the rules to benefit her. If she continues to build on it, she will be the only one on that branch of the blockchain. It will become really obvious that her branch (or fork) of the blockchain is illegitimate.

Now, if a majority of miners (as measured by computing power) collude, they could all intentionally build in the invalid block and make the fork appear as the legitimate trunk of the Bitcoin blockchain. That is known as a *51 percent attack*. In a large blockchain network such as Bitcoin, the amount of resources required to accumulate such computing power to reach 51 percent is enormous. With that kind of computing power, a potential attacker is economically better off following the rules to mine new Bitcoin blocks instead of trying to attack and destroy the Bitcoin value for everyone.

> **Note**
> A 51 percent attack is a way for the community to reach consensus to accept a block with invalid transactions.

Proof of Stake (PoS)

While PoW is a great invention that has been proven secure in the real world, it also suffers from many problems. It requires enormous amounts of computing power to perform wasteful computational work to artificially make it economically unfeasible for potential attackers. It encourages everyone to participate in the mining process, causing consensus to be slow to emerge and converge. When there are multiple competing blocks, it takes a long time (an hour or more) for the system to settle on a consensus branch.

To solve PoW's problems, a new consensus mechanism called *proof of stake* was proposed. A PoS system allows a straight vote for each new block by the network's stakeholders (account holders for the blockchain's native cryptocurrency or token). The proposer of a new block is randomly chosen. Your voting power is proportional to the tokens you hold in your account. With voting, the blockchain can achieve finality in each block with a minimal amount of computation. The proposer of an accepted new block receives an award in the blockchain's native cryptocurrency.

This process is called *minting* new cryptocurrency as opposed to POW's *mining*. A PoS system is typically much more performant than a PoW system. Examples of large public PoS blockchains include the following:

- The Casper project (https://github.com/ethereum/casper) aims to transform the Ethereum blockchain from a PoW system to a PoS system. Once completed, it will be the largest PoS blockchain ecosystem in the world.

- The QTUM blockchain (https://qtum.org/) is designed to be a PoS blockchain based on a Bitcoin-like infrastructure.

Note

An interesting side effect of a PoS cryptocurrency is that stakeholders are encouraged to *stake* their tokens to participate in the voting process and receive new block awards. They are financially dis-incentivized to trade their tokens. That decreases the "money" supply and could make such cryptocurrency more valuable in the market.

The voting mechanism in a PoS system is the subject of intense research and innovation. Specifically, the system must assume uncooperative or even malicious voters. This is commonly known as the Byzantine Generals Problem in game theory. A voting mechanism that can be mathematically proven to withstand up to one-third of fraudulent voters has to be Byzantine fault tolerant (BFT). BFT consensus engines are now widely used in blockchain design.

However, a plain PoS system also has significant shortcomings. Here are some examples:

- Participants could have nothing to lose by voting yes on invalid block proposals. Some kind of penalty (or *slashing*) must be introduced to "punish" misbehaving participants.

- Voting itself is a technical endeavor few people master, as the performance and security requirements are high for a high-performance network.

- Allowing all stakeholders (even ones with a single token) to vote could result in the same performance degradation seen in PoW systems.

- The large voting power from large stakeholders could result in a concentration of power over time.

A few improvements to PoS have been suggested. A leading candidate is called *delegated proof of stake* (DPoS).

Delegated Proof of Stake (DPoS)

A DPoS system has only a limited number of validators who can propose and vote on new blocks. Stakeholders can "delegate" their cryptocurrencies to validators they choose, and validators will vote on their behalf. That allows validators to become professional operators (similar to a mining pool in a PoW system) and can be subject to penalties if they vote for invalid blocks (or are careless and hacked). Examples of DPoS blockchains include the following:

- The Bitshares project (https://bitshares.org/) is the pioneer of the DPoS concept. It is a public blockchain with 21 elected validators.

- The Cosmos project (https://cosmos.network/) is a public network of blockchains all built on the Tendermint DPoS consensus engine that can exchange information with each other. We will cover Cosmos in later chapters.

- The CyberMiles project (http://cybermiles.io/) is a public blockchain network specifically optimized for smart contracts and compliant token issuance for commercial businesses. We will use CyberMiles as an example of blockchain system design in later chapters.

In political economy terms, DPoS is similar to a representative democracy with landowner (or property owner) suffrage.

- Validators, or representatives, are delegated by the community to decide the day-to-day questions, such as the consensus for each block and each transaction, to maintain the integrity of the ledger (no double spend) and the smart contract executions.

- The right to vote on representatives is given to participants who hold a certain form of property. This property represents a commitment to the community and also a loss of liquidity. In this case, the crypto tokens that represent the value of the blockchain network as a whole are the property. This model resembles the historical landowner suffrage.

Notice that, similar to the democratic system, the property (or tokens) is used only for staking a delegate. The staked tokens are locked by the network to prevent trading and are made available for penalties. The ownership of the staked tokens is never transferred to the validator.

In the end, the purpose of the blockchain is to reach consensus. It is natural for us to model consensus after representative democracy mechanisms that human society has used for thousands of years.

Conclusion

In this chapter, I explained how economic engineering works hand in hand with software engineering to secure blockchain networks. Such a trustless network requires, and also enables, valuable cryptocurrencies to function.

3

Your First Blockchain App

The easiest way to get started with blockchain application development is to use the open source BUIDL tool—an online integrated development environment (IDE) that works in any modern web browser. Just go to http://buidl.secondstate.io/ and start coding! BUIDL provides a comprehensive coding environment for creating and deploying end-to-end blockchain applications (Figure 3.1). You can create an entire blockchain application inside BUIDL, from smart contracts on the back end to HTML on the front end, and everything in the middle.

For beginners and experts alike, BUIDL takes much of the complexity and guesswork out of blockchain development and allows you to focus on coding. It does not require any software

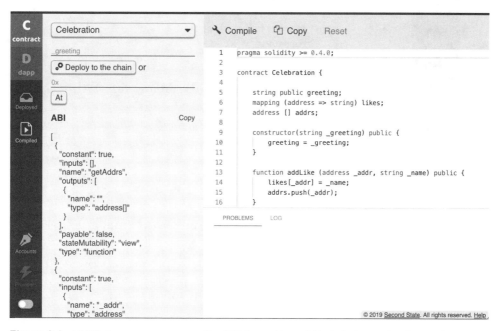

Figure 3.1 BUIDL is an open source online IDE for end-to-end blockchain app development.

download or installation. It eliminates the need for developers to deal with wallets, private keys, cryptocurrencies, and lengthy transaction confirmation. Yet, it deploys your applications on live public blockchains and makes the application accessible to anyone you share to.

In this chapter, you will learn to create your first blockchain application and then share it with the world. We will walk through key concepts behind blockchain applications, also known as *decentralized apps (dapps)*.

Smart Contract

In short, a *smart contract* is the back-end service code that lives on the blockchain. Once deployed, external applications can invoke functions and code inside a smart contract to perform tasks and record the results on the blockchain through consensus. The most popular programming language to write smart contracts is the Solidity language pioneered by Ethereum. In this example, let's create a simple smart contract and deploy it with BUIDL.

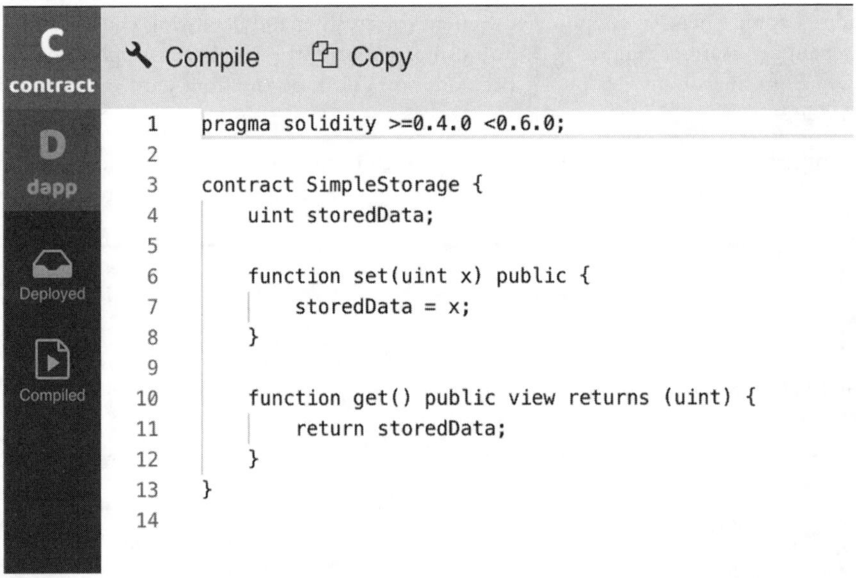

```
C
contract

D
dapp

Deployed

Compiled

⚒ Compile      ⎘ Copy

1    pragma solidity >=0.4.0 <0.6.0;
2
3    contract SimpleStorage {
4        uint storedData;
5
6        function set(uint x) public {
7            storedData = x;
8        }
9
10       function get() public view returns (uint) {
11           return storedData;
12       }
13   }
14
```

Figure 3.2   A simple smart contract in BUIDL

Load BUIDL in your web browser. You will see a simple smart contract already in the online editor window (Figure 3.2).

The contract simply allows you to store a number on the blockchain. You can view or update the stored number by calling its functions get() and set(). The code is as follows. The Solidity syntax should be familiar to most developers as it is similar to JavaScript.

```
pragma solidity >=0.4.0 <0.6.0;

contract SimpleStorage {
  uint storedData;
```

```
  function set(uint x) public {
    storedData = x;
  }

  function get() public view returns (uint) {
    return storedData;
  }
}
```

Click the **Compile** button to compile the contract. A sidebar will open to show you the compiled application binary interface (ABI, a JSON-based artifact used by the blockchain to facilitate remote function calls) and the bytecode of the contract (Figure 3.3).

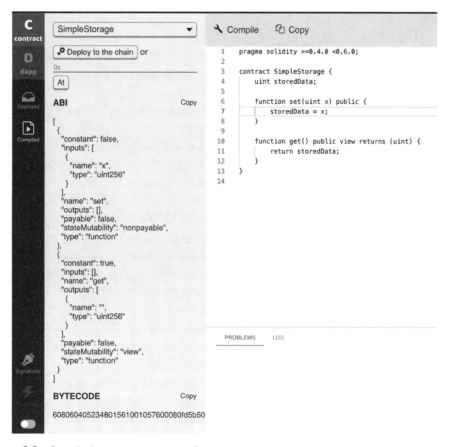

Figure 3.3   Compiled smart contract ready for deployment

Next, you can click the **Deploy to the chain** button in the left panel to instantiate and deploy the contract to a public blockchain. You can interact with deployed contracts by calling their public methods from inside BUIDL. For example, you can set the contract's `storedData` value and click the **Transact** button to save the value onto the blockchain; then click the **Call** button to see the value in the LOG panel (Figure 3.4).

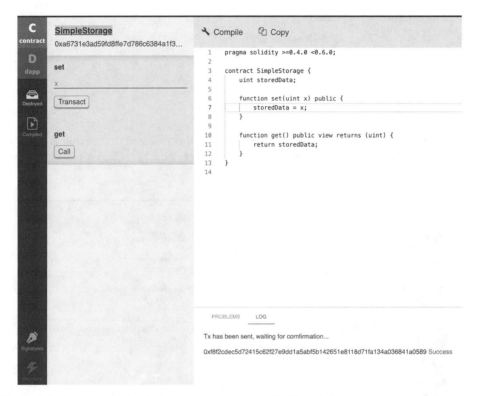

Figure 3.4   Interacting with a deployed smart contract on the blockchain

You have probably noticed that the BUIDL IDE deploys to the Second State DevChain by default. This is an Ethereum-compatible public blockchain designed for improving the developer experience. For example, the DevChain has a block time of one second, and all transactions are confirmed as soon as the block is produced. DevChain smart contracts have a fast interaction time of one second instead of a confirmation time of minutes or even hours on the public Ethereum blockchain. The "gas price" on the DevChain is zero, and hence you do not need to worry about getting crypto tokens for pay for "gas."

Furthermore, since the DevChain requires no gas or cryptocurrency, the address or account on the blockchain serves only as an ID for the caller of smart contract functions. BUIDL automatically generates five addresses for you to use. You can see them on the **Accounts** tab (Figure 3.5). You can set any of them as your own default address. If you already have an address, you can also import it into BUIDL. All address private keys are managed locally in your computer's browser cache. BUIDL does not require you to have any crypto wallet, and hence it works on any browser, including smartphone browsers. You can truly code anywhere.

Once your smart contract is written, you can deploy it to any Ethereum-compatible blockchain including the Ethereum mainnet and testnets. You can do that directly from within BUIDL. Please see Chapter 4 as well as the BUIDL documentation for details.

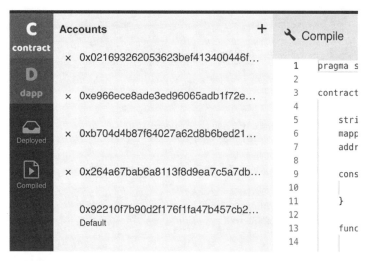

Figure 3.5   Addresses/accounts in BUIDL

Front-End HTML

Next click the **dapp** tab to work on the web application that interacts with the smart contract on the blockchain. The HTML front end of the application is simple. It displays two buttons that allow users to invoke the two corresponding smart contract functions (Figure 3.6).

```
<button id="s">Set Data</button>
<button id="g">Get Data</button>
```

Figure 3.6   The HTML editor on the dapp tab

It is also possible to add CSS and JavaScript library resources to the HTML via the **Resources** tab in BUIDL (Figure 3.7).

JavaScript and web3.js

The HTML web page displays the UI of the dapp. The web application makes function calls against the smart contract via the JavaScript web3.js library (Figure 3.8).

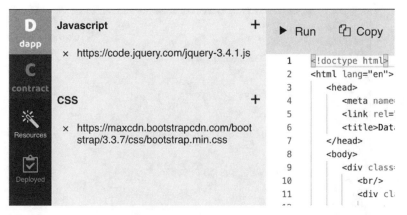

Figure 3.7   Resources of the HTML web app

```
/* Don't modify */
var abi = [{"constant":false,"inputs":[{"name":"x","type":"uint256"}],"name":"set","outputs":
var bytecode = '608060405234801561001057600080fd5b5060df8061001f6000396000f300608060405260043
var cAddr = '0xdc6ac5fb540fa517beca41a17b502a3ce82460ee';
/* Don't modify */

var instance = null;
window.addEventListener('web3Ready', function() {
  var contract = web3.ss.contract(abi);
  instance = contract.at(cAddr);
});

document.querySelector("#s").addEventListener("click", function() {
  var n = window.prompt("Enter the number:");
  n && instance.set(n);
});
document.querySelector("#g").addEventListener("click", function() {
  instance.get(function(e,d) {
    console.log(d.toString());
    alert(d.toString());
  });
});
```

Figure 3.8   The JavaScript editor on the dapp tab

The JavaScript has several sections. The `/* Don't modify */` section is populated by the BUIDL tool. It contains code to instantiate the contract you just deployed via BUIDL. The contract instance and its operations are all defined in the `web3.js` library.

The event handler for the Set Data button shows how to call the smart contract's `set()` function in a transaction from JavaScript.

```
document.querySelector("#s").addEventListener("click", function() {
  var n = window.prompt("Input the number:");
  n && instance.set(n);
});
```

The event handler for the Get Data button calls the smart contract's get() function and displays the result.

```
document.querySelector("#g").addEventListener("click", function() {
  console.log(instance.get().toString());
});
```

The web3.js library supports the JavaScript front end to make remote function calls against smart contracts deployed on blockchains.

In Action

To run the dapp, click the **Run** button in BUIDL. You will see the dapp UI in the right panel. You can click the **Set Data** button to store a number, and you can click the **Get Data** button to retrieve the stored number. Figure 3.9 shows the dapp in action.

Now you have a dapp running on a public blockchain!

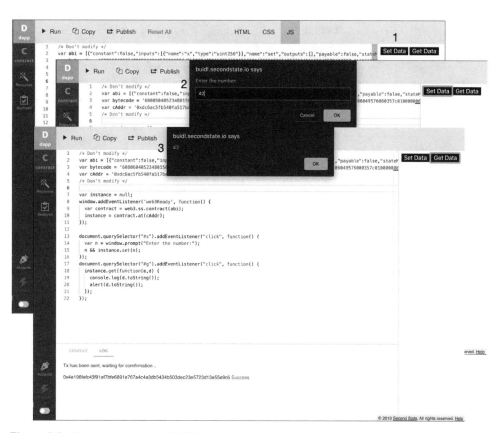

Figure 3.9   Running the dapp in BUIDL

Share Your Dapp

Since the Second State DevChain is a public blockchain, you can share your dapp with other people, and they will be able to access it, too. Just click the **Publish** button. BUIDL will package the application front end into a single HTML file and upload it to a public web site. Once it is done, BUIDL shows a Launched link (Figure 3.10). Click that link to open the dapp web site. You can now share this link with anyone.

Figure 3.10   Publishing your dapp from BUIDL

You can also download and save the HTML file from that Launched link onto your local computer hard drive. You can put the HTML file on any web host and make it accessible to the world. There are many free services to host your HTML files.

When users come to the web page to interact with your dapp, they will see a small gadget at the bottom of the page that allows the user to select her blockchain address (Figure 3.11). Note that all those addresses are automatically generated, and the selected address serves as the user's on-chain ID.

You can also import your own address private key or use your address in MetaMask wallet.

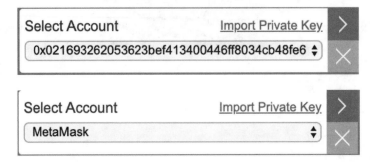

Figure 3.11   Managing addresses in the dapp

As we mentioned, the Second State DevChain requires no gas, and all those addresses can have zero balance in cryptocurrency. In an enterprise environment, each user might have a unique address as an ID. In such environment, you might need to provision addresses and private keys for your authorized users.

Conclusion

In this chapter, I showed you how to create and deploy your first blockchain dapp using the BUIDL tool. The dapp you just built is compatible with the Ethereum protocol. In the next part, I will discuss the Ethereum protocol and its applications.

Part II

An Introduction to Ethereum

In this part of the book, I introduce one of the most important public blockchains today, Ethereum. In terms of market cap, Ethereum is second only to the Bitcoin blockchain. Since Ethereum was the first blockchain that pioneered the concept of smart contracts, many public and private blockchains today are compatible with Ethereum to leverage the Ethereum developer community. In that regard, Ethereum is not just a public blockchain. It is a protocol many other blockchains conform to.

Hence, for developers, it is important to understand how Ethereum works and how to write applications (i.e., smart contracts and decentralized applications) on it. The chapters in this part will discuss how to build Ethereum-compatible smart contracts and applications from the ground up. It is important to note that there are several Ethereum-compatible blockchains you can use to develop and deploy Ethereum applications, ESPECIALLY for applications optimized for specific business use cases.

Then, in Part III of the book, I will further explore the inner workings and future plans of Ethereum.

4

Getting Started

While it is possible to write software programs for the Bitcoin blockchain, few people do because of the limited programming functionality supported on the Bitcoin network.

Ethereum is the first large-scale blockchain network that supports sophisticated application development. Ethereum's ambition is to become the "world's computer." Through autonomous software programs, known as *smart contracts*, the Ethereum blockchain can be programmed to automatically execute transactions when certain conditions are met. To support this, Ethereum natively supports a Turing complete programming language (Solidity) and virtual machine (Ethereum Virtual Machine [EVM]), making it possible to program a wide range of applications.

For programmers, writing smart contract code to run on the Ethereum blockchain is the first step into the world of blockchain application development. As Ethereum continues to gain popularity and value, programming Ethereum applications has become a necessary and valuable skill.

In this chapter, we will start with a simple "Hello, World!" smart contract on Ethereum. We walk through the entire process to deploy and then interact with it on one of the Ethereum's test networks using popular tools. This example aims to get you started with Ethereum as quickly as possible. The subsequent chapters will go deeper into those concepts and alternative tools.

> **Note**
>
> It is often beneficial to develop your applications on an Ethereum-compatible blockchain rather than the Ethereum blockchain itself. You have seen the Second State DevChain as a clear example of a fast Ethereum-compatible blockchain. Later in this book, we will use the CyberMiles public blockchain as another Ethereum-compatible alternative for developers. The CyberMiles public blockchain is optimized for e-commerce applications. But at the same time, it is fully compatible with Ethereum languages and tools with faster execution speed, faster transaction confirmation time (10s), and much lower cost (1,000 times cheaper). You can learn more in Chapter 14.

The BUIDL Way

In Chapter 3, I introduced you to the BUIDL open source integrated development environment (IDE). It works with all Ethereum-compatible blockchains including the Ethereum mainnet and testnet. Let's set up BUIDL to work with Ethereum. Open the BUIDL web app at http://buidl.secondstate.io/ and click the **Providers** tab in the lower-left corner of the browser window (Figure 4.1).

Ethereum Mainnet

You should configure the web3 and ES (Elasticsearch) providers to public Ethereum nodes, as shown below. Or you can launch the following URL to have everything auto-configured for Ethereum. https://buidl.secondstate.io/eth

- *ES provider*. Set this to https://eth.search.secondstate.io/. The ES provider is a smart contract search engine that provides real-time data from the Ethereum network. You can learn more in Chapter 11.

- *Web3 provider*. Set this to https://mainnet.infura.io/. This is a public Ethereum blockchain node provided by Infura. Infura requests regular users to register an API key in order to use their services. Please do so and set your own mainnet.infura.io URL with your API key here. Alternatively, you could use a community-provided web3 provider such as https://main-rpc.linkpool.io/ or https://eth.node.secondstate.io/.

- *Chain ID*: Set this to 1 for the Ethereum mainnet.

- *Custom Tx gas*: Check this box so that BUIDL uses the specified gas price when creating contracts and calling contract functions.

- *Gas price*: Set this to 10000000000 (wei, or 10 Gwei) as the default gas price used by BUIDL. You can use the Ethereum Gas Tracker to see the current gas price on the network (https://etherscan.io/gasTracker). The higher gas price you are willing to pay, the faster your transactions can be confirmed.

- *Gas limit*: Set this to 8000000, which is the current block gas limit for Ethereum.

> **Note**
>
> Since the Ethereum mainnet can be extremely congested from time to time, you should be prepared to pay a high gas price (as much as $10 USD just to deploy a contract or call a function), and you could wait hours for the transaction to confirm. I recommend that most developers develop and even deploy on much faster and cheaper blockchains such as the Ethereum Classic or CyberMiles.

Now we have configured BUIDL to pay gas when deploying and calling smart contracts on Ethereum. BUIDL creates five random accounts for each user and then uses the default selected account to interact with the blockchain (Figure 4.2). So, you need an ETH balance in the default account. Just send some ETHs from your wallet or exchange accounts to your BUIDL default account. Or, you can use the + button next to Accounts to import an ETH account from other wallets.

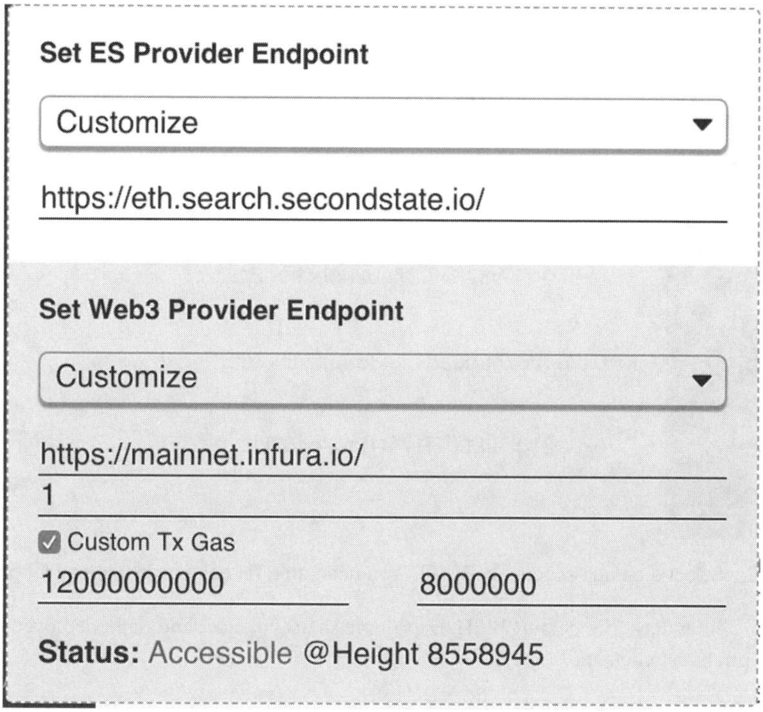

Set ES Provider Endpoint

Customize   ▼

https://eth.search.secondstate.io/

Set Web3 Provider Endpoint

Customize   ▼

https://mainnet.infura.io/
1
☑ Custom Tx Gas
12000000000   8000000

Status: Accessible @Height 8558945

Figure 4.1   Configuring BUIDL to work with the Ethereum mainnet

> **Note**
>
> BUIDL has a built-in wallet that manages account private keys. However, BUIDL can only sign transactions and pay gas from its accounts. It is designed for application development. BUIDL is not a general-purpose wallet, and I do not recommend maintaining more than 0.1 ETH balance in it.

That's all you need in the contract tab. You can now write a smart contract, click the **Compile** and **Deploy to the chain** buttons to deploy it to Ethereum, and then use the BUIDL user interface (UI) to call any function on the deployed contract.

Finally, on the dapp tab of BUIDL, you need to add gasPrice and gas parameters to all web3 transactions. You are safe to use BUIDL's default web3.ss package here, as it contains all web3.eth objects and functions. Here is an example:

```
instance.set(n, {
  gas: 100000,
  gasPrice: 10000000000
}, function (e, result) {
  // ... ...
});
```

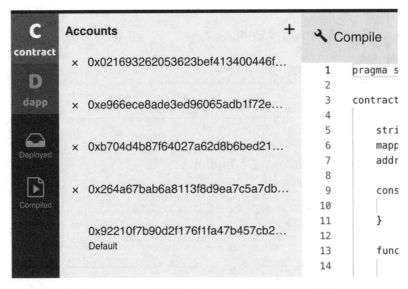

Figure 4.2   Select a default account in BUIDL. You need an ETH balance in it to pay for gas.

That's it. You now have the default BUIDL example smart contract and dapp deployed on the Ethereum public blockchain.

Ethereum Classic Mainnet

If you are not willing to pay $10 USD and wait hours for every contract call, you can use the Ethereum Classic blockchain to deploy your applications. The Ethereum Classic blockchain is one of the most reputable and stable blockchain networks in the world, and it is fully compatible with the Ethereum protocol. Its native cryptocurrency, ETC, costs a fraction of ETH. The Ethereum Classic blockchain is seldom congested, and hence a 10 Gwei gas price (pennies) typically results in transaction confirmation in less than a minute. To configure BUIDL to use the Ethereum Classic mainnet, use the following settings. Or you can launch the following URL to have everything auto-configured for Ethereum Classic. https://buidl.secondstate.io/etc

- *ES provider*: Set this to https://etc.search.secondstate.io/.
- *Web3 provider*: Set this to https://www.ethercluster.com/etc.
- *Chain ID*: Set this to 61 for the Ethereum Classic mainnet.
- *Custom Tx gas*: Check this box.
- *Gas Price*: Set this to 10000000000 (wei, or 10 Gwei) as the default gas price used by BUIDL.
- *Gas Limit*: Set this to 8000000.

In addition, the current Ethereum Classic blockchain requires Solidity compiler version 0.4.2.

You must configure that for BUIDL by using URL parameter /?s042 when launching BUIDL.

Send some ETC to your BUIDL account as gas. You can now compile, deploy, and call your smart contract on the Ethereum Classic blockchain.

CyberMiles Mainnet

The CyberMiles public blockchain is an Ethereum-compatible blockchain that is much faster (a ten-second transaction confirmation time) and cheaper than both ETH and ETC. You can read more about it in Chapter 14. To configure BUIDL to use the CyberMiles mainnet, configure the following settings. Or you can launch the following URL to have everything auto-configured for CyberMiles. https://buidl.secondstate.io/cmt

- *ES provider*: Set this to https://cmt.search.secondstate.io/.

- *Web3 provider*: Set this to https://rpc.cybermiles.io:8545/.

- *Chain ID*: Set this to 18 for the CyberMiles mainnet.

- *Custom Tx gas*: Check this box.

- *Gas Price*: Set this to 5000000000 (wei, or 5 Gwei) as the default gas price used by BUIDL.

- *Gas Limit*: Set this to 8000000.

Send some CMT to your BUIDL account as gas. You can now compile, deploy, and call your smart contract on the CyberMiles blockchain.

> **Note**
>
> Ethereum, Ethereum Classic, and CyberMiles all have testnets for developers to try their applications without spending real money. However, from my experience, testnet tokens are difficult to come by, and the test dapps are difficult to share, as few users have testnet wallets or tokens. The testnet is also often unreliable and runs different software than the mainnet. For CyberMiles, the cost of transactions is less than 1 cent. It is a good choice even for development purposes.

The Hard Way

The key benefit of BUIDL is that it is easy to use and allows fast development cycles. But it also hides some important concepts from the application developer. In this section, we will take a step back and use more traditional Ethereum developer tools to explain the concepts behind Ethereum.

Metamask Wallet

The Metamask wallet is a Chrome browser extension to manage your Ethereum blockchain accounts. It stores and manages your private keys to those accounts on your computer (i.e., a wallet for private keys and, by extension, cryptocurrency stored in those accounts). For developers, Metamask is a great tool since it integrates with other development tools and allows you to interact with Ethereum accounts programmatically.

First, make sure you have the latest Google Chrome browser installed. You can get it at https://www.google.com/chrome/.

Next, follow the instructions on the Metamask web site (https://metamask.io/) to install Metamask on your Chrome browser.

Now, you should see the Metamask icon on your Chrome toolbar. Click it to bring up its UI. You should create a password for your Metamask wallet (Figure 4.3). This is important since your password protects your account's private keys stored on this computer. Once you create the password, Metamask will give you a 12-word recovery phase. That is the only way for you to recover the password, so keep it safe!

Figure 4.3   Creating a password for your Metamask wallet

For development purposes, select the top-left drop-down list in the Metamask UI, and select the Ropsten Test Network (Figure 4.4), which is an Ethereum public blockchain maintained for testing purposes.

You will also need to create an account on the Ropsten testnet to store your ETH cryptocurrency there. Select the person icon at the top right of the Metamask UI, and select **Create Account** (Figure 4.5, left). Metamask will create an account address and its associated private key for you. You can click an account in the UI and get its address in the clipboard or export its private key (Figure 4.5, right). You can name this account so that you can access it in the Metamask UI later. You can also use Metamask to manage mainnet ETHs, which can be traded on exchanges for U.S. dollars. But to do that, you should make sure that your computer is physically secure since real money will be at stake.

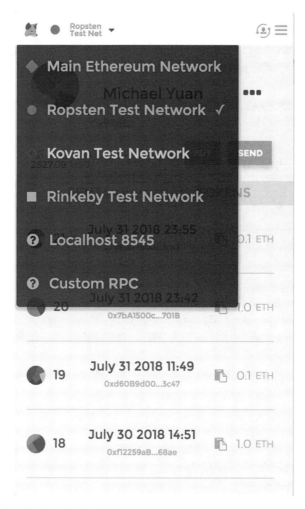

Figure 4.4   Selecting the Ropsten testnet

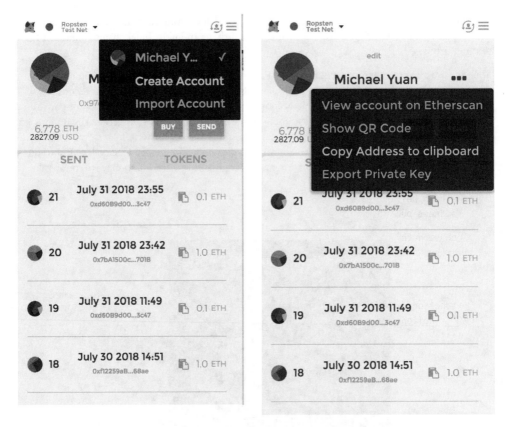

Figure 4.5   Creating a new account on the Ropsten testnet and getting the account address

Of course, you still need to fund your account with some Ropsten testnet ETH to use it. Go to the public Ropsten faucet (http://faucet.ropsten.be:3001/) and request 1 testnet ETH for your address! The Ropsten testnet ETH can be used only on the testnet. It is not traded in any exchanges and can disappear at any time when the Ropsten testnet is retired. Unlike the mainnet ETH, Ropsten ETH has zero monetary value.

Now you have set up Metamask and are ready to interact with your first Ethereum smart contract on the Ropsten testnet!

Remix

Remix the Ethereum IDE for developers to experience smart contracts on the Ethereum block-chain. Remix is completely web-based. Just go to its web site to load the web app: http://remix.ethereum.org/.

> **Note**
>
> The Remix IDE is similar to the contract tab in BUIDL, except that BUIDL does not require any external wallet like Metamask.

In the code editor to the right, let's enter a simple smart contract. The following is an example of the "Hello, World!" smart contract. It is written in a special JavaScript-like programming language known as Solidity.

```
pragma solidity ^0.4.17;

contract HelloWorld  {

    string helloMessage;
    address public owner;

    constructor () public {
        helloMessage = "Hello, World!";
        owner = msg.sender;
    }

    function updateMessage (string _new_msg) public {
        helloMessage = _new_msg;
    }

    function sayHello () public view returns (string) {
        return helloMessage;
    }

    function kill() public {
        if (msg.sender == owner) selfdestruct(owner);
    }
}
```

The "Hello, World!" smart contract has two key methods.

- The `sayHello()` method returns a greeting to its caller. The greeting is initially set to "Hello, World!" when the smart contract is deployed.

- The `updateMessage()` method allows the method caller to change the greeting message from "Hello, World!" to another message.

Hit the **Start to compile** button in the right panel to compile this contract (Figure 4.6). It will generate the bytecode and application binary interface (ABI) to be used later.

Next, on the Run tab of Remix (Figure 4.7), you can connect Remix to your Metamask account via the Injected Web3 drop-down box. Remix will automatically detect your existing Metamask accounts. If your Ropsten address does not show up here, try logging out and then back into Remix.

Figure 4.6   Compiling an Ethereum smart contract in Remix

> Compile   Run   Settings   Analysis   Debugger   Support

| Environment | Injected Web3 | ⚡ Ropsten (3) | ⇕ | **i** |

| Account | 0x97d...73ceb (7.778611759 ether) | ⇕ | 🗐 ⊕ |

| Gas limit | 3000000 |

| Value | 0 | wei | ⇕ |

HelloWorld   ⇕

Deploy

Load contract from Address   At Address

Transactions recorded: ⓪   ⌄

Deployed Contracts   🗑

Currently you have no contract instances to interact with.

Figure 4.7   Injecting Metamask into Remix

You should now see options to deploy the smart contract to the blockchain. Click the **Deploy** button to deploy the contract to the blockchain. Since you have selected a Ropsten address to inject into this Remix session, the contract will be deployed on the Ropsten testnet. At this time, Metamask will pop up and ask you to send a gas fee from your existing account address (Figure 4.8). The gas fee is required by the Ethereum network to pay for the network service required to deploy your contract.

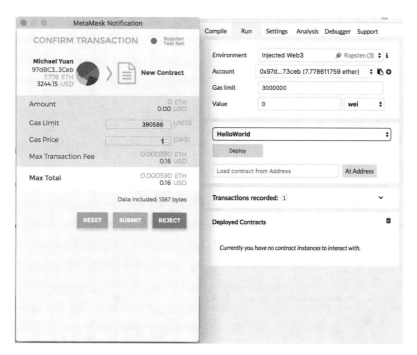

Figure 4.8   Paying a gas fee to deploy the contract

After you submit the Metamask request, wait for a few minutes for the Ethereum network to confirm the deployment of your contract. The contract deployment address will be shown in the confirmation, and the deployed contract and its available functions will be available on the Run tab in Remix as well (Figure 4.9).

If you have already deployed the smart contract on the Ropsten testnet, you already know the deployed address of the contract. You can simply enter the contract address in the box next to the At Address button and click the button. This configures Remix to use an already-deployed contract. No gas fee is needed in this case.

Once Remix is connected to your deployed contract, it shows the contract functions on the Run tab. You can enter a new greeting next to the updateMessage button and click the button to update the message. Since Ethereum network storage is required to store the updated message, you will again be prompted to pay a gas fee through Metamask.

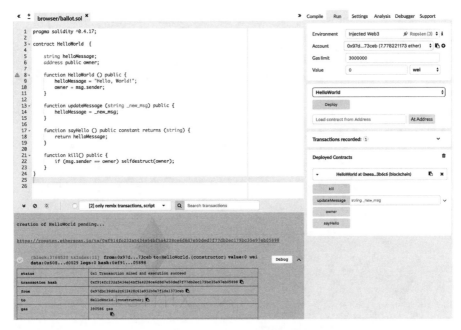

Figure 4.9   The contract is now deployed, and the available methods are shown.

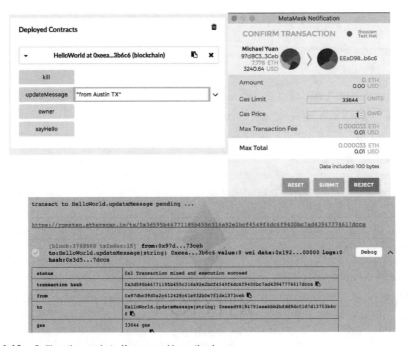

Figure 4.10   Calling the updateMessage() method

Figure 4.11 Calling the sayHello() method

Once the network confirms the message update, you will again see a confirmation message (Figure 4.10). After the updateMessage() method is confirmed, you can call sayHello() from Remix (Figure 4.11), and you will see the updated message. The sayHello() function does not alter the blockchain state. It can be executed by a local node connected to Remix and does not affect any other node on the network. It can be executed without any need for gas fees.

The Remix IDE is easy to use. It is an excellent choice for beginners. As your development skill advances, there are additional tools you can use to develop and deploy smart contracts. Chapter 6 has more details.

Web3

While Remix is a great tool, it is too hard for regular people. To make your smart contracts available to the general public, you typically need to build a web-based UI. For that, you need the web3 JavaScript library to interact with the Ethereum blockchain.

> **Note**
>
> The dapp tab in BUIDL injects a preconfigured web3 instance into the JavaScript program in BUIDL.

Once Metamask is installed, it automatically injects a custom instance of the web3 object into the page's JavaScript context. Method calls that require private keys will automatically prompt the user to select an account, and Metamask will use the selected private key to sign the transaction before sending it to the Ethereum network.

The overall structure of a web3 dapp is a JavaScript function that starts when the web page loads (i.e., the following onPageLoad() function). The JavaScript function manages the application state and makes function calls to the smart contract on the blockchain. Because of network delay and confirmation requirements for blockchain operations, all web3 API calls are asynchronous. So, we use the web3 callback API to handle the return values. Notice that if you need to make one smart contract call after another, you must nest those calls. The following code snippet shows the structure of the JavaScript function. The `myFunc()` and `anotherFunc()` calls can happen in parallel at the same time, while the `secondFunc()` call must happen after `myFunc()` returns.

```javascript
var onPageLoad = function () {
  web3.eth.getAccounts(function (e, address) {
    if (e) {
      // ...
    } else {
      contract = web3.eth.contract(abi);
      instance = contract.at(contract_address);
      instance.myFunc (params..., function (e, r) {
        if (e) {
          // ...
        } else {
          return_value_0 = r[0];
          return_value_1 = r[1];
          // ...
          // show the UI based on the return values

          // Make a subsequent call after myFunc
          instance.secondFunc (params..., function (e2, r2) {
            // update the UI based on the r2 return values
          }
        }
      });

      instance.anotherFunc (params..., function (e, r) {
        if (e) {
          // ...
        } else {
          // show results on UI
        }
      });
    }
  });
}
```

The "Hello, World!" example, however, does not require complex sequences of smart contract function invocations. It just needs to invoke one contract function and then update the web UI. The source code for the `helloworld.html` file is shown here:

```html
<!DOCTYPE html>
<html lang="en">
  <head>
    <script>
      window.addEventListener('load', function() {
        var hello = web3.eth.contract(...).at("...");
```

```
            var new_mesg = location.search.split('new_mesg=')[1];
            if (new_mesg === undefined || new_mesg == null) {
            } else {
              new_mesg = decodeURIComponent(new_mesg.replace(/\+/g, '%20'));

              web3.eth.getAccounts(function (error, address) {
                if(!error) {
                  hello.updateMessage(new_mesg, {
                      from: address.toString()
                  }, function(e, r){
                    if(!e)
                      document.getElementById("status").innerHTML =
                        "<b>Submitted to blockchain</b>. " +
                        "New message will take a few sec to show up! " +
                        "<a href=\"helloworld_europa.html\">Reload page.</a>";
                  });
                }
              });
            }

            hello.sayHello(function(error, result){
              if(!error)
                document.getElementById("mesg").innerHTML = result;
            });
          })
      </script>
    </head>

    <body>
    <h2>Hello World</h2>
      <form method=GET>
        New message:<br/><br/>
        <input type="text" size="40" name="new_mesg"/><br/><br/>
        <input type="submit"/>
        <p id="status"/>
      </form>
      <p>The current message is: <span id="mesg"/></p>
    </body>
  </html>
```

Notice the web3.eth.contract(...).at("...") line. The at() function takes the contract's deployment address on the blockchain as a parameter. You can find it on the Run tab's Deployed Contracts section, as shown in Figures 4.9 and 4.10. The contract function takes a JSON structure known as the contract's ABI. You can find that by clicking the Details button on the Compile tab. You can copy the entire ABI section to your computer's clipboard by clicking the clipboard icon. Alternatively, the WEB3DEPLOY section's first line of code shows the contract function's ABI parameter all on one line (Figure 4.12).

The web application now allows users to interact with the "Hello, World!" smart contract directly from the Web (Figure 4.13). To submit a new message, the app requires Metamask to send gas

```
ABI  ❏  ❷
  ▸ 0:
  ▸ 1:
  ▸ 2:
  ▸ 3:
  ▸ 4:
```

```
WEB3DEPLOY  ❏  ❷

var helloworldContract = web3.eth.contract([{"constant":false,"inputs":[{"name":"_new_
```

Figure 4.12   Finding the ABI

1

Hello World

New message:

[This is an updated contract]

[Submit]

The current message is: Hello, World

2

MetaMask Notification

CONFIRM TRANSACTION   ● Ropsten Test Net ▾

Michael Yuan
97dBC3...3Ceb   8bC27c...7E9C
9.997 ETH
6798.32 USD

Amount	0 ETH
	0.00 USD
Gas Limit	51660 UNITS
Gas Price	1 GWEI
Max Transaction Fee	0.000051 ETH
	0.03 USD
Max Total	0.000051 ETH
	0.03 USD

Data Included: 100 bytes

[RESET] [SUBMIT] [REJECT]

3

Hello World

New message:

[   ]

[Submit]

Submitted to blockchain. The new message might take a few seconds to show up! Reload page.

The current message is: Hello, World

4

Hello World

New message:

[   ]

[Submit]

The current message is: This is an updated contract

Figure 4.13   Using the Metamask wallet to write to a contract

fees as it calls the `updateMessage()` function on the contract. Notice that all web3 functions are nested and invoked asynchronously. You can read more about dapp development in Chapter 7.

Using Metamask with web3.js is probably the best way to get started with Ethereum application development. But for the average web user, installing and using Metamask is a significant barrier of entry. As you have seen, the BUIDL IDE provides a light-weight wallet on the dapp web page, which is probably sufficient for users who just need to pay gas for their interactions with the Ethereum blockchain. Or, we could design the application so that a centralized server pays for gas on behalf of users (see Chapter 8).

Conclusion

In this chapter, I explained how to build, deploy, and use a smart contract on Ethereum-compatible blockchains. We used tools such as Metamask, Remix, and web3 to get started. In the next several chapters, we will explore the key concepts behind Ethereum, software tools involved in its operation, inner workings of smart contracts, alternative development tools, and the software stack for decentralized applications. We will tie everything together with a new dapp that showcases the capability of smart contracts in Chapter 16.

5

Concepts and Tools

In the previous chapter, I showed you how to build, deploy, and interact with an Ethereum smart contract. However, by focusing on graphical user interface (GUI) tools, we have also left many concepts and points unexplained.

In this chapter, I will explain how to run and interact with an Ethereum node. In the process, you will learn critical concepts behind the design, implementation, and operation of the Ethereum blockchain. Those concepts also apply to Ethereum-compatible blockchains.

Ethereum Wallet and Basic Concepts

To use Ethereum, you first need an Ethereum wallet to hold your ETH coins. Like Bitcoin, anyone can create an "account" on the Ethereum blockchain to hold and transact ETH coins. An account is uniquely identified by a pair of public and private keys. A *key* is a long string of seemingly random numbers and characters. The key pair can be randomly generated on your own computer.

- The Ethereum account number is directly derived from the public key. If someone wants to send you some ETHs, all they need is the account number.

- The private key is used to identify the owner of this account. When you need to move ETH out of the account (i.e., to spend it or transfer to another account), you will need the private key. Without the private key, the Ethereum miners will deem the transaction invalid and refuse to include it in the blockchain.

Now you see that it is critical to safeguard your private key. If someone else gets hold of it, that person will have full authority over the ETHs in that account. And if you somehow lose the private key, you will forever lose control over the ETHs in your account—the ETHs will remain in the account for the world to see, but no one can move or spend them without the private key.

All the wallet does is store and manage your public/private key pair. It often also provides a UI for you to manage ETHs in your account using the underlying public/private key pair. The wallet can be a completely stand-alone piece of software (or even hardware). Or, it can be a web application that stores your keys on their servers. Here are some notable wallets for Ethereum:

- Mist is the official wallet software from the Ethereum development team. You can install and run it on your own computer. It is more than just a wallet, though; it is a "blockchain browser" that includes a full Ethereum node. For example, you can upload smart contract code using Mist. That also means Mist requires more than 4GB of RAM and more than 100GB of hard drive space to run. It takes 24 to 48 hours for Mist to start the first time as it needs to download the entire blockchain history.

- Parity is another fully featured GUI Ethereum client. It competes against Mist. It is supposed to be faster than Mist. But still, it needs to download the entire blockchain to run a full Ethereum node.

- Metamask, covered in Chapter 4, is a Chrome-based wallet. It stores the private keys on your computer with the Chrome browser. Hence, physical security of your computer is important for Metamask wallets.

- The imToken mobile app is a wallet for your smartphone. You can create key pairs (accounts) in the app and use the app to send and receive ETH to and from your accounts in the wallet. The imToken app does not download the blockchain itself. It starts instantly and is ready for use.

- Tezer and Ledger are USB key-sized hardware devices that store and manage your keys. They typically work in tandem with a computer program. The computer program provides the UI to check balances and create transactions. When it needs to sign a transaction, it passes to the USB device to complete it. The private key never leaves the USB device.

- Coinbase is a web-based wallet, which also provides banking services to convert your ETHs to and from U.S. dollars. Almost all crypto exchanges have wallets for you to deposit and withdraw coins.

> **Note**
>
> If you are running a wallet application on your own PC/mobile/dedicated hardware device, you must be responsible for the physical safety of the device. Do not lose your private key!

> **Note**
>
> Ethereum-compatible blockchains also have their own wallet applications. For example, the CyberMiles blockchain has its own Metamask-like Chrome extension wallet, as well as a stand-alone mobile wallet application, called CyberMiles App, which can run web3-based dapps. Learn more in Appendix A.

If the wallet manages only the public/private key pairs, what about the coins and tokens stored in those accounts? Are your coins in your wallet? The answer is no, your tokens or coins are not in your wallet. Remember that the blockchain is a ledger system. It records all the transactions and balances associated with all accounts in the system. So, the wallet needs to manage only your account credentials, and the tokens or coins in your account can be found on the blockchain itself.

Etherscan

The Etherscan web site is a useful tool to look into the internal states of the Ethereum blockchain. You can use it to look up and review every transaction recorded on the blockchain and, by extension, the balance and history of every account. On its front page, you can see the latest blocks and the transactions within them (Figure 5.1).

> **Note**
>
> Most blockchains also have their own blockchain explorer. For example, the CyberMiles public blockchain has https://www.cmttracking.io/, which shows not only transactions but also data related to its delegated proof of stake operations. Learn more in the Appendix.

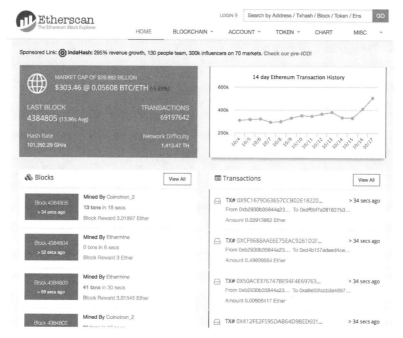

Figure 5.1   Latest blocks and transactions in Etherscan

Wallets or exchanges can also display transactions to or from your account. Etherscan shows the accounts and fund involved, as well as whether the transaction is validated by blockchain miners (Figure 5.2).

Figure 5.2   Drilling into a transaction

Of course, as a developer, it is not enough just to have accounts and ETHs. We want to run the blockchain software, mine ETH coins, and execute our own smart contracts.

The TestRPC

To study and develop applications for Ethereum, you need access to the Ethereum Virtual Machine (EVM). Ideally, you would run a full Ethereum node on the blockchain and communicate with the blockchain network through that node. However, a full Ethereum node is expensive. For developers, it is much easier to get started with the TestRPC. I will discuss how to run Ethereum full nodes later in this chapter.

Note

To run a full Ethereum node and join the Ethereum network, you will need to run a full Ethereum client, download the entire transaction history of the Ethereum blockchain (more than 100GB worth of data), and then start "mining" ETH to participate in the process of validating transactions and creating new blocks on the blockchain. This is a big commitment and requires a significant amount of computing resources. Even then, you are unlikely to mine any ETH successfully—with ETH traded at above $150, mining competition is fierce. Since most tasks on the public Ethereum blockchain require ETH to complete, you will need to purchase ETH just to start experimenting with it. Again, at $150+ per ETH, that is an expensive learning process.

For developer testing of Ethereum application programming interface (API) functions and smart contract programming, you can use a simulator that simply answers all Ethereum API calls but does not incur the cost of actually building a blockchain network. The TestRPC is just such a simulator. The TestRPC was originally developed as a volunteer open source project. It was later acquired by the company behind the open source Truffle framework for smart contract development (renamed to Ganache CLI; see https://github.com/trufflesuite/ganache-cli).

You should first make sure that node.js and its package manager npm, are installed on your machine. You can install them from https://www.npmjs.com/get-npm. On most Linux distributions, you can use the system package manager to install them as well. For example, the following command installs node.js and npm on a CentOS/RedHat/Fedora Linux system:

```
$ sudo yum install epel-release
$ sudo yum install nodejs npm
```

Next, let's install the Ganache CLI using the npm package manager.

```
$ sudo npm install -g ganache-cli
```

You can start the TestRPC server from the command line. It will randomly create ten accounts (pairs of public key addresses and private keys). All the accounts are unlocked by default for easy testing.

```
$ ganache-cli
Ganache CLI v6.0.3 (ganache-core: 2.0.2)

Available Accounts
==================
(0) 0xbaea21140ce33f0fa7046692f61a4238eaa407e3
(1) 0x944205dcdaeeb097870925ea26e159f6b6dab4c1
(2) 0x1f62a96f38d5247815dd4ed2d18ed9e228c06d40
(3) 0x6235ca5d31c476b649b8517ce24f428db34e8446
(4) 0xa13feaf894f1ae33e321c78c396a3eaf2048a621
(5) 0xee3a90f6403853b57a7a325cccee0e6120cb39f2
(6) 0x889dd868cc580080e1e809fd38ca1b5ff2aef017
(7) 0xb0e664c4732d7c065b4f20e461cfc89ce5598119
(8) 0x3c183932b2d9c0aedb611cc89c210ab71e7d3f4c
(9) 0xf3deac45c47e48620571108b9a9320aacd7518fe

Private Keys
==================
(0) 75af4be053b6da9b6ae6af0dd137de406bb6405779be056ffa5861873346a54f
(1) 112ff21d135f28273c3185c6d519f3c4f38907418448ac875443206eed25eb39
(2) 28b5b6d6d04d38be899f69bb9ce6335d75b30daaea4476c9f16e75cb638076b9
(3) 122a12f40411b5fd66c354493d3ec9e83d66f14071e47bdfc9a0b747d1040344
(4) 6e062a75413f9632d33f1520e0b4246e05edde517caf4b1657c6d652d324dc06
(5) 71212db8910dabd3d5399470bb8ea37a29ffdb2402a2b03d9144d7bea6a5cfda
(6) 301283f708770350180a2b00e5f8092f43238d23fd2249397f5a185d5a9ecc1f
(7) 7cfc7dba9c475fc7f394507ea1e9fd3d8604b288a058477b684f9a58a9176f33
```

```
(8)  14f259263d41a1e5986c588f4ae9bc93b6e56c4734ed7046394a7b1d37aba094
(9)  4aceb1f8a42c36a50402d0e679d0666a61bb4786ef7196c98b5cd3e0f6992b5b

HD Wallet
==================
Mnemonic:  foot silly tag melt require tuition soon become frequent tell forest
satisfy
Base HD Path:  m/44'/60'/0'/0/{account_index}

Listening on localhost:8545
```

You can start the TestRPC node with the same set of accounts every time, and you can give each account an initial balance as well.

```
$ ganache-cli --account="0x99cf2f6...,1234000000000000000000"
--account="0xa295df7...,3141590000000000000000"
Ganache CLI v6.0.3 (ganache-core: 2.0.2)

Available Accounts
==================
(0)  0xd61a8f9afaaa3f12e75781c3a1e271c2744442ba
(1)  0x9f37a44226a4c65336ceacbd608ea248fca5453c

Private Keys
==================
(0)  99cf2f6a09d3ba6491e838ac62edcd1b8df5507056a89c87e495948a2211c9c4
(1)  a295df779395bb57b38765a592374d56d0d4a259d54fb8f5cfad2f35b90ae8cd

Listening on localhost:8545
```

The TestRPC is a fully featured Ethereum simulator. It is much faster than any live Ethereum node because it does not perform the actual work of creating, mining, and synchronizing blocks. That makes it ideally suited for fast turnaround development cycles.

Interacting with Ethereum via GETH

Once the TestRPC node starts or the full Ethereum node is synchronized to the blockchain, you can use the GETH program to connect to it and send commands and interactions to the network. All you need to do is to attach the GETH command to the node by specifying the node's IP address. If the node is running locally (e.g., a TestRPC node on the local machine), you can simply use localhost for the IP address.

```
$ geth attach http://node.ip.addr:8545
```

GETH opens an interactive console in the new terminal, and you can use the Ethereum JavaScript API to access the blockchain. For instance, the following commands will create a new account to hold virtual currency on this network. Just repeat it a few times, and you will see a few accounts in the eth.accounts list. As mentioned earlier, each account consists of a pair of private and public keys. Only the public key is recorded on the blockchain in every transaction that involves this account.

```
> personal.newAccount()
Passphrase:
Repeat passphrase:
"0x7631a9f5b7af9705eb7ce0679022d8174ae51ce0"
> eth.accounts
["0x7631a9f5b7af9705eb7ce0679022d8174ae51ce0", ...]
```

When you create or unlock accounts from the GETH console, the private key of the account is stored in the keystore file on the attached node's file system. On a live Ethereum node (i.e., not the TestRPC), you can start mining and deposit the ethers you mine to one of your accounts. For the TestRPC, you will have ETHs in your initial accounts, and you can skip this step.

```
> miner.setEtherbase(eth.accounts[0])
> miner.start(8)
true
> miner.stop()
True
```

Next, you can send some of your ethers from one account to another. If your GETH console is attached to a live Ethereum node, you will need access to the sender account's private key via the keystore and passphrase on the node. If you are attached to TestRPC either via localhost or remotely, you can skip the account unlocking calls, as all accounts are unlocked by default in the TestRPC. On a console attached to a live Ethereum node, if you do not call the unlockAccount() method first, the sendTransaction() method will ask for your passphrase to unlock the account for you.

```
> personal.unlockAccount("0x7631a9f5b7af9705eb7ce0679022d8174ae51ce0")
Unlock account 0x7631a9f5b7af9705eb7ce0679022d8174ae51ce0
Passphrase:
true
> eth.sendTransaction({from:"0x7631a9f5b7af9705eb7ce0679022d8174ae51ce0",
to:"0xfa9ee3557ba7572eb9ee2b96b12baa65f4d2ed8b",
value: web3.toWei(0.05, "ether")})
"0xf63cae7598583491f0c9074c8e1415673f6a7382b1c57cc9b06cc77032f80ed3"
```

The last line is the transaction ID for the transaction to send 0.05 ETH between the two accounts. Using a tool like Etherscan, you will be able to see a record of this transaction on the blockchain.

Interacting with Ethereum via web3

The GETH interactive console is convenient to test and experiment with the Ethereum blockchain using the JavaScript API methods. But to access the Ethereum blockchain from an application, you can use the JavaScript API directly from a web page.

The web page in Figure 5.3 shows an application that queries an Ethereum account's balance. The user enters an account address, and the JavaScript API retrieves and displays the account balance.

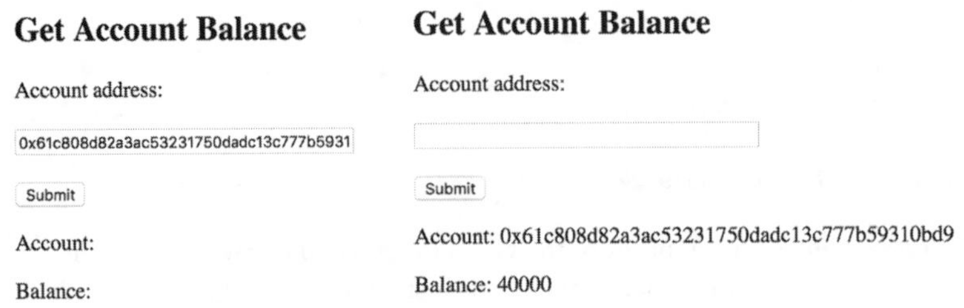

Get Account Balance

Account address:

```
0x61c808d82a3ac53231750dadc13c777b5931
```

Submit

Account:

Balance:

Get Account Balance

Account address:

```
                                        
```

Submit

Account: 0x61c808d82a3ac53231750dadc13c777b59310bd9

Balance: 40000

Figure 5.3   A demo page for web3.js

Via the web3.js library provided by the Ethereum project, the JavaScript on the page first connects to an Ethereum node. Here, you can put in your own Ethereum node (e.g., `http://node.ip.addr:8545`) or a public node INFURA provides (see the following example). For a local TestRPC node, you can simply use the `http://localhost:8545` URL.

```
web3 = new Web3(new Web3.providers.HttpProvider(
  "https://mainnet.infura.io/"));
```

Then the JavaScript uses web3.js functions to query the address. These are the same JavaScript method calls we can make in the GETH console.

```
var balanceWei = web3.eth.getBalance(acct).toNumber();
var balance = web3.fromWei(balanceWei, 'ether');
```

Our demo application queries the account balance. The balance is public information and does not require any account private key. If your web3.js application needs to send ETH from one account to another, you will need access to the sending account's private key. There are several ways to do this, and I will cover them in Chapter 8.

Running an Ethereum Node

While the TestRPC is great for beginners, to truly understand the Ethereum blockchain, you should run your own node. Only through your own node can you examine the blocks and access all the functionalities the blockchain offers. In this section, I will discuss how to run a node on the Ethereum public network. It requires a significant amount of computing resources, such as a 24/7 available server and Internet connection, as well as at least a few hundred gigabytes of disk space to store the blockchain data. If you are on a development team (e.g., in a company), it is sufficient to run a single node for all the team members to access. To get started, download the official Ethereum client software GETH to your computer.

```
https://geth.ethereum.org/downloads/
```

The official GETH program is written in the GO programming language. It is simply a compiled binary executable program that you can run from the command line.

```
$ geth version
Geth
Version: 1.7.1-stable
```

If you start GETH with all the default options, you will be connected to the public Ethereum blockchain. To start the node in noninteractive node and keep it running in the background after the current user logs out, use NOHUP.

```
$ nohup geth &
```

It will take hours and many gigabytes of RAM and disk space to download and sync the entire blockchain history. So, it is probably a good idea to start GETH on the official Ethereum test network. That will cut down on the initial startup time and resources significantly, but still you need to prepare to wait for several hours even to sync the testnet.

```
$ geth --testnet --fast
```

> **Note**
>
> The ether cryptocurrency (ETH) you mine or receive on testnet or your private network has no value. It can be used only for network testing purposes. You cannot exchange it on the open market.

As I mentioned earlier in this section, you need only one running Ethereum node for the entire development team. The GETH client on the running Ethereum node manages its own keystore on the machine's local file system. All the accounts created through this node will have their private keys stored in this file, and each private key will be protected by a passphrase. The keystore file is located in the following directories. You can copy the keystore file to another node and access the accounts from the new node. You can also extract the private key from the keystore and sign your transactions to access the account from any node on the Ethereum blockchain network.

- Linux: `~/.ethereum/keystore`
- Mac: `/Library/Ethereum/keystore`
- Windows: `%APPDATA%/Ethereum`

Companies like INFURA (https://infura.io/) provide public Ethereum nodes on the Internet. This saves you the trouble and significant resources required by running a node. However, the public nodes cannot store private keys for security reasons. Specifically, you have to use signed transactions to access accounts.

Running a Private Ethereum Network

For developers, it is often a good idea just to start your own private Ethereum test network. The following command starts the first node on the private network from scratch (i.e., block 0, or the *genesis*):

```
$ geth --dev console
```

> **Note**
>
> There are many command-line options for geth that you can use to customize your private network. For example, you could pass a genesis.json file to the geth init command and specify the following: peer nodes on the network, initial coin balances for selected accounts, difficulty in mining new coins, and so on.

Running a single node network is oftentimes sufficient for development tasks. But sometimes you do need a real network with multiple nodes. To start a new peer node, find out the identity of your current (first) node in the interactive console.

```
> admin.nodeInfo
{
  enode: "enode://c74de1...ce@[::]:55223?discport=0",
  id: "c74de1...ce",
  ip: "::",
  listenAddr: "[::]:55223",
  name: "Geth/v1.7.0-stable-6c6c7b2a/linux-amd64/go1.7.4",
  ports: {
    discovery: 0,
    listener: 55223
  },
  protocols: {
    eth: {
      difficulty: 131072,
      genesis: "0xe5be...bc",
      head: "0xe5...bc",
      network: 1
    },
  ...
```

With the enode ID, you can start a second peer node from another computer. Notice that the [::] in the enode ID is your node's IP address. So, you will need to replace it with the IP address of the first node.

```
geth --bootnodes "enode://c74de1...ce@192.168.1.3:55223"
```

You can now start more peer nodes. The `bootnodes` parameter can take multiple enode addresses separated by commas. Alternatively, you can start each node in the console mode, use `admin.nodeInfo` to figure out the enode ID for each, and then use `admin.addPeer` to connect each node to each other.

```
> admin.addPeer("enode://c74de1...ce@192.168.1.3:55223")
True
> net.peerCount
1
```

Each new node will start by downloading and syncing the complete blockchain from the private network. They can all mine ethers and validate transactions on the network.

Conclusion

In this chapter, I discussed the basic concepts behind Ethereum and how to set up your own private Ethereum blockchain. Of course, Ethereum does much more than creating and transacting the ETH cryptocurrency. The core idea of Ethereum is the smart contract, which we will explore in the next chapter.

6

Smart Contracts

The most important feature of the Ethereum blockchain is its ability to execute software code known as *smart contracts*. Now, we already have many distributed computing networks. Why do we need a blockchain to act as a distributed computer? The answer is decentralized and trusted autonomous execution. With the Ethereum blockchain, you do not need to trust anyone to correctly execute your code. Instead, a community of network participants (Ethereum miners) will all execute your smart contract code and reach a consensus that the results are correct.

In this chapter, I will first revisit the "Hello, World!" smart contract to illustrate how an Ethereum smart contract works under the hood. I will then provide a high-level overview of the design features of smart contract languages like Solidity to help you get a head start on Solidity programming. I will also cover how to build and deploy smart contracts using the open source framework and tools. While I will continue to cover graphical user interface (GUI) tools, I will focus on command-line power tools that are more suitable for professional developers in this chapter.

"Hello, World!" Again

The idea behind smart contracts is software code that is, once written, guaranteed to get executed correctly. In this section, let's review a simple smart contract. It works as follows:

- Anyone can submit the smart contract code to the Ethereum blockchain. Ethereum miners validate the code, and if most of them agree (i.e., reach consensus), the code will be saved on the blockchain. The smart contract now has an address on the blockchain, as if it is an account.

- Anyone can then call any public method on the smart contract at that blockchain address. The blockchain nodes will all execute the code. If most of them agree on the results of the code execution, the changes made by the code will be saved on the blockchain.

> **Note**
>
> Ethereum network nodes are responsible for executing those smart contracts and reaching consensus on the correctness of their results. The nodes perform this work in exchange for Ethereum's native cryptocurrency, called *ether* (ETH), in each transaction. The transaction fee, called *gas*, is paid by the "from" account specified by the method caller.

In this chapter, I will again use the "Hello, World!" example to further illustrate how smart contracts work and how to interact with them using different tools. The contract is written in the Solidity programming language. The filename is `HelloWorld.sol`. The most important requirement of a smart contract is that it must produce the same result when executed on different node computers. That means it cannot contain any random functions or even floating-point math as floating-point numbers are represented differently on different computer architectures. The Solidity language is designed to be completely unambiguous in the programs it expresses.

```
pragma solidity ^0.4.17;

contract HelloWorld  {

    string helloMessage;
    address public owner;

    function HelloWorld () public {
        helloMessage = "Hello, World!";
        owner = msg.sender;
    }

    function updateMessage (string _new_msg) public {
        helloMessage = _new_msg;
    }

    function sayHello () public view returns (string) {
        return helloMessage;
    }

    function kill() public {
        if (msg.sender == owner) selfdestruct(owner);
    }
}
```

The "Hello, World!" smart contract has two key functions.

- The `sayHello()` function returns a greeting to its caller. The greeting is initially set to "Hello, World!" when the smart contract is deployed. It is a view method indicating that it does not change the state of the smart contract and hence can be executed locally on any Ethereum node without gas fees.

- The `updateMessage()` function allows the method caller to change the greeting from "Hello, World!" to another message.

The "Hello, World!" smart contract maintains an internal state (`helloMessage`) that can be modified by the public function `updateMessage()`. The key feature of blockchain technology is that each function call is executed by all nodes on the network, and any change to the helloMessage state must be agreed upon by at least the majority of validators or miners on the network before it can be recorded on the blockchain. In turn, every change of the `helloMessage` state is recorded in the blockchain. Any interested party can review the blocks and find out all recorded change histories for `helloMessage`. That level of transparency ensures that the smart contract cannot be tampered with.

It is important to note that the `sayHello()` function can be executed on any Ethereum node the caller has access to. It looks up information from the blockchain and does not change the blockchain state. It affects no other nodes in the network. Hence, the Ethereum blockchain does not require a gas fee for view function calls like `sayHello()`.

On the other hand, the `updateMessage()` function causes state changes across all nodes in the Ethereum network. It can take effect only when nodes on the blockchain all execute it and reach consensus on the results. Hence, the `updateMessage()` function call requires a gas fee. The results of the `updateMessage()` function call also takes a rather long time (up to ten minutes on Ethereum) to take effect since the blocks containing the results need to be confirmed and added to the blockchain by miner nodes.

Learning Smart Contract Programming

This book does not intend to be a Solidity tutorial. Solidity is a JavaScript-like language. It is also unique and different from JavaScript in many important ways. Details of the Solidity syntax are ever-evolving and outside the scope of this book. I encourage you to learn the Solidity language from its official documentation at https://solidity.readthedocs.io/.

However, it is important to understand the high-level design features of Solidity as they are generally applicable to all smart contract languages. Understanding the design will give you a head start on learning Solidity as its quirkiness will now make sense.

Consensus vs. Nonconsensus Code

As you have seen from the "Hello, World!" smart contract's `sayHello()` and `updateMessage()` functions, there are clearly two types of code in a smart contract.

- One type of code, like the `updateMessage()` function, requires consensus. These functions must be precise and produce deterministic behaviors (i.e., no random numbers or floating-point numbers) since all nodes must produce the same results. They are also slow, require long confirmation time, and are expensive to execute both in terms of computing resources (all nodes must run them) and in gas fees.

- The other type of code, like the `sayHello()` function, does not require consensus. These functions can be executed by a local node and hence do not require gas. It is not a problem even if different nodes return different results from the same function (i.e., precision loss for floating-point numbers).

In Solidity variables have the reference types `memory` and `storage` to indicate whether the values should be saved on the blockchain. Functions that do not modify the blockchain state (nonconsensus) should be labeled as view functions. Functions that do not even read the blockchain state (purely computational) should be labeled as pure functions.

It is clear that the virtual machine can provide many more functionalities and performance optimizations for nonconsensus code. However, the current design of the Solidity language is dominated by the need of consensus code. As a result, it lacks many basic features that could be easily provided for the nonconsensus part of the system, such as a string library, JSON parser, complex data structure support, and so on.

I view this as a flaw of Solidity. In the future Ethereum 2.0, the WebAssembly-based new virtual machines (including the Second State Virtual Machine) could solve this problem by supporting multiple commonly used programming languages for nonconsensus code. That would make the blockchain truly a computing platform rather than just a decentralized state machine.

Data Structures

Besides the primitive types, such as `int`, `uint`, and `address`, the Solidity language supports the `array` data type. In fact, the `string` data type is internally implemented as an array. However, the array type is also difficult to work with. For example, the computational cost for iterating over an array depends on the size of the array. It could be expensive and is difficult to estimate before the function execution. That is why Solidity supports only limited string operations out of the box.

For structured data, I recommend using the `struct` data type to group multiple related data fields. For collections, I recommend using the `mapping` data type to build key/value stores. The mapping structure has the advantage of fixed computational cost for adding, removing, or looking up elements from the collection.

Function Parameters and Return Values

While `struct` and `mapping` are widely used inside smart contracts, you can pass only primitive types into and out of contract functions. The contract function's input and return values are both tuples of limited length. Ethereum extension (as well as EVM 2.0) projects are working on different ways to relax such constraints, especially for nonconsensus view functions.

For now, to pass complex data objects to a function, you could encode the data into a string format (e.g., a CSV) and then parse the string inside the contract. However, because of the lack of high-performance string libraries in Solidity, this is also difficult and gas expensive.

Payable Functions

One of the unique features of a smart contract language is functions that can receive payments. In Solidity, you can label any contract function as `payable`. A `payable` function automatically requires consensus. It can be invoked only via a transaction that gets recorded in the blockchain. The caller can attach an ETH `value` to the transaction. The ETHs will be transferred from the caller's address to the contract address upon execution of this function.

The contract can also have a default `payable` function. It is called when an address makes a regular ETH transfer to the contract address without making an explicit function call.

The contract can access its own fund through the `this.balance()` function and transfer funds to other addresses through the `<address>.transfer(amount)` function.

Calling Other Contracts

A contract function can call functions in another contract deployed at a different address. The caller contract needs to know the callee contract's ABI and address.

This feature allows us to build proxy contracts, where function implementations can be changed or upgraded because we can update the proxy to point to different implementing contracts. Some well-known smart contracts, such as the GUSD contract, are written this way.

In this section, I discussed some unique design features of the Solidity language, compared with traditional programming languages. It should get you started on learning Solidity. As a first-generation smart contract programming language, Solidity has many shortcomings, especially with regard to nonconsensus functions and programs. Ethereum extensions such as the Lity project are working on better solutions (see Chapter 14).

Building and Deploying the Smart Contract

In this section, I will use the "Hello, World!" contract as an example to show how to build and deploy an Ethereum smart contract. Let's start with the standard Solidity tools.

Solidity Tools

While you can install and use a JavaScript version of the Solidity compiler, I recommend you install the fully featured C++ version. You can do it easily with Linux distributions' package managers. Here is how to do it using the `apt-get` package manager on Ubuntu:

```
$ sudo add-apt-repository ppa:ethereum/ethereum
$ sudo apt-get update
$ sudo apt-get install solc
```

The `solc` command takes a Solidity source file as input and outputs the compiled bytecode as well as the ABI definition as a JSON string.

```
$ solc HelloWorld.sol
```

The output from the command is a large JSON structure that gives information about compiler errors and results. You can find the following under the HelloWorld contract:

- The compiled EVM bytecode as a hex string in the `evm/bytecode/object field`
- The associated ABI definition in the `abi` field
- The recommended gas costs in the `gasEstimates` field

Next, you can deploy this contract from GETH and obtain an address on the blockchain for the deployed contract instance. You can run the following command in the GETH console attached to an Ethereum blockchain network or the TestRPC:

```
> var owner = "0xMYADDR"
> var abi = ...
> var bytecode = ...
> var gas = ...
> personal.unlockAccount(owner)
... ...
> var helloContract = eth.contract(abi)
> var hello = helloContract.new(owner, {from:owner, data:bytecode, gas:gas})
```

Once the contract is mined and recorded on the blockchain, you should be able to query for its address.

```
> hello.address
"0xabcdCONTRACTADDRESS"
```

You need to record and save the ABI and contract address. As you have seen, those two pieces of information are needed when you retrieve this contract instance later in another program.

The BUIDL Integrated Development Environment (IDE)

While the command-line compiler tool is fundamental to Solidity smart contract development, many developers prefer to use graphical user interface (GUI) tools for a more visual development experience. The BUIDL IDE is by far the easiest GUI tool to compile and deploy Solidity smart contracts.

First, you need to configure BUIDL to work with Ethereum blockchains via the **Providers** tab (see Figure 6.1). Then, send a small amount of ETH (e.g., 0.1 ETH) to the default address on the **Accounts** tab so that BUIDL can pay gas fees to Ethereum on your behalf. See more details in Chapter 4.

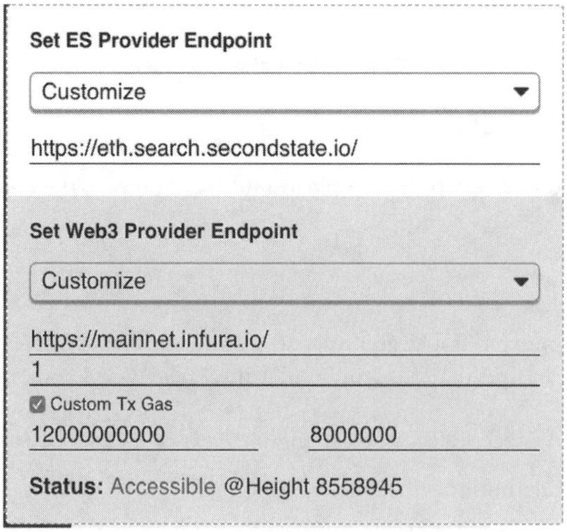

Figure 6.1   Configuring BUIDL to work with Ethereum

Next, type your Solidity code into the editor in the contract section, and hit the **Compile** button. You will be able to see the compiled ABI and bytecode in the side panel (see Figure 6.2).

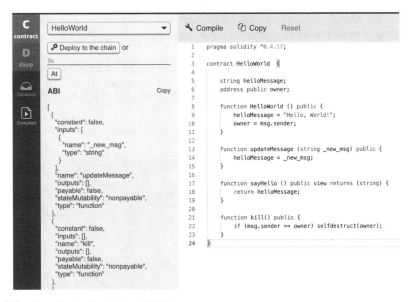

Figure 6.2   Compiled artifacts from BUIDL

Of course, you can also copy the ABI and bytecode and paste them into your other tools to use.

The Remix IDE

Remix is a web-based IDE for Solidity smart contracts from the Ethereum Foundation. You can access it in your web browser: http://remix.ethereum.org/.

You can simply enter Solidity source code into the text box, and the IDE will compile it for you. The compiler output is shown by clicking the **Details** button next to the contract name (Figure 6.3).

Figure 6.3   The Remix IDE compiles a Solidity smart contract.

As you can see in Figure 6.4, the IDE provides the ABI and bytecode results from the compiler, as well as a GETH script to deploy the contract for your convenience.

BYTECODE 🔲 ❷

```
{
    "linkReferences": {},
    "object": "6060604052341561000f57600080fd5b604080519081016040528060d81526020017f48(
    "opcodes": "PUSH1 0x60 PUSH1 0x40 MSTORE CALLVALUE ISZERO PUSH2 0xF JUMPI PUSH1 0x0
    "sourceMap": "28:488:0:-;;;113:108;;;;;;;;;154:30;;;;;;;;;;;;;;;;;;;:12;:30;;;;;;;;;;
}
```

ABI 🔲 ❷

▸ 0:
▸ 1:
▸ 2:
▸ 3:
▸ 4:

WEB3DEPLOY 🔲 ❷

```
var helloworldContract = web3.eth.contract([{"constant":false,"inputs":[{"name":"_new_m
var helloworld = helloworldContract.new(
    {
      from: web3.eth.accounts[0],
      data: '0x6060604052341561000f57600080fd5b604080519081016040528060d81526020017f4486
      gas: '4700000'
    }, function (e, contract){
    console.log(e, contract);
    if (typeof contract.address !== 'undefined') {
        console.log('Contract mined! address: ' + contract.address + ' transactionHash
    }
})
```

Figure 6.4   Clicking the Details button shows the ABI, bytecode, and a deployment script for the smart contract.

Truffle Framework

The Truffle Framework significantly streamlines and simplifies the process of building and deploying smart contracts. We recommend it for complex smart contracts as well as for automated building and testing in professional software development settings.

The Truffle framework builds on the node.js framework. So, you should first make sure that node.js and its package manager, npm, are installed on your machine. You can install them at https://www.npmjs.com/get-npm. On most Linux distributions, you can use the system package manager to install them as well. For example, the following command installs node.js and npm on a CentOS/RedHat/Fedora Linux system:

```
$ sudo yum install epel-release
$ sudo yum install nodejs npm
```

Next, let's install the Truffle framework using the npm package manager.

```
$ sudo npm install -g truffle
```

Next, you can create a basic project structure using the truffle command.

```
$ mkdir HelloWorld
$ cd HelloWorld
$ truffle init
$ ls
contracts        test             truffle.js
migrations       truffle-config.js
```

Now you can create a HelloWorld.sol file in the HelloWorld/contracts directory. The file content was listed earlier in this chapter, and you can also get it from the sample project on GitHub. In addition, create a migrations/2_deploy_contracts.js file to indicate that the HelloWorld contract needs to be deployed by Truffle. The content of the 2_deploy_contracts.js file is as follows:

```
var HelloWorld = artifacts.require("./HelloWorld.sol");

module.exports = function(deployer) {
  deployer.deploy(HelloWorld);
};
```

You will also need to update the truffle.js file, which configures the deployment targets. The following truffle.js example has two targets: one for the TestRPC on the localhost, and one for an Ethereum testnet node on the local network.

```
module.exports = {

  networks: {
    development: {
      host: "localhost",
      port: 8545,
      network_id: "*" // Match any network id
    },
    testnet: {
      host: "node.ip.addr",
      port: 8545,
      network_id: 3, // Ropsten,
      from: "0x3d113a96a3c88dd48d6c34b3c805309cdd77b543",
      gas: 4000000,
      gasPrice: 20000000000
    }
  }
};
```

To compile and build the smart contract, you can use the following command:

```
$ truffle compile
Compiling ./contracts/HelloWorld.sol...
Compiling ./contracts/Migrations.sol...
Writing artifacts to ./build/contracts
```

The previously mentioned contract ABI, when constructing a contract object from the blockchain address, is a JSON object in the `build/contracts/HelloWorld.json` file.

```
{
  "contractName": "HelloWorld",
  "abi": [
    ... ...
  ],
  ... ...
}
```

Finally, you have two deployment options. The first option is to deploy to the TestRPC. You must have the TestRPC running on the same machine. Run the following command to deploy the `HelloWorld` contract to the TestRPC:

```
$ truffle migrate --network development

Using network 'development'.

Running migration: 1_initial_migration.js
  Deploying Migrations...
  ... 0x22cbcdd77c162a7d72624ddc52fd83aea7bc091548f30fcc13d745c65eab0a74
  Migrations: 0x321a5a4ee365a778082815b6048f8a35d4f44d7b
Saving successful migration to network...
  ... 0xcb2b363e308a22732bd35c328c36d2fbf36e025a06ca6e055790c80efae8df13
Saving artifacts...
Running migration: 2_deploy_contracts.js
  Deploying HelloWorld...
  ... 0xb332aee5093195519fa3871276cb6079b50e51308ce0d63b58e73fb5331016fc
  HelloWorld: 0x4788fdecd41530f5e2932ac622e8cffe3247caa9
Saving successful migration to network...
  ... 0x8297d06a8112a1fd64b2401f7009d923caa553516a376cd4bf818c1414faf9f9
Saving artifacts...
```

The second option is to deploy to a live Ethereum blockchain network. However, since this costs gas, you will need to unlock an account with an ETH balance first. You can use GETH attached to the testnet node to do this. The unlocked address is the one specified in the `testnet/from` field in the `truffle.js` file. Please see Chapter 5 to review GETH account unlocking commands.

```
$ ./geth attach http://node.ip.addr:8545 (http://172.33.0.218:8545/)
Welcome to the Geth JavaScript console!
```

```
modules: eth:1.0 miner:1.0 net:1.0 personal:1.0 rpc:1.0
> personal.unlockAccount("0x3d113a96a3c88dd48d6c34b3c805309cdd77b543", "pass");
true
```

Then deploy to the testnet using `truffle`.

```
$ truffle migrate --network testnet

Using network 'testnet'.

Running migration: 1_initial_migration.js
  Deploying Migrations...
  ... 0x958a7303711fbae57594959458333b4c6fb536c66ff392686ca8b70039df7570
  Migrations: 0x7dab4531f0d12291f8941f84ef9946fbae0a487b
Saving successful migration to network...
  ... 0x0f26814aa69b42e2d72731651cc2cdd72fca32c19f82073a76461b76265e564a
Saving artifacts...
Running migration: 2_deploy_contracts.js
  Deploying HelloWorld...
  ... 0xc97646bcd00f7a3d1745c4256b334cdca8ff965095f11645144fcf1ec002afc6
  HelloWorld: 0x8bc27c8129eea739362d786ca0754b5062857e9c
Saving successful migration to network...
  ... 0xf077c1158a8cc1530af98b960d90ebb3888aa6674e0bcb62d0c7d4487707c841
Saving artifacts...
```

Finally, you can verify the contract deployed on the live network at this address:
https://ropsten.etherscan.io/address/0x8bc27c8129eea739362d786ca0754b5062857e9c

Calling Smart Contract Functions

Now that you have deployed the "Hello, World!" smart contract on the blockchain, you should be able to interact with it and call its public functions.

The BUIDL IDE

Once you have configured the BUIDL IDE to work with the Ethereum blockchain and have hit the **Compile** button to compile your Solidity smart contract, you are ready to deploy it.

Hit the **Deploy to the chain** button (see Figure 6.5) to deploy the smart contract onto the Ethereum blockchain. The deployed contracts are available on the Deployed tab. You can click to open any of them and interact with the public functions directly from inside BUIDL.

The Remix IDE

As I showed in Chapter 4, the Remix IDE can build a UI for a smart contract given the ABI and contract address. All public functions of the contract are listed in the UI. Functions that result in blockchain state changes (e.g., require gas to operate) are labeled as red buttons (Figure 6.6).

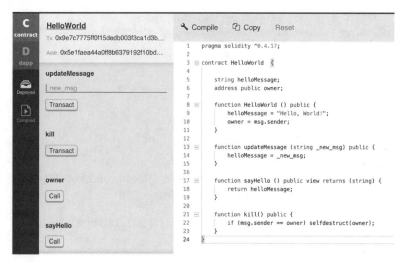

Figure 6.5   Calling functions on a deployed Ethereum smart contract

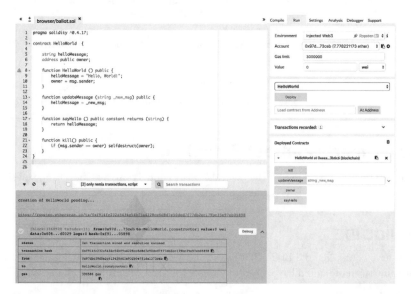

Figure 6.6   A smart contract UI built by Remix

Functions that do not result in state changes (i.e., view methods) are labeled as blue buttons. You can pass call parameters to functions in the input boxes next to each button.

The Remix UI is convenient, but it cannot be automated and hides details of the transactions. To fully understand how smart contracts are executed on the blockchain, I recommend you interact with the functions directly on a blockchain node. In the case of Ethereum, it is a node running GETH connected to the mainnet or testnet.

> **Note**
>
> As shown in Chapter 4, you can use the web3.js JavaScript library to build applications that work in tandem with the Metamask wallet to call smart contract methods. But web3.js does not help you with interactive development and debugging of the smart contract itself.

GETH Console

GETH is a GO language-based client for Ethereum. You can run GETH in a mode that attaches itself to an Ethereum node (or the TestRPC for local testing). See Chapter 5 for how to run an Ethereum node yourself using GETH.

```
$ geth attach http://node.ip.addr:8545
```

In the console, you can now create an instance of the contract via the `eth.contract().at()` method. You need two pieces of information. Both of them come from the tool you use to build and deploy your smart contract to the blockchain, which I will cover in the next section.

- The JSON parameter to the `contract()` method is known as the ABI. When you build the smart contract, the compiler outputs the ABI. In the case of the Truffle framework, the ABI is located in the `build/contracts/HelloWorld.json` file's abi JSON field, with all line breaks removed.

- The `at()` method parameter is the address to this specific instance of the smart contract. That is, you can deploy the same smart contract class multiple times, and each time the Ethereum blockchain will create a unique address for it.

```
> var abi = [ { "constant": false, "inputs": [ { "name": "_new_msg",
"type": "string" } ], "name": "updateMessage", "outputs": [], "payable":
false, "stateMutability": "nonpayable", "type": "function" },
{ "constant": false, "inputs": [], "name": "kill", "outputs": [],
"payable": false, "stateMutability": "nonpayable", "type": "function" },
{ "constant": true, "inputs": [], "name": "owner", "outputs": [ { "name":
"", "type": "address" } ], "payable": false, "stateMutability": "view",
"type": "function" }, { "constant": true, "inputs": [], "name":
"sayHello", "outputs": [ { "name": "", "type": "string" } ], "payable":
false, "stateMutability": "view", "type": "function" }, { "inputs": [],
"payable": false, "stateMutability": "nonpayable", "type":
"constructor" } ]
> var helloContract = eth.contract(abi)
> var hello = helloContract.at("0x59a173...10c");
```

The `sayHello()` method on the contract instance does not change the blockchain state. So, it is "free" and immediately executed by the node connected to our GETH console.

```
> hello.sayHello()
"Hello, World!"
```

.

The `updateMessage()` method, on the other hand, changes the contract's internal state on the blockchain. It must be executed by all the miners and gets recorded on the blockchain once most miners reach consensus. Because of that, it's execution requires gas (in ETH) to pay the miners for their effort. The gas is provided by an account specified on the method call.

If your GETH console is connected to the TestRPC, you should already have unlocked accounts. But if you are connected to a real Ethereum node, you can use the following command in the GETH console to create a new Ethereum account and then send ETH to this account from one of your wallets:

```
> personal.newAccount("passphrase")
```

Next, the account must be unlocked so that we can "spend" its ETH as gas.

```
> personal.unlockAccount("0xd5cb83f0f83af60268e927e1dbb3aeaddc86f886")

Unlock account 0xd5cb83f0f83af60268e927e1dbb3aeaddc86f886
Passphrase:true
... ...

> hello.updateMessage("Welcome to Blockchain", {from:
"0xd5cb83f0f83af60268e927e1dbb3aeaddc86f886"})
"0x32761c528f426993ba980fdd212f929857a8bd392c98896a4e4a898077223c07"
> hello.sayHello()
"Welcome to Blockchain"
>
```

While the gas fee is small, it is necessary. If your account specified in the method call has zero balance and cannot pay gas, the function call will fail. The changed state of the contract will be finalized across all blockchain nodes when the transaction is confirmed by the miners. The confirmation could take several minutes on the Ethereum blockchain, degrading the user experience. On Ethereum-compatible blockchains like CyberMiles, the confirmation time could be as fast as seconds. That is a compelling reason to develop and deploy Ethereum applications on alternative compatible blockchains (learn more in Appendix A).

A New Language

While the Solidity language is currently the most widely used programming language for Ethereum smart contract development, it is also hard to use and has many design flaws. Specifically, it lacks safeguards and logical separations commonly available in modern programming languages. It is easy to make human errors in Solidity.

In fact, a large-scale code audit has revealed about 100 obvious bugs for every 1,000 lines of Solidity code. That is astonishingly high as most Solidity code is for smart contracts that actually manage financial assets. In contrast, nonfinancial business software typically contains 10 bugs per 1,000 lines of code.

To address Solidity's problems, the Ethereum community is developing a new experimental language for smart contract programming called Vyper. It is designed for human readability and auditability. It removes some confusing features from Solidity and should produce safer smart contracts with fewer bugs.

While Vyper is in early beta and the design is still changing, it is possibly the future of Ethereum development. In this section, I will show how to rewrite the Solidity "Hello, World!" example in Vyper and how to deploy it. The following is the Vyper code for the smart contract. You will notice that the Vyper smart contract is similar to the Python language. The filename is `HelloWorld.v.py`. The filename suffix is `.py` to allow development tools to highlight its syntax using Python rules. If that is a concern, you can also use the `.vy` suffix.

```
#State variables
helloMessage: public(bytes32)
owner: public(address)

@public
def __init__(_message: bytes32):
    self.helloMessage = _message
    self.owner = msg.sender

@public
def updateMessage(newMsg: bytes32):
    self.helloMessage = newMsg

@public
@constant
def sayHello() -> bytes32:
    return self.helloMessage

@public
def kill():
    if msg.sender == self.owner:
        selfdestruct(self.owner)
```

To install the Vyper compiler, you will need Python 3.6 or newer. Since Vyper is still an evolving technology, the official documentation suggests building from the source. You can find the latest instructions at https://vyper.readthedocs.io/en/latest/installing-vyper.html.

Once you have the Vyper application installed, you can run it as any other compiler. The following command will output the hex string of the compiled bytecode of the contract:

```
$ vyper HelloWorld.v.py
```

The following command will output the JSON string of the ABI for the contract:

```
$ vyper -f json HelloWorld.v.py
```

With both the bytecode and ABI, you can use GETH to deploy the smart contract to Ethereum or the TestRPC.

```
> var owner = "0xMYADDR"
> var abi = ...
> var bytecode = ...
> var gas = ...
```

```
> personal.unlockAccount(owner)
... ...
> var helloContract = eth.contract(abi)
> var hello = helloContract.new(owner, {from:owner, data:bytecode, gas:gas})
```

Now, similar to Remix, there is also an online compiler for Vyper contracts: https://vyper.online/ (Figure 6.7). You can type in your Vyper source code and let the web application compile it into bytecode (Figure 6.8) and ABI (Figure 6.9).

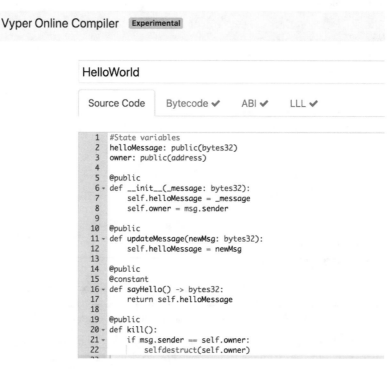

Figure 6.7   A web-based Vyper compiler, vyper.online

Figure 6.8   The compiled bytecode from vyper.online

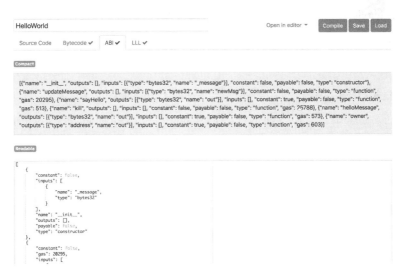

Figure 6.9   The ABI interface generated by vyper.online

More Smart Contract Languages

While the Vyper language is similar to Python, it cannot be called Python since it removes some important features from the Python language to make its programs deterministic. All blockchain node computers must produce the same result when executing the smart contract code in order to reach consensus. Therefore, no general-purpose computer programming language can be used directly for smart contract programming. The language must be modified to produce entirely deterministic behavior.

The new generations of blockchain virtual machines are leveraging state-of-the-art virtual machine technologies such as the WebAssembly (Wasm) virtual machine. For example, the next Ethereum Virtual Machine will be based on WebAssembly and called Ethereum Flavored WebAssembly (eWASM). Another large public blockchain, EOS, already has a WebAssembly-based virtual machine.

Those new-generation virtual machines are commonly based on the LLVM technology that supports optimization across the entire application lifecycle from compile time to link time to runtime. LLVM uses an intermediate representation (IR) code format between the application source code and machine bytecode to support a "language-agnostic" compiler infrastructure. The IR allows the virtual machine to support multiple source code programming languages on the front end. Indeed, LLVM already supports 20+ programming languages. Solidity and Vyper are also evolving to become compatible with the LLVM IR. For example, the open source SOLL project is developing an LLVM-based Solidity compiler for the next generation of blockchain virtual machines. See https://github.com/second-state/soll.

However, because of the unique constraints of smart contract programming, it is impossible to expect mainstream programming languages to be fully supported on blockchain virtual machines. When EOS says that its smart contract programming language is C++, it means a modified version of C++ that produces deterministic programs. It will be a major effort to modify and reform mainstream programming languages to support smart contract programming. So, in the near future, I think Solidity will continue to be the dominant smart contract programming language.

Conclusion

In this chapter, I explained what a smart contract is, how to program it, and how to interact with it. I covered both the Solidity language and the upcoming Vyper language for smart contract programming. Using open source tools, we explored different options to test and deploy the smart contract onto Ethereum blockchain networks. Of course, Solidity and Vyper still have their limitations. I will cover an alternative programming language called Lity, which is fully backward compatible with Solidity but attempts to address some of the most glaring problems, in Chapter 14.

7

Decentralized Applications (Dapps)

In the previous chapter, we discussed the concept of smart contracts and how to interact with them on the Ethereum blockchain. However, tools like GETH, Truffle, and even Remix and Metamask are geared toward developers or expert users. For regular users to access blockchain applications, there is still much work around the user interface (UI), user experience (UX), and supporting infrastructure.

The Internet took off when the user experience of web applications started to match client-server applications on closed networks. Only after that point did the open and decentralized advantages of the Internet start to matter. The Internet excels at enabling open ecosystems that orchestrate multiple data and service providers. But such ecosystems are useful only when the users are willing to use web applications. Similarly, decentralized and autonomous smart contracts can be mass adopted only when the application user experience is on par with regular web applications. Enter *dapps*.

The purpose of a decentralized application is to provide UIs for smart contracts and other blockchain functionalities. Ideally, a dapp is a rich client application downloaded onto the user's device. It ties together multiple back-end services, including the blockchain service. A dapp is typically a JavaScript application that can be downloaded from any web server (i.e., there is no central server that can be shut down) and relies on the decentralized blockchain for its data and logic functionalities.

In this chapter, I discuss architectural design and best practices for blockchain dapps through some notable success stories.

> **Note**
>
> Dapp development on Ethereum is a chore. It requires you to set up Metamask, Remix, web3, a web server, maybe even an Ethereum node, and a flurry of infrastructure tools just to write the first line of code. And the standard Ethereum dapp is not going to work on mobile devices out of the box.

> On the other hand, BUIDL is a complete dapp development environment that requires almost no setup. BUIDL applications can be published to the Web and accessed from mobile devices. Learn more about BUIDL in Chapter 3 and Chapter 4.

Dapp Stack

Once we have built and tested the smart contracts, it is time to build the dapp UI for users to interact with the smart contracts. The idea here is that unlike a web application that depends on a central server for logic and data, a dapp can save user data locally and utilize multiple back-end services, including the blockchain service, to achieve decentralization (Figure 7.1).

The dapp typically runs in the user's device as a client-side JavaScript application. Its primary function is to provide a user interface. It interacts with the blockchain smart contracts for core data and application logic. It could also interact with other public or even local services to store and manage off-chain data. The most important difference between a dapp's off-chain data and a regular web app's central server is that the dapp's server data can be replicated and replaced when needed. There is no single point of failure in a dapp infrastructure.

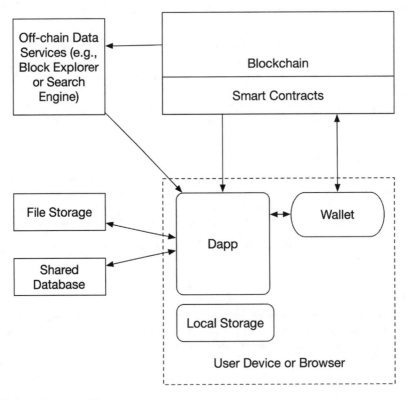

Figure 7.1   The dapp architecture

For example, the dapp can utilize the device's HTML5 local storage API to store data specific to users on this device.

You can write a dapp in any client-side JavaScript framework. Popular examples include jQuery and ReactJS. In the Truffle project, you can find templates (https://truffleframework.com/boxes) for creating dapps for popular JavaScript frameworks.

The web3 Library

The JavaScript application connects to the blockchain services via a library called web3.js (https://github.com/ethereum/web3.js/). Currently, web3.js supports only the Ethereum blockchain, and it has not reached version 1.0. Yet it is already by far the most popular library to connect dapps to blockchain services. The web3 library provides the following features:

- Send or transfer fund from one address to another
- Deploy smart contracts
- Call public functions on deployed smart contracts
- Estimate the gas fee for contract function calls
- Query a contract or address status

The web3.js library requires a private key to sign transactions it sends to the blockchain. As you have seen, blockchain account private keys are stored and managed by wallet applications; the web3.js library should be used in junction with a compatible wallet application. The wallet is also known as a *web3 provider*. It is up to the dapp JavaScript code to detect the availability and validity of a web3 provider. Metamask is a web3 provider for Ethereum. The "Hello, World!" web application from Chapter 4 is an example of a web3 dapp that works in tandem with Metamask.

> ### Note
>
> In addition to the more popular web3.js, the ethereumJS library (https://ethereumjs.github.io/) can sign Ethereum transactions without a wallet application. However, to do so, the JavaScript code must have access to the account private key. It provides a JavaScript library (https://github.com/ethereumjs/ethereumjs-wallet) to implement your own embedded wallet inside the dapp.

> ### Note
>
> Cross-blockchain applications like Scatter (https://get-scatter.com/) act like wallets but are designed to run dapps.

External Services

As I have described, dapps store only core logic and data on blockchain smart contracts. It is too slow and too expensive to store large amounts of data on the blockchain. Most applications also require media files, databases, and other off-chain data to function. The dapp could use online services to store and manage data. Here are some examples:

- The IPFS (https://ipfs.io/) is a blockchain-based media file storage and exchange service protocol. Dapps can store large user files on IPFS and make them accessible everywhere.

- Swarm (https://ethersphere.github.io/swarm-home/) is a file storage and sharing solution built on top of Ethereum.

- GitHub (https://github.com/), Dropbox (https://www.dropbox.com/), or Google Drive (https://www.google.com/drive/) are examples of traditional Internet file storage and sharing services that can be accessible by individual dapp users. You can use GitHub or Dropbox web sites to serve dapp JavaScript files directly from an individual user's accounts.

- Database as a service (DBaaS) providers such as Microsoft Azure SQL (https://azure.microsoft.com/en-us/services/sql-database/), AWS Relational Database Service (https://aws.amazon.com/rds/), Google BigQuery (https://cloud.google.com/bigquery/), and MongoDB Atlas (https://www.mongodb.com/cloud/atlas) are examples of database services that can be utilized by dapps to store application data.

- An off-chain data service is a query interface to search and browse blockchain data, such as transactions, accounts, and smart contract function calls. It is potentially much more powerful, versatile, and scalable than calling the view functions to get smart contract data. This approach is discussed in more detail in Chapter 10.

A common design practice to ensure the safety and validity of off-chain data is to store the data's hash in on-chain smart contracts.

A dapp is more complex than most web applications. From the start, you need to design which part of the application is based on blockchain smart contracts, which part utilizes off-chain server-side data, and which part is the client-side UI. Each of those elements requires its own software stack to function and communicate with the rest of the application.

Dapp Showcases

Because of Ethereum's slow confirmation time (up to ten seconds) and high gas fees for executing smart contract functions, successful Ethereum dapps so far are all financial applications that do not require frequent user interactions.

Uniswap

One of the most polished Ethereum dapps is the Uniswap exchange. It is a decentralized crypto token exchange. The idea is that some people will make initial contributions to a liquidity pool (as market makers) and earn a share of the trading fees. All other traders will trade against the liquidity pool based on a simple pricing formula of supply and demand. If a token becomes scarce in the liquidity pool, its price against the ETH will increase, incentivizing holders to sell it back to the liquidity pool. This mechanism allows trading to happen in a completely automated manner without matching for counter parties. The entire Uniswap system is a set of smart contracts on the Ethereum blockchain. The application state is completely stored in and managed by the contracts.

The Uniswap project has developed a polished UI (Figure 7.2) to interact with its underlying smart contracts. The UI is completely written in web3 JavaScript and is fully internationalized. Through the dapp UI, novice users can contribute to the liquidity pool and earn fees for their crypto deposits or can immediately start trading pairs of ERC20 tokens.

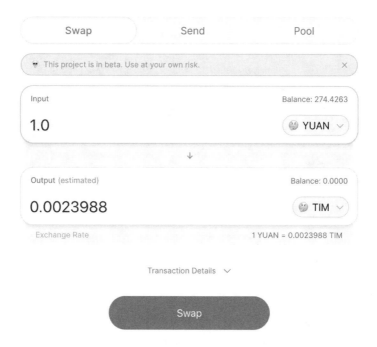

Figure 7.2   The Uniswap UI

The interesting aspect of the Uniswap dapp is that it is truly decentralized. All the application logic and its data are stored on the Ethereum blockchain. Anyone can create a web site to host the JavaScript dapp, and all those copies of dapps will behave the same way as they all get their logic and data from the blockchain. In Uniswap, Ethereum has truly become a "computer" back end.

CryptoKitties

The CryptoKitties game took over Ethereum by storm in late 2017. It gave rise to the idea of crypto collectibles and nonfungible tokens, which later become the ERC721 specification.

CryptoKitties are unique digital entities that exist on the Ethereum blockchain. They are data in smart contracts. Their uniqueness is guaranteed by the contract code. Each CryptoKittie has an associated owner address. CryptoKitties can then by bought, sold, and traded on the blockchain.

The interesting thing about CryptoKitties is that they are visually appealing (Figure 7.3). The dapp UI design visualizes the unique features of each digital entity. That contributed significantly to CryptoKitties' success.

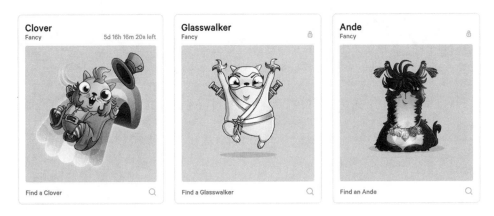

Figure 7.3   CryptoKitties

Gambling Games

Gambling games are popular dapps. They are great use cases for smart contracts, with transparent rules and betting pools. They also benefit greatly from largely unregulated cryptocurrencies.

However, gambling games are often interactive in nature, requiring users to bet often in response to other people's real-time bets. Ethereum's slow confirmation time represents a great barrier for this type of game. Faster blockchains such as EOS and Tron, which is itself a fork from Ethereum, are now blockchains specialized in gambling dapps.

Interactive Dapps

Most Internet applications are interactive. For Ethereum blockchains to support interactive applications, performance is an important factor. The Lity project creates high-performance extensions to the Ethereum protocol and tools. It enables us to create interesting interactive dapps. See Chapter 16 for several complete examples.

Conclusion

A dapp is typically a web3 application that runs in tandem with a wallet application. It interacts with smart contracts on the blockchain for essential data and core application logic. It can also use local storage or third-party services to store and manage nonessential data that is private to the user or could be regenerated by the public. In the next chapter, I will discuss how applications use blockchain data services, in addition to blockchain transactions, to provide a rich user experience.

8

Alternatives to Dapps

The concept of dapps is compelling and native to blockchain technology's most obvious use cases, such as peer-to-peer financing. However, the world is never binary. There are also many blockchain application use cases that could fit into the model of traditional web applications. Those are typically use cases where the public or consortium blockchain's transparency and immutability can add value to an existing business. The application only needs the blockchain as a feature and does not need to decentralize the entire application itself. A payment processor for e-commerce web sites to accept cryptocurrencies is a good example. A crypto asset exchange (crypto to crypto or crypto to fiat) is another example.

For those applications, we need to make blockchain transactions and/or make smart contract function calls from a server. To do that, the accounts' private keys or keystores and passwords must be managed on the server side.

- For new transactions, it is obvious since the sender account needs to use its private key to authenticate the funds transferring out of it.

- For modifying contract states, an Ethereum-compatible blockchain requires the party requesting the change to pay a "gas fee" for network maintainers (miners) to validate the request and record the change in new blocks. That also requires transferring funds (a gas fee) out of the requestor's account and hence requires its private key.

In this chapter, we explore how to access Ethereum-compatible blockchain functionalities from a web app. The basic approach is to use a web3-compatible library but without a client-side wallet like Metamask.

JavaScript

The node.js framework enables JavaScript applications to be deployed on the server side. It is hence conceivable to use the web3.js library (or the compatible web3-cmt.js library) in a node.js server application.

The Full-Node Wallet

The first approach is to use a fully synchronized Ethereum node as the "wallet" for the application. The GETH (Ethereum) or Travis (CyberMiles) software running the node is able to manage keystores (i.e., the web3.personal package), sign transactions, and broadcast transactions to other blockchain nodes. Through the blockchain node's Remote Procedure Call (RPC) interface, external applications can interact with the blockchain.

You will need to synchronize a full Ethereum (or Ethereum-compatible blockchain, such as CyberMiles) node behind a firewall. The node should turn on RPC services (i.e., the Ethereum default port 8545) so that the server-side web application can access it behind the firewall. It is important that the node's port 8545 be completely blocked by the firewall and available only inside the firewall, as illustrated in Figure 8.1.

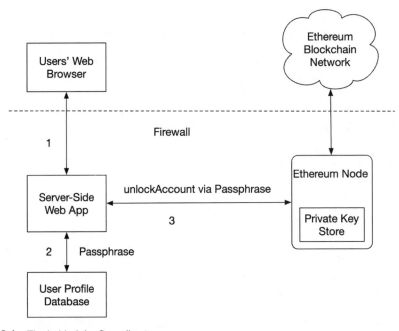

Figure 8.1   The behind-the-firewall setup

The following code example shows how to call the HelloWorld contract's `updateMessage()` function (see Chapter 4) to record a new state in helloMessage onto the blockchain and pay its gas fees. We assume that the web3.js instance on the node.js server is attached to an Ethereum node that already has the keystore containing an account private key. The account has a sufficient balance to pay the gas fee for this transaction. You just need to unlock the account using its passphrase.

```
web3 = new Web3(new Web3.providers.HttpProvider(
            "http://node.ip.addr:8545"));
web3.personal.unlockAccount("...", pass);
hello.updateMessage(new_mesg);
```

Of course, storing the keystores on the node is still insecure. A single misconfigured firewall setting might expose the node's port 8545 to attackers. Attackers could easily gain access to all private keys on the server as they are unlocked by the web application.

Raw Transactions

The second approach is to create signed raw transactions and then simply use web3.js to broadcast the transaction onto a blockchain node. In this setup, the blockchain node could be a third-party hosted node outside of the firewall, such as an Infura node. The blockchain node does not store any private key or keystore. The web application itself, however, manages the private keys it needs in a database table. Figure 8.2 illustrates the architecture of this design.

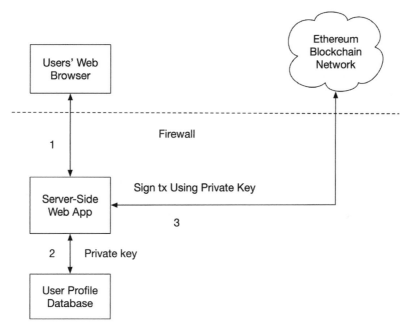

Figure 8.2 Application-managed private keys

Signing raw transactions is beyond the scope of web3.js. We use the EthereumJS library here to work in conjunction with web3.js. In particular, the `ethereumjs-tx` project provides ways to sign transactions using private keys. The private keys are typically stored in database tables in this case.

The following code shows how to deploy the HelloWorld smart contract on Ethereum using a signed raw transaction. The gas fee is paid from the account, and the application has access to the private key.

```
const Web3 = require("web3");
const Tx = require('ethereumjs-tx')
web3 = new Web3(new Web3.providers.HttpProvider(
          "http://node.ip.addr:8545"));

var account = "0x1234"; // Ethereum account address
var key = new Buffer('private key', 'hex');

var abi = // ABI of Hello World
var bytecode = // Bytecode of Hello World

var create_contract_tx = {
    gasPrice: web3.toHex(web3.eth.gasPrice),
    gasLimit: web3.toHex(3000000),
    data: bytecode,
    from: account
};

var tx = new Tx(create_contract_tx);
tx.sign(key);

var stx = tx.serialize();
web3.eth.sendRawTransaction('0x' + stx.toString('hex'), (err, hash) => {
    // ... Test if success
});
```

The next example shows how to call the **updateMessage()** function on the contract:

```
const Web3 = require("web3");
const Tx = require('ethereumjs-tx')
web3 = new Web3(new Web3.providers.HttpProvider(
          "http://node.ip.addr:8545"));

var account = "0x1234"; // Ethereum account address
var key = new Buffer('private key', 'hex');

var abi = // ABI of Hello World
var contract_address = "0xabcd";
var contract = web3.eth.contract(abi).at(contract_address);
var data = contract.updateMessage.getData(msg);
var nonce = web3.eth.getTransactionCount(account);

var call_contract_tx = {
    nonce: web3.toHex(nonce),
    gasPrice: web3.toHex(web3.eth.gasPrice),
```

```
        gasLimit: web3.toHex(3000000),
        from: account,
        to: contract_address,
        value: '0x00',
        data: data
    };

    var tx = new Tx(call_contract_tx);
    tx.sign(key);

    var stx = tx.serialize();
    web3.eth.sendRawTransaction('0x' + stx.toString('hex'), (err, hash) => {
        // ... Test if success
    });
```

The EthereumJS library is much more than just `ethereumjs-tx`. It provides the JavaScript to manage private keys, keystores, and wallets. It would be useful if you are doing extensive key management and low-level programming on your own.

Python and Others

While JavaScript is the native language for web3.js, many developers do not like to use JavaScript on server applications. Because of that, there are other programming languages' implementations of the web3 library. For example, web3.py is a Python implementation of web3. The following code shows how to decrypt and construct a private key from a GETH keystore file. You can store the content of this keystore file in a database table, and its password in another database table.

```
with open('filename') as keyfile:
    encrypted_key = keyfile.read()
    private_key = w3.eth.account.decrypt(encrypted_key, password)
```

With the private key in place, the code segment next illustrates how to construct a raw transaction in web3.py to transfer ETH from one account to another.

```
from web3 import Web3

tx = {\
    'to': '0xABCD',\
    'value': w3.toWei('10', 'ether'),\
    'gas': 2000000,\
    'gasPrice': w3.toWei('2', 'gwei'),\
    'nonce': 0\
}

private_key = b"\xyz123"
signed = w3.eth.account.signTransaction(transaction, private_key)
tx_hash = w3.eth.sendRawTransaction(signed.rawTransaction)
```

The next example shows how to use web3.py to make a smart contract function call:

```
from web3 import Web3

contract_address = ="0xWXYZ"
contract = w3.eth.contract(address=contract_address, abi=HELLO_ABI)
nonce = w3.eth.getTransactionCount('0xABCD')
tx = contract.functions.updateMessage(\
    'A new hello message'\
).buildTransaction({\
    'gas': 70000,\
    'gasPrice': w3.toWei('2', 'gwei'),\
    'nonce': nonce\
})

private_key = b"\xyz123"
signed = w3.eth.account.signTransaction(tx, private_key)
tx_hash = w3.eth.sendRawTransaction(signed.rawTransaction)
```

There is obviously a lot more to the web3.py library, and it is substantially different from web3.js when it comes to the exact API usages. I encourage interested readers to review its documentation at https://web3py.readthedocs.io. Furthermore, there are other programming language choices for web3.

- *The PHP web3*: https://github.com/formaldehid/php-web3

- *The Java web3*: https://github.com/web3j/web3j

Since web applications vary a lot depending on the development framework you choose, I will leave it as an exercise for you to work out your own web applications.

Conclusion

In this chapter, I discussed how to build server-side applications that interact with blockchains and smart contracts. Those applications require central servers to function and hence are less decentralized than the dapps discussed in Chapter 7. However, for the short term, incorporating decentralized features into otherwise centralized applications could be the most plausible path for the mass adoption of blockchain applications.

Part III

Ethereum in Depth

In the previous part, I introduced you to the concepts and tools for Ethereum smart contract and dapp development. In the next several chapters, we will dive deeper into Ethereum. We will look into how smart contract data and states are stored in the Ethereum blockchain and how smart contract developers could make use of such data. We will also look into best practices to secure smart contracts, which is a major issue the community faces today. Finally, we will review the Ethereum road map on what's coming for developers.

Inside Ethereum

By Tim McCallum

In the previous chapters, you learned how to interact with the Ethereum blockchain from the outside as a client. The chapters covered topics such as executing transactions, developing and deploying smart contracts, and developing dapps using tools like the web3 library. However, to truly understand how Ethereum works and perhaps modify its behavior for your own purposes, we will need to look deeper beneath the external interface of the blockchain platform.

In this chapter, I deconstruct Ethereum to provide you with an understanding of its data storage layer, and I introduce the concept of blockchain state. Also, I cover the theory behind the Patricia trie data structure and demonstrate Ethereum's concrete implementation of tries using Google's LevelDB database. From this point, you will be able to execute transactions and explore how Ethereum's state responds to activities such as transactions.

What Is Blockchain State?

Bitcoin's *state* is represented by its global collection of unspent transaction outputs (UTXOs). The transfer of value in Bitcoin is actioned through transactions. More specifically, a Bitcoin user can spend one or more UTXOs by creating a transaction and adding one or more UTXOs as the transaction's input.

A full explanation of UTXOs is beyond the scope of this chapter. However, I mention UTXOs in the following paragraphs to point out a fundamental difference between Bitcoin and Ethereum. Specifically, the following two Bitcoin examples will provide contrast between Bitcoin's UTXO model and Ethereum's world state.

First, Bitcoin UTXOs cannot be partially spent. If a Bitcoin user spends 0.5 Bitcoin (using her only UTXO, which is worth 1 Bitcoin), the user has to deliberately self-address (send herself) 0.5 Bitcoins (BTC) in return change (Figure 9.1). If the user doesn't send change, she will lose the 0.5 Bitcoin change to the Bitcoin miner who mines her transaction.

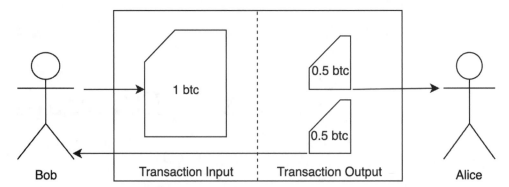

Figure 9.1   Sending a partial Bitcoin

Second, at the most fundamental level, Bitcoin does not maintain user account balances. With Bitcoin, a user simply holds the private keys to one or more UTXOs at any given point in time (Figure 9.2). Digital wallets make it seem like the Bitcoin blockchain automatically stores and organizes user account balances and so forth. This is not the case.

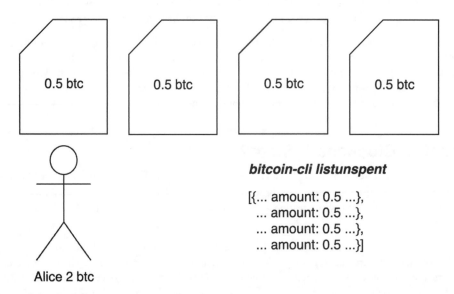

Figure 9.2   Computing account balance for Bitcoin

A user account balance in Bitcoin is an abstract notion. Realistically, a user's account balance is the sum total of each individual UTXO (for which that user holds the corresponding private key), as shown in Figure 9.3. The key that a user holds can be used to individually sign/spend each of the UTXOs.

Figure 9.3   A Bitcoin wallet aggregates UTXOs to show account balances.

The UTXO system in Bitcoin works well, in part, because digital wallets are able to facilitate most of the tasks associated with transactions. This includes but is not limited to the following:

- Handling UTXOs
- Storing keys
- Setting transaction fees
- Providing return change addresses
- Aggregating UTXOs (to show available, pending, and total balances)

Interestingly, a backup of a nondeterministic wallet (like the Bitcoin core wallet pictured in Figure 9.3) provides only a snapshot of the UTXOs (at that point in time). If a user performs any transactions (sending or receiving), the original backup that the user made will be out-of-date.

To summarize, you now know the following:

- The Bitcoin blockchain does not hold account balances.
- Bitcoin wallets hold keys to UTXOs.
- If included in a transaction, an entire UTXO is spent (in some cases partially received as change in the form of a new UTXO).

Next, let's look into the Ethereum blockchain.

Ethereum State

In contrast to the previous information, the Ethereum world state is able to manage account balances and more. The state of Ethereum is not an abstract concept. It is part of Ethereum's base protocol layer. Ethereum is a transaction-based state machine; in other words, it's a technology on which all transaction-based state machine concepts can be built.

Storing state data on each Ethereum node allows for light clients that do not necessarily need to download the entire blockchain to function. Light clients just need access to the state database on a node to get the current state of the entire system and send in transactions to alter the state. That enables a whole range of applications to be developed on the Ethereum blockchain efficiently. Without stored data on nodes and light clients, most smart contracts or dapp use cases would be impossible.

For example, an interesting idea mentioned in the Ethereum white paper is the notion of a savings account. In this scenario, two users (perhaps a husband and wife, or business partners) can each withdraw 1 percent of the account's total balance per day. This idea is mentioned in the "Further Applications" section of the white paper, but it's interesting because it, in theory, could be implemented as part of Ethereum's base protocol layer (as opposed to having to be written as part of a second-layer solution or third-party wallet). You may recall the discussion about Bitcoin UTXOs earlier in this chapter. UTXOs are blind to blockchain data, and as discussed, the Bitcoin blockchain does not actually store a user's account balance. For this reason, the base protocol layer of Bitcoin is far less likely (or perhaps unable) to implement any sort of daily spend limits.

Next, let's look into the actual structure of the Ethereum state data store.

Data Structure

Let's start at the beginning. As with all other blockchains, the Ethereum blockchain begins life at its own genesis block. From this point (genesis state at block 0) onward, activities such as transactions, contracts, and mining will continually change the state of the Ethereum blockchain. In Ethereum, an example of this is an account balance (stored in the state trie, as shown in Figure 9.4), which changes every time a transaction, in relation to that account, takes place.

Importantly, data such as account balances is not stored directly in the blocks of the Ethereum blockchain. Only the root node hashes of the transaction trie, state trie, and receipts trie are stored directly in the blockchain.

You will also notice, from Figure 9.4, that the root node hash of the storage trie (where all of the smart contract data is kept) actually points to the state trie, which in turn points to the blockchain. I will zoom in and cover all of this in more detail soon.

There are two vastly different types of data in Ethereum: permanent data and ephemeral data. An example of permanent data is a transaction. Once a transaction has been fully confirmed, it is recorded in the transaction trie and never altered. An example of ephemeral data is the balance of a particular Ethereum account address. The balance of an account address is stored in the state trie and is altered whenever transactions against that particular account occur. It makes sense that

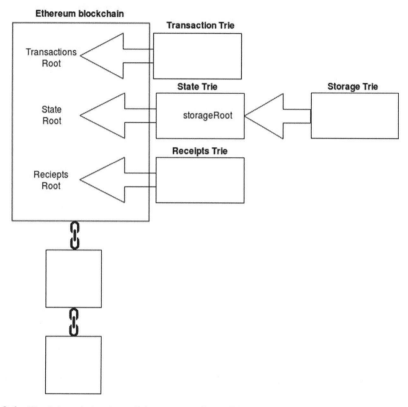

Figure 9.4   The internal structure of data storage in an Ethereum node

permanent data, such as mined transactions, and ephemeral data, such as account balances, should be stored separately. Ethereum uses trie data structures (as broadly outlined earlier) to manage data. The next section will take a detour and provide a quick overview on tries.

Trie (or Tree)

A *trie* (or tree) is a well-known data structure that is used for storing sequences of characters. Ethereum exclusively uses what is known as the "practical algorithm to retrieve information coded in alphanumeric" (Patricia) trie. The main advantage of the Patricia trie is its compact storage. We will now analyze the inner workings of the standard (more traditional) trie versus the Patricia trie.

Standard Trie

Figure 9.5 shows the structure of a standard trie that stores words. Each character in the word is a node in the tree, and each word is terminated by a special null pointer.

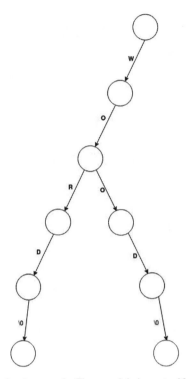

Figure 9.5   A standard trie storing two words. The special character \0 represents the null pointer.

Rules for Adding a Word to the Trie

We follow the search path for the word we are adding. If we encounter a null pointer, we create a new node. When we have finished adding our word, we create a null pointer (terminator). When adding a (shorter) word that is contained in another (longer) word, we just exhaust all of the characters and then add a null pointer (terminator).

Rules for Deleting a Word from the Trie

We search for a leaf (the end of a branch) on the trie that represents the string (which we want to delete). We then start deleting all nodes from the leaf back to the root of the trie—unless we hit a node with more than one child; in this case, we stop.

Rules for Searching for a Word in the Trie

We examine each of the characters in the string for which we are searching and follow the trie for as long as it provides our path (in the right sequence). If we encounter a null pointer before exhausting all the characters in the string (which we are searching for), then we can conclude that the string is not stored in the trie. On the contrary, if we reach a leaf (the end of a branch) and that path (from the leaf back to the root of the trie) represents our string, we conclude that the string is stored in the trie.

Patricia Trie

Figure 9.6 shows the structure of a Patricia trie that stores words. The storage is more compact than the standard trie. Each word is terminated by a special null pointer.

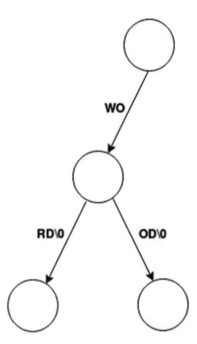

Figure 9.6   A Patricia trie storing two words

Rules for Adding a Word to the Patricia Trie

Patricia tries group all common characters into a single branch. Any unusual characters will constitute a new branch in the path. When adding a word to a Patricia trie, we exhaust all the characters and then add the null pointer (terminator), as shown in Figure 9.7.

Rules for Deleting a Word from the Patricia Trie

This is the same as with a traditional trie, except for when deleting nodes (from the leaf back to the root), we must ensure that all parent nodes must be in possession of at least two child nodes. It is okay for a single child node to just have characters and a null pointer (this occurs in Figure 9.7, at the end of every word). It is also okay for a single node to just have a null pointer (this occurs if a shorter word is contained in a longer word). See Figure 9.7, which illustrates how *wood* and *wooden* coexist in the same trie.

Importantly, when deleting from a trie, a path cannot be left with a parent node that connects to just a single child node. If this occurs (when deleting, we need to concatenate the appropriate characters to resolve this). This is illustrated in Figure 9.8 (where we delete the word from the trie).

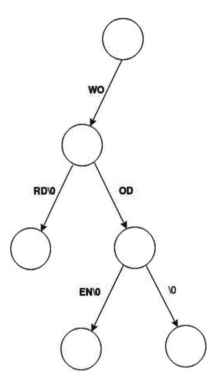

Figure 9.7   Adding a word (*wooden*) to the Patricia trie

Rules for Searching for a Word in the Patricia Trie

The rules for searching the Patricia trie are the same as for searching the standard trie.

Similarities between the Trie and Patricia Trie

The runtime "O" for adding is O(mN), where "m" is the length of the string we are adding and "N" is the size of the available alphabet.

The runtime for deleting is O(mN), where "m" is the length of the string we want to delete and "N" is again the size of the available alphabet.

The runtime for searching is O(m), where "m" is the length of the string we are searching for.

Main Difference between the Trie and Patricia Trie

The main advantage of using the Patricia trie is in relation to storage.

The storage requirement "O" for the standard trie is O(MN), where "M" is the total length of all strings in the trie and "N" is the size of the available alphabet.

The storage requirement "O" for the Patricia trie is O(nN+M), where "n" is the number of strings stored in the Patricia trie, "N" is the size of the available alphabet, and "M" is the total length of all strings in the trie.

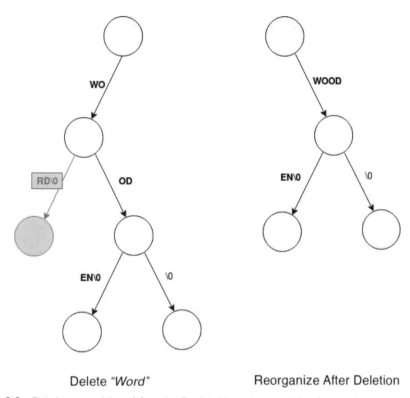

Delete "*Word*"   Reorganize After Deletion

Figure 9.8 Deleting a word (*word*) from the Patricia trie and reorganizing it

In short, you will have noticed a marked difference in the depth of the tries. The Patricia trie is less deep (shallower). This is because of the Patricia trie's ability to group common characters (and concatenate null pointers to leaves).

Modified Merkle Patricia Trie

In the Ethereum state database, the data is stored in a modified Merkle Patricia trie, which means the root node of the trie is a hash of the data in its leaves. This design makes the state database on each node resistant to tampering, just like the blockchain itself.

Every function (put, update, and delete) performed on a trie in Ethereum utilizes a deterministic cryptographic hash. Further, the unique cryptographic hash of a trie's root node can be used as evidence that the trie has not been tampered with.

For example, any changes to a trie's data, at any level (such as increasing an account's balance), will completely change the root hash. This cryptographic feature provides an opportunity for light clients (devices that do not store the entire blockchain) to quickly and reliably query the blockchain; in other words, does account 0x…4857 have enough funds to complete this purchase at block height 5044866?

Trie Structure in Ethereum

Let's look at the state, storage, and transaction tries in a bit more depth.

State Trie: The One and Only

There is one, and one only, global state trie in Ethereum. This global state trie is constantly updated. The state trie contains a key-value pair for every account that exists on the Ethereum network.

- The *key* is a single 160-bit identifier (the address of an Ethereum account).

- The *value* in the global state trie is created by encoding the following account details of an Ethereum account (using the recursive-length prefix [RLP] encoding method): nonce, balance, storageRoot, codeHash.

The state trie's root node (a hash of the entire state trie at a given point in time) is used as a secure and unique identifier for the state trie; the state trie's root node is cryptographically dependent on all internal state trie data. The state trie's root node is stored in the Ethereum block header corresponding to the time when the state trie was updated (see Figure 9.9) and can be queried from the block (Figure 9.10).

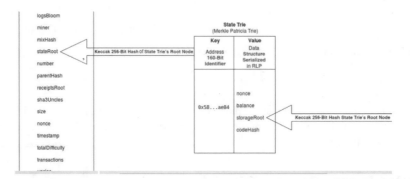

Figure 9.9   Relationship between the state trie (LevelDB implementation of a Merkle Patricia trie) and an Ethereum block

```
size: 533,
stateRoot: "0x8c77785e3e9171715dd34117b047dffe44575c32ede59bde39fbf5dc074f2976",
timestamp: 1517107395,
totalDifficulty: 3021121,
transactions: [],
transactionsRoot: "0x56e81f171bcc55a6ff8345e692c0f86e5b48e01b996cadc001622fb5e363b421",
uncles: []
```

Figure 9.10   Showing the trie roots

Storage Trie: Where the Contract Data Lives

A storage trie is where all the contract data lives. Each Ethereum account has its own storage trie. A Keccak 256-bit hash of the storage trie's root node is stored as the storageRoot value in the global state trie (Figure 9.11).

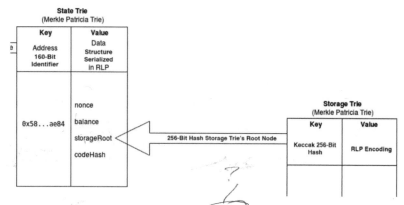

Figure 9.11   State trie—Keccak 256-bit hash of the state trie's root node stored as the stateRoot value in a given block

Transaction Trie: One per Block

Each Ethereum block has its own separate transaction trie. A block contains many transactions. The order of the transactions in a block is of course decided by the miner who assembles the block. The path to a specific transaction in the transaction trie is via the RLP encoding of the index of where the transaction sits in the block. Mined blocks are never updated; the position of the transaction in a block never changes. This means that once you locate a transaction in a block's transaction trie, you can return to the same path over and over to retrieve the same result. Figure 9.12 shows how the transaction trie's root hash is stored in an Ethereum block header.

Concrete Examples of Tries in Ethereum

The main Ethereum clients use two different database software solutions to store their tries. Ethereum's Rust client, Parity, uses RocksDB. Ethereum's Go, C++, and Python clients all use LevelDB.

RocksDB is out of scope for this book. Let's explore how three out of the four major Ethereum clients utilize LevelDB.

LevelDB is an open source Google key-value storage library that provides, among other things, forward and backward iterations over data, ordered mapping from string keys to string values, custom comparison functions, and automatic compression. The data is automatically compressed using Snappy, an open source Google compression/decompression library. While Snappy does not aim for

Figure 9.12   The transaction trie stores data about each transaction in a block.

maximum compression, it aims for very high speeds. LevelDB is an important storage and retrieval mechanism that manages the state of the Ethereum network. As such, LevelDB is a dependency for the most popular Ethereum clients (nodes) such as go-ethereum, cpp-ethereum, and pyethereum.

> **Note**
>
> While the implementation of the trie data structure can be done on disk (using database software such as LevelDB), it is important to note that there is a difference between traversing a trie and simply looking at the flat key-value database.

To learn more, we have to access the data in LevelDB using the appropriate Patricia trie libraries. To do this, we will need an Ethereum installation (see Chapter 5). Once you have set up your Ethereum private network, you will be able to execute transactions and explore how Ethereum's state responds to network activities such as transactions, contracts, and mining. In the next section, I will provide code examples and screen captures from an Ethereum private network.

Analyzing the Ethereum Database

As mentioned previously, there are many Merkle Patricia tries (referenced in each block) within the Ethereum blockchain: state trie, storage trie, transaction trie, and receipts trie.

To reference a particular Merkle Patricia trie in a particular block, we need to obtain its root hash as a reference. The following commands allow us to obtain the root hashes of the state, transaction, and receipt tries in the genesis block:

```
web3.eth.getBlock(0).stateRoot
web3.eth.getBlock(0).transactionsRoot
web3.eth.getBlock(0).receiptsRoot
```

If you want the root hashes of the latest block (instead of the genesis block), please use the following command:

```
web3.eth.getBlock(web3.eth.blockNumber).stateRoot
```

We will be using a combination of the `nodejs`, `level`, and `ethereumjs` commands (which implements Ethereum's VM in JavaScript) to inspect the LevelDB database. The following commands will further prepare our environment (in Ubuntu Linux):

```
cd ~
sudo apt-get update
sudo apt-get upgrade
curl -sL https://deb.nodesource.com/setup_9.x |
sudo -E bash - sudo apt-get install -y nodejs
sudo apt-get install nodejs
npm -v
nodejs -v
npm install levelup leveldown rlp merkle-patricia-tree --save
git clone https://github.com/ethereumjs/ethereumjs-vm.git
cd ethereumjs-vm
npm install ethereumjs-account ethereumjs-util --save
```

Get the Data

From this point, running the following code will print a list of the Ethereum account keys
(which are stored in the state root of your Ethereum private network). The code connects to
Ethereum's LevelDB database, enters Ethereum's world state (using a stateRoot value from a block
in the blockchain), and then accesses the keys to all accounts on the Ethereum private network
(Figure 9.13).

```
<Buffer 15 f5 e0 eb 04 db 31 de 72 ff b4 b9 64 0f c9 12 49 af 60 74 d9 8d a1 e1 1f 50 d2 a3 37 55 39 05>
<Buffer be 13 87 9f 13 52 0d 22 33 92 ef 63 74 24 42 b4 56 0c be b7 3f 1d 7e 20 80 96 5f 91 de a5 25 fd>
<Buffer 31 98 3a 89 3e 98 1c b4 1a 9f 3e 49 7e a1 fa 5e 1e 4d 60 fe 18 41 f4 7b 35 af e2 f2 da 85 d1 38>
```

Figure 9.13   Raw data read from the trie in LevelDB

```
//Just importing the requirements
var Trie = require('merkle-patricia-tree/secure');
var levelup = require('levelup');
var leveldown = require('leveldown');
var RLP = require('rlp');
var assert = require('assert');

//Connecting to the leveldb database
var db = levelup(leveldown(
    '/home/user/geth/chaindata'));

//Adding the "stateRoot" value from the block so that
//we can inspect the state root at that block height.
var root = '0x8c777…2976';

//Creating a trie object of the merkle-patricia-tree library
var trie = new Trie(db, root);

//Creating a nodejs stream object so that we can access the data
var stream = trie.createReadStream()
```

```
//Turning on the stream
stream.on('data', function (data){
  //printing out the keys of the "state trie"
  console.log(data.key);
});
```

> **Note**
>
> Interestingly, accounts in Ethereum are added to the state trie only once a transaction has taken place (in relation to that specific account). For example, just creating a new account using geth account new will not include that account in the state trie, even after many blocks have been mined. However, if a successful transaction (one that costs gas and is included in a mined block) is recorded against that account, then and only then will that account appear in the state trie. This is clever logic that protects against malicious attackers continuously creating new accounts and bloating the state trie.

Decoding the Data

You will have noticed that querying LevelDB returns encoded results. This is because Ethereum uses its own specially modified Merkle Patricia trie implementation when interacting with LevelDB. The Ethereum wiki provides information about the design and implementation of both Ethereum's modified Merkle Patricia trie and RLP encoding. In short, Ethereum has extended the trie data structures described earlier. For example, the modified Merkle Patricia trie contains a method that can shortcut the descent (down the trie) through the use of an extension node.

In Ethereum, a single modified Merkle Patricia trie node is one of the following:

- An empty string (referred to as NULL)
- An array that contains 17 items (referred to as a *branch*)
- An array that contains two items (referred to as a *leaf*)
- An array that contains two items (referred to as an *extension*)

As Ethereum's tries are designed and constructed with rigid rules, the best way to inspect them is through the use of computer code. The following example uses ethereum.js. The following code (when provided with a particular block's stateRoot as well as an Ethereum account address) will return that account's correct balance in a human-readable form (Figure 9.14):

```
Account Address: 0xcccc6b46fa5606826ce8c18fece6f519064e6130b
Balance: 300000
```

Figure 9.14   The decoded results

```
//Mozilla Public License 2.0
//Getting the requirements
var Trie = require('merkle-patricia-tree/secure');
var levelup = require('levelup');
var leveldown = require('leveldown');
var utils = require('ethereumjs-util');
var BN = utils.BN;
var Account = require('ethereumjs-account');

//Connecting to the leveldb database
var db = levelup(leveldown('/home/user/geth/chaindata'));

//Adding the "stateRoot" value from the block
//so that we can inspect the state root at that block height.
var root = '0x9369577...73028';

//Creating a trie object of the merkle-patricia-tree library
var trie = new Trie(db, root);

var address = '0xccc6b46fa5606826ce8c18fece6f519064e6130b';
trie.get(address, function (err, raw) {
    if (err) return cb(err)
    //Create an instance of an account
    var account = new Account(raw)
    console.log('Account Address: ' + address);
    //Decode and present the account balance
    console.log('Balance: ' + (new BN(account.balance)).toString());
})
```

Read and Write the State LevelDB

So far, I have shown how to access the Ethereum state's LevelDB database using JavaScript on a local node. If you are familiar with GO and can work with Ethereum source code, there is an easier way. You could just import the go-ethereum source code in GO and call its functions to read and even modify the LevelDB database. The write function will not only change the values in the nodes but also update the root hash to reflect the changes. Specifically, the functions are in the following source code file:

```
https://github.com/ethereum/go-ethereum/blob/master/core/state/statedb.go
```

It contains methods such as GetBalance, AddBalance, SubBalance, and SetBalance to operate on the account balances. However, changing the state LevelDB in this way will change the data on only one node and will likely cause this node to go out of sync with the rest of the nodes on the network. The right way to change the state is to follow how go-ethereum processes a transaction and records it on the blockchain. That is out of scope for this book.

Conclusion

In this chapter, I demonstrated that Ethereum has the ability to manage its state. This clever up-front design has many advantages, allowing for light clients and many different kinds of dapps that do not need to run the entire blockchain. It is important to understand the inner workings of Ethereum to write great smart contracts and applications on the Ethereum platform.

## 10

Blockchain Data Services

The previous chapter explained how the blockchain stores state data in block-based databases. The data is organized into a tree structure, and each block has a timestamp. This structure makes it easy to add new data (new blocks) and almost impossible to delete or change anything in old blocks, hence securing the blockchain data. However, while you can easily list each block's content (i.e., transactions), it is hard to get longitudinal or aggregated views of the blockchain state. As a result, it is hard to search the blockchain data based on an address or specific actions performed by an address. Yet, many blockchain applications require the capability to search and analyze blockchain data.

A common design pattern for dapps is to call `view` functions in smart contracts to query data stored in the contract. However, such an approach is hard to scale since you need a full blockchain node to execute every `view` request, and the data query is limited by the data structure supported by the smart contract (i.e., no SQL or JSON queries). By harvesting smart contract data into a data warehouse and enabling rich queries on the data warehouse, we could potentially build much more complex and scalable dapps.

In this chapter, I discuss how to build normalized databases for blockchain data so that they can be easily searched, analyzed, and browsed.

Blockchain Explorers

Almost every blockchain requires a data explorer so that users can search and browse transactions and account addresses on the blockchain. The blockchain explorers and the data services they provide are now part of standard infrastructure for every blockchain project.

- For Bitcoin and compatible Bitcoin Cash (BCH) blockchains, there are many, including https://explorer.bitcoin.com/btc and https://btc.com/.

- For the Ethereum blockchain, the most well-known one is https://etherscan.io/.

- For the EOS blockchain, there are https://bloks.io/ and https://eospark.com/, among others.

- For the CyberMiles blockchain, there is https://www.cmttracking.io/.

Each blockchain explorer provides information that is specific to its blockchain. For example, explorers for proof-of-work (PoW) blockchains like Bitcoin and Ethereum provide information such as hash rate and mining awards. Explorers for delegated proof-of-stake (PoS) blockchains like EOS and CyberMiles provide information such as block producer/validator nodes, voting power, and inflation awards. Explorers for smart contract platforms such as Ethereum, EOS, and CyberMiles provide information about smart contracts as well as assets held or issued by those smart contracts.

Figure 10.1, Figure 10.2, and Figure 10.3 show screenshots from Etherscan. They provide insights into the global state, transactions, and smart contracts on the Ethereum blockchain. Figures 10.4 and 10.5 illustrate how the CMTTracking web site provides delegated PoS information for the CyberMiles blockchain in real time. Such information is not applicable for the Ethereum blockchain, as Ethereum uses PoW mining for consensus.

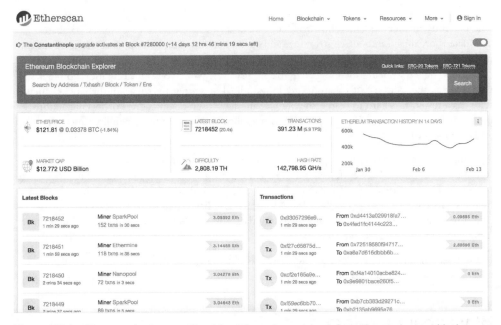

Figure 10.1 Etherscan front page with pricing information, mining information, and recent blocks

The explorer can also provide off-chain information related to the crypto assets on the blockchain. For example, it could provide the current pricing, trading volume, and market cap for the crypto assets. It could associate blockchain accounts and smart contracts with identities in the real world. It could monitor accounts belonging to key ecosystem players, such as exchanges and super nodes to detect and report trading signals. Those data services are of broad interest from users, traders, investors, and government regulators.

Those explorers, especially open source explorers, are also decentralized applications. Everyone with the source code can deploy their own explorer service. All the data is from the blockchain and other distributed sources, such as pricing aggregators. There is no single point of failure to shut down the explorer software.

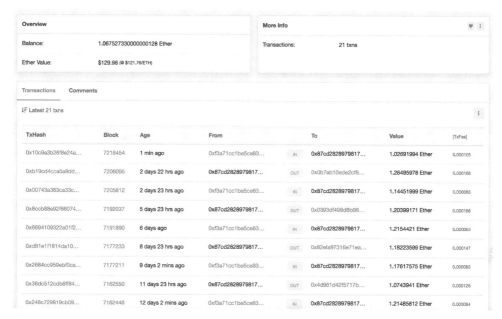

Figure 10.2   Etherscan page for an account and its transactions

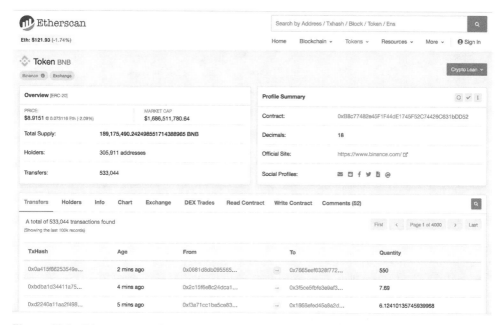

Figure 10.3   Etherscan page for a smart contract that issues an ERC20 asset

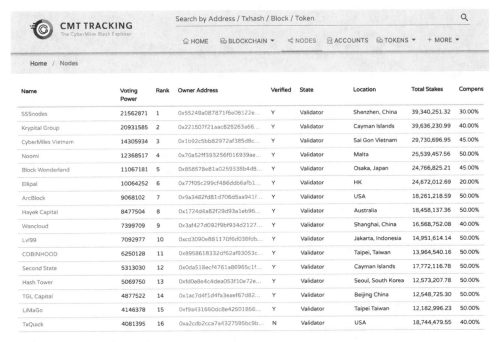

Name	Voting Power	Rank	Owner Address	Verified	State	Location	Total Stakes	Compens
SSSnodes	21562871	1	0x55249a087871f6e08122e...	Y	Validator	Shenzhen, China	39,340,251.32	30.00%
Krypital Group	20931585	2	0x221507f21aac826263a66...	Y	Validator	Cayman Islands	39,636,230.99	40.00%
CyberMiles Vietnam	14305934	3	0x1b92c5bb82972af385d8c...	Y	Validator	Sai Gon Vietnam	29,730,696.95	45.00%
Noomi	12368517	4	0x70a52ff393256f016939ae...	Y	Validator	Malta	25,539,457.56	50.00%
Block Wonderland	11067181	5	0x858578e81a0259338b4d8...	Y	Validator	Osaka, Japan	24,766,825.21	45.00%
Ellipal	10064252	6	0x77f05c299cf486ddb6afb1...	Y	Validator	HK	24,672,012.69	20.00%
ArcBlock	9068102	7	0x9a3482fd81d706d5aa941f...	Y	Validator	USA	18,261,218.59	50.00%
Hayek Capital	8477504	8	0x1724d4a82f29d93a1eb96...	Y	Validator	Australia	18,458,137.36	50.00%
Wancloud	7399709	9	0x3af4d092f9bf934d2127...	Y	Validator	Shanghai, China	16,568,752.08	40.00%
Lvl99	7092977	10	0xcd3090e881170f6d036fdb...	Y	Validator	Jakarta, Indonesia	14,951,614.14	50.00%
COBINHOOD	6250128	11	0x8958618332df62af93053c...	Y	Validator	Taipei, Taiwan	13,964,540.16	50.00%
Second State	5313030	12	0x0da518ecf4761a86965c1f...	Y	Validator	Cayman Islands	17,772,116.78	50.00%
Hash Tower	5069750	13	0xfd0e8e4c4dea053f10e72e...	Y	Validator	Seoul, South Korea	12,573,207.78	50.00%
TGL Capital	4877522	14	0x1ac7d4f1d4fa3eaef67d82...	Y	Validator	Beijing China	12,548,725.30	50.00%
LiMaGo	4146378	15	0xf9a431660dc8e42501856...	Y	Validator	Taipei Taiwan	12,182,996.23	50.00%
TxQuick	4081395	16	0xa2cdb2cca7a4327595bc9b...	N	Validator	USA	18,744,479.55	40.00%

Figure 10.4   CMTTracking page for CyberMiles validator nodes, their status, voting power, and compensation rate for people who stake in them

Figure 10.5   CMTTracking page showing validator information, stakes, and awards

Figure 10.6 illustrates the overall architecture of a typical blockchain explorer. It consists of a harvester and a query interface. The harvester retrieves data from the blockchain, normalizes it, associates individual records with off-chain sources, and then saves the data in a database.

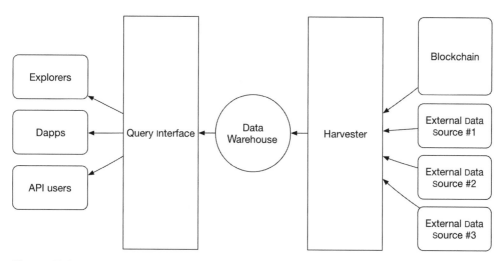

Figure 10.6   The blockchain data explorer architecture view

The query interface provides a search engine and visualization tools to chart the data. It could also support API services for automated queries.

In the next sections, I will go into the technology stacks of the blockchain explorer software and discuss how you might improve existing explorers and develop specialized data services for your own applications.

Harvesting Data

The harvester application must have access to a full blockchain node. This is a node that contains the entire blockchain history data from the genesis block to the current head, not just the current account states. The node runs continuously and stays in sync with the blockchain's current head block. I recommend you run and sync a full node yourself just for the harvester to use since the harvester's data quality depends on the availability of the node. With your own node, the harvester could also potentially access the databases inside the blockchain software to directly extract data as opposed to going through the blockchain's Remote Procedure Call (RPC) service interface. Figure 10.7 illustrates the architecture of the harvester.

The key component in the harvester is a scheduler. It runs every few seconds to retrieve information from the blockchain node. The scheduler's running time interval should be shorter than the block time to make sure that it always gets the latest block information. There are a variety of technology choices for the scheduler.

- For Linux-based systems, you can use cron jobs to run the harvester application in fixed intervals.

- If the harvester is a Java application, you can use the Quartz Scheduler to run worker jobs at fixed intervals (www.quartz-scheduler.org/).

- If the harvester is a node.js JavaScript application, you can use the egg.js framework for scheduled workloads (https://eggjs.org/).

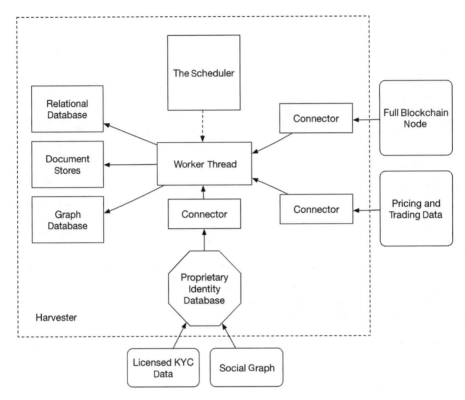

Figure 10.7   The blockchain data harvester

The scheduler runs a workload to retrieve data through the following means. You could build each of them into a connector that plugs into the harvester.

- *RPC connector to the node*: For Ethereum-compatible blockchains (e.g., CyberMiles), this is the RPC service available via port 8545. This connector is typically done through a web3-compatible library.

- *Database connector to LevelDB*: This is used to directly access the databases on the node to read data that is potentially not available (or too cumbersome) from the RPC connector.

- *Web services connectors*: This is used to access external services such as pricing and market intelligence data from the CoinMarketCap API (https://coinmarketcap.com/api/).

- *Local database connectors*: This is used to access potentially proprietary data stored on the harvester's local servers. Examples include proprietary databases that associate blockchain accounts with names, entities, and exchanges, including known criminals.

Once the data for each block is retrieved from the connectors, the harvester runs a data warehouse operation to combine, clean, and normalize the data. The data is organized into a set of logical schema and saved.

- Structured results such as blocks, accounts, and transactions can be saved into a relational database with well-defined schema to ensure data integrity and query efficiency.

- Unstructured data such as events generated from smart contracts or bytecodes and hashes can be saved on NoSQL document stores such as MongoDB and Cassandra.

> **Note**
>
> The Google Blockchain ETL is a fully integrated blockchain data warehousing solution. It uses the Google Cloud Composer to orchestrate the harvesting process. It starts by making RPC requests to export blockchain data into comma-separated value (CSV) files and then loads the CSV files into the Google BigQuery table. The data can then be queried from BigQuery. The drawback, however, is that it is not a real-time solution. The data is harvested and ingested every 24 hours. And it relies on the Google Cloud infrastructure.

In the rest of this section, we look into various data types the harvester can collect and normalize for later queries.

Transactions and Accounts

Most blockchain platforms provide standard RPC interfaces to get a list of transactions by block height. From there, the harvester can get details from each transaction, including the from/to accounts, transfer amount, gas amount, success status, and data associated with the transaction, such as smart contract function calls.

All those data elements are highly structured. They can be normalized into a relational database with account addresses acting as keys. For example, we could query all transactions from and to a specific account. The harvester application could perform internal data integrity checks by adding up all the transactions for each account and compare them with the account balances reported by the blockchain RPC.

Awards

Most blockchains also "create" crypto tokens over time to award entities that run computer servers to secure the blockchain network. That is called *block awards*. For (PoW) blockchains, miners compete for the right to create the next block. The winner is awarded certain amounts of tokens. For various PoS blockchains, including delegated proof-of-stake (DPoS) blockchains, the validators or block producers were assigned duties to produce the next block while all other nodes validate and agree on the block's content. The block award goes to the block producer or is divided according to stake or voting power.

The harvester needs to understand the algorithm to distribute block awards and creates database entries for such events indexed by account addresses. This data is also highly structural and relational. The harvester can verify its computed block awards distribution against account balances from the blockchain itself.

Off-Chain Identities

A key use case of the blockchain data service is to understand the flow and exchange of digital assets. It is often important to associate a blockchain address with real-world entities that hold its private key. Since blockchain transactions are transparent, once you know the real identity of an address, it is often possible to figure out the identity of any addresses that ever transferred in and out of the known address.

> **Note**
>
> The only "anonymous" addresses on blockchain are miner accounts from PoW blockchains. However, once a miner starts to spend or exchange tokens with known addresses, the miner's identity could be revealed.

The association between off-chain entities and blockchain addresses can come from multiple sources.

- *Data sharing agreement with crypto exchanges*: Most crypto exchanges require know your customer (KYC) checks for all their users. They have broad reach and knowledge of blockchain account address ownership as users deposit and withdraw tokens from or into their own addresses.

- *Data sharing agreement with initial coin offering (ICO) projects*: Many ICO projects conduct KYC checks for all their initial contributors. They have knowledge of each contributor's source and deposit addresses.

- *Data sharing agreement with crypto payment processors and e-commerce merchants*: When users use crypto tokens to pay for goods and services in the real world, they leave a trail that we can follow (e.g., shipping address) to determine the identity of the accounts related to the real-world transaction.

- *Data mining from social media*: When crypto projects run marketing campaigns, it often provides airdrops to followers on social media. Such airdrops require users' addresses.

While the association between blockchain addresses and their off-chain owners' identities is structured and relational, the transactions linking one blockchain address to the next are not relational. The harvester could put the known address associations into a relational database and put connected transactions into a graph database, such as Neo4j, for further analysis and queries.

> **Note**
>
> Monitoring known exchange addresses and large token holders' addresses can help you predict market movements. For example, if a large account holder withdraws his stake at a DPoS block producer/validator and moves the tokens to an exchange account, you can anticipate increased selling pressure in the near future.

Inside Smart Contracts

Ethereum-compatible blockchains are foremost smart contract platforms. The smart contract bytecode and their data structure can be arbitrary. Hence, smart contract data is unstructured, and it has been difficult to track the function execution and state changes in the blockchain.

> **Note**
>
> Etherscan and other Ethereum-compatible blockchain explorers have long provided the ability to verify user/community-submitted smart contract source code against its bytecode on the blockchain. That helps the community verify that the source code and behavior of such contracts are indeed as advertised. But, this method provides no insights into the execution of functions and data inside the smart contracts.

A smart contract can write permanent data to the blockchain by declaring and then emitting an event. Emitted event log data will remain intact indefinitely, even if that particular smart contract and its global state have been completely removed using the previously mentioned opcode `0xff`, known as *self-destruct*.

> **Note**
>
> The cost of writing to event logs is comparatively cheaper than writing to the blockchain's global state. For example, it costs around 40,000 gas to write a single address and a single uint to the blockchain's state. Alternatively, it costs only about 1,000 gas to write that same single address and uint to the blockchain's event logs.

The following example in Solidity (and Lity) shows how to define an event in your smart contract:

```
event pointBalanceUpdated(address indexed endUser, uint256 amount);
```

As you can see, to declare the event, we simply type the word `event` followed by the name of the event. Then we pass in some data types and data names (in this case, the data types of `address` and `uint256`, which relate to the data names `endUser` and `amount`, respectively).

You will notice that we have deliberately specified, in this declaration, that the `endUser` data be indexed. Essentially, indexing a parameter allows for efficient searching later. Up to three parameters per event declaration can be indexed.

It is wise to index data, such as account addresses, because it's likely that you will be searching for information based on a particular account address. It is not a great idea to index other types of data, such as arbitrary amounts (i.e., integers such as 1 or 10). It is completely unnecessary to include (in your event logs) any information that can be easily retrieved using predefined global variables or functions (e.g., `block.number`). Variables like `block.number` are included in standard transaction receipts by default. Let's now emit the event declared earlier, as shown here:

```
emit pointBalanceUpdated(msg.sender, pointValue);
```

As you can see from the previous code, to emit an event, you simply type `emit` followed by the name of the event (which was declared in the previous code snippet). The data to be included in the event log is passed in during a function's execution. The order in which data is passed into the `emit` command must match the order of the data, as shown in the event declaration.

The following code shows the entire smart contract, thereby providing context for the previous snippets:

```solidity
pragma solidity ^0.4.0;

contract EventLogCreator{

    // Contract variables
    mapping(address => uint256) private pointBalances;

    // Event
    event pointBalanceUpdated(address indexed endUser, uint256 amount);

    // Function which adds points and emits
    function addPoints(uint256 pointValue) public {
        pointBalances[msg.sender] += pointValue;
        emit pointBalanceUpdated(msg.sender, pointValue);
    }

    // Function that returns points which are mapped to a certain address
    function getPoints(address userAddress) public constant returns(uint256){
        return pointBalances[userAddress];
    }
}
```

Now, every time a user calls the addPoints() function on this contract, the pointBalanceUpdated event is emitted. The event is recorded in transaction receipts when you query a transaction via RPC. In fact, the web3 library provides an even easier way to query past events, as shown here:

```
var events = await web3ContractInstance.getPastEvents(eventName, {
    filter: {},
    fromBlock: lastIndexedBlock,
    toBlock: target
});
```

The harvester receives JSON objects in the events array in the previous code. Each event JSON object looks like the following. Please note that I'm showing a more complex event from the Uniswap exchange deployed on the CyberMiles blockchain here, as opposed to the simple event described earlier.

```json
{
    "address" : "0x09cabEC1eAd1c0Ba254B09efb3EE13841712bE14",
    "blockHash" : "0x249ac ... b2",
    "blockNumber" : 6848001,
    "logIndex" : 10,
    "removed" : false,
    "transactionHash" : "0x453a2 ... 60",
    "transactionIndex" : 14,
    "id" : "log_327a5bb5",
    "returnValues" : {
      "0" : "0x00dEe1F836998bcc736022f314dF906588d44808",
```

```
        "1" : "109494525547445255474",
        "2" : "1216943725441155089",
        "buyer" : "0x00dEe1F836998bcc736022f314dF906588d44808",
        "tokens_sold" : "109494525547445255474",
        "eth_bought" : "1216943725441155089"
      },
      "event" : "EthPurchase",
      "signature" : "0x7f409 ... 05",
      "raw" : {
        "data" : "0x",
        "topics" : [
          "0x7f409 ... 05",
          "0x00000 ... 08",
          "0x00000 ... 32",
          "0x00000 ... 11"
        ]
      }
    }
  }
}
```

The JavaScript Object Notation (JSON) object can be deconstructed and saved into a relational database. Or, it can be saved directly into a JSON-aware document store for future queries. In this way, we can now harvest data directly from inside smart contract function calls.

In this next chapter, I will discuss how to directly harvest and track public data from smart contracts using a search engine approach.

Query Interface

With the harvester in place, it is now possible to query the databases and provide data services to end users. A web-based UI can be built with any modern JavaScript user interface (UI) framework in front of those back-end data query services. The UI simply makes asynchronous data requests to the query interface.

But more interestingly, the query interface can be used as web services for all applications, not just for the blockchain explorer. For example, a dapp could query blockchain and generate charts or maps.

SQL Query

You can use SQL to query data from the relational databases the harvester builds. For example, it is now easy to find transactions that originate from a specific address, transactions that call a specific smart contract function, or transactions that block awards from a certain period of time.

JSON Query

Perhaps more interestingly, you can query JSON objects directly from tools like Elasticsearch. Here is an example query for Uniswap exchange events in the smart contract event log:

```json
{
"query": {
  "bool": {
     "must": [{
        "match": {
          "name": "TokenPurchase"
        }
     },
     {
        "match": {
          "jsonEventObject.address": "0x09ca ... 14"
        }
     }]
    }
  },
  "_source": ["name", "jsonEventObject.returnValues.buyer",
    "jsonEventObject.blockNumber"],
  "highlight": {
    "fields": {
      "title": {}
    }
  }
}
}
```

The result would look something like this:

```json
{
  "total": 1885,
  "max_score": 1.648463,
  "hits": [{
    "_index": "uniswap_exchange_events",
    "_type": "event",
    "_id": "0xe26e ... fe",
    "_score": 1.648463,
    "_source": {
      "name": "TokenPurchase",
      "jsonEventObject": {
        "returnValues": {
          "buyer": "0xbc8dAfeacA658Ae0857C80D8Aa6dE4D487577c63"
        },
        "blockNumber": 6630726
      }
    }
  }, {...},{...}]
}
```

The Elasticsearch framework is a powerful search engine framework. We have found that it works well with blockchain data.

GraphQL

Another promising query interface for blockchain data is GraphQL, an open source query language and execution engine that originally was developed by Facebook. Leading implementations of GraphQL for blockchain data include TheGraph (https://thegraph.com/) and Arcblock's OCAP. In this section, let's look into how TheGraph handles GraphQL queries. You could simply use its hosted service to query data from the public Ethereum blockchain or build your own using its open source software (https://github.com/graphprotocol).

TheGraph provides, among many other things, a mechanism for a dapp to directly fetch and consume only the exact amount of data that the dapp actually requires, at any given time. Here is an example of a GraphQL query for TheGraph:

```
{
    transactions(first: 1) {
        event
    }
}
```

Right off the bat, we can see that TheGraph is different from a traditional RESTful web service, in that this GraphQL query is not written in valid JSON. In fact, this GraphQL syntax is more lightweight than JSON because it does not have to specify whole `key:value` pairs, such as `{"event": true}`, and so forth.

As examples, let's use TheGraph to query Uniswap exchange smart contracts deployed on the Ethereum blockchain. To echo the earlier discussion in this chapter, TheGraph has already harvested event logs from Ethereum smart contracts and is making this data available for GraphQL queries. The previous GraphQL query translates to "Considering all of the Uniswap transactions to date, please give me only the name of the first event log that was ever emitted." The response is as follows:

```
{
    "data": {
        "transactions": [{
            "event": "AddLiquidity"
        }]
    }
}
```

The response is, in fact, valid JSON. You also will notice that this data is minimalistic. We can build on this first query by expanding the query to ask for not only the event but also the block number.

```
{
    transactions(first: 1) {
        block
        event
    }
}
```

The following result shows that the event was mined into block 6629139:

```
{
    "data": {
        "transactions": [{
            "block": "6629139",
            "event": "AddLiquidity"
        }]
    }
}
```

Another way that we can achieve/confirm this is to return all the event logs, ordered by block number in ascending order.

```
{
    transactions(orderBy: block, orderDirection: asc) {
        block
        event
    }
}
```

The query returns the following result:

```
{
    "data": {
        "transactions": [{
                "block": "6629139",
                "event": "AddLiquidity"
            },
            // ... data extracted for display purposes
        }
    ]
}
```

As TheGraph demonstrates, GraphQL could be an important tool for providing blockchain data to end-user applications.

Google BigQuery

As discussed earlier in this chapter, the Google Blockchain ETL project is a fully integrated data warehouse solution to ingest data from multiple blockchains into Google BigQuery tables. The data schema is designed to be unified across multiple blockchains. On all its blockchain data sets, the Google Blockchain ETL project supports the "double entry book" view that lists cryptocurrency transactions in traditional accounting formats.

You can then make queries against the data set using any query language that BigQuery supports, including SQL-like queries. For example, the following query verifies an account balance is indeed the sum of its transactions:

```
WITH double_entry_book AS (
    -- debits
```

```
SELECT
  array_to_string(inputs.addresses, ",") as address
, inputs.type
, -inputs.value as value
FROM `bigquery-public-data.crypto_bitcoin.inputs` as inputs
UNION ALL
-- credits
SELECT
  array_to_string(outputs.addresses, ",") as address
, outputs.type
, outputs.value as value
FROM `bigquery-public-data.crypto_bitcoin.outputs` as outputs
)
SELECT
    address
,   type
,   sum(value) as balance
FROM double_entry_book
GROUP BY 1,2
ORDER BY balance DESC
LIMIT 1000
```

The following query shows the frequency of different transaction fees on the Bitcoin blockchain:

```
SELECT
  ROUND((input_value - output_value)/ size, 0) AS fees_per_byte,
  COUNT(*) AS txn_cnt
FROM
  `bigquery-public-data.crypto_bitcoin.transactions`
WHERE TRUE
  AND block_timestamp >= '2018-01-01'
  AND is_coinbase IS FALSE
GROUP BY 1
```

The Google Blockchain ETL project provides a SQL-like cloud-based data warehousing solution for blockchain data. You can customize it to fit your own needs.

What's Next?

From a design perspective, let's briefly think back to the days of the Simple Object Access Protocol (SOAP). While SOAP facilitated communication between disparate machines, it also relied on a set of predefined application data types that were essentially a permanent structure. Any changes (for example, updates to the software application or changes to the static configuration) would disrupt or render the previously working interoperability inoperable. Simply put, SOAP is a rigid protocol.

Representational State Transfer (REST), on the other hand, introduced essentially an architectural style. Systems that conformed to all six architectural constraints were considered RESTful. Further, web services that adhered to the architectural constraints were considered RESTful APIs.

Still, in design mode, while it is tempting to explore ways in which we can, say, improve JSON compression (between the data provider and the dapp) and so forth, thinking like this takes us down the path of a protocol—a protocol that enforces that both sides have to agree on a predefined set of rules and that forces the client side (in this case the dapp) to perform additional work (unzipping, decoding, etc.).

Taking more of an architectural design viewpoint, would it be more effective, in terms of flexibility and interoperability, to focus on conventions as opposed to static configuration? We must remember that smart contract developers can create their own custom event logs that can emit one to many variables of various data types. Do we want to be setting up static configuration for each contract that is deployed in the blockchain network? Is human-driven static configuration sustainable? Can it be avoided altogether through the use of strong conventions and machine automation?

The next wave of blockchain architecture is rising, and right now there are big opportunities. I believe that upcoming blockchain data providers and explorer projects should do the following:

- Provide a mechanism to autonomously harvest a smart contract's event log data based purely on an application binary interface (ABI) file and a smart contract's address
- Automatically assign correct data field types (based solely on the smart contract's ABI)
- Require only a minimal amount of configuration and automated schema generation as per the previous point
- Provide sufficient internal querying, filtering, and logic to produce the most succinct responses
- Automatically/dynamically offer autocomplete syntax to the calling software
- Provide a variety of default visual front-end display portals
- Provide a library of built-in analytics (not only to explore trends, correlations, and so forth, but also to generate data sets for machine learning)
- Provide a mechanism to interoperate with ubiquitous business software, file formats, and content management and software development applications

This is an exciting time. We have an unprecedented amount of information, documentation, and software available, as well as the appropriate decentralized infrastructure to test and deploy your projects on.

Conclusion

In this chapter, I discussed how to build a blockchain data service. The blockchain explorers are pioneers in this space, but there is much more that can be done both on the harvesting side and on the query side. I believe that advanced off-chain storage and querying of blockchain data, especially smart contract execution data, is going to be a key component in the dapp ecosystem as well. In the next chapter, I will cover a new data service that provides real-time updates to public states of smart contracts. The data service is provided over a JavaScript library that complements web3.

## 11

Smart Contract Search Engine

The first-generation blockchain data browsers were focused primarily on providing snapshots of transaction details. For example, in the case of Bitcoin, they displayed verbatim records of structured data, as well as the results of valid transactions executed at the rigid base protocol layer.

The unprecedented rise of smart contracts, with customized data fields and unique internal programmable logic, has brought about the need for a new mechanism, one that can provide an easy way to search and visualize this new rich, unstructured blockchain data.

This mechanism is analogous to the rise of search engines while the Web grew in the 1990s. However, blockchain networks are unique in that they record all data in a time series of transactions. Smart contract data needs to be indexed and made available to both end users and machines in real time. Traditional web search engine technology is seldom used in the blockchain world because the World Wide Web and blockchain networks are fundamentally different. In this chapter, I will introduce an open source smart contract search engine. I will then discuss how to leverage it to power new types of dapps.

Introduction to the Smart Contract Search Engine

There are many ways to build a search engine for blockchain data. In this chapter, we focus on the open source search engine built by Second State. It works with all Ethereum-compatible blockchains and is production ready. Most important, it serves as an example for the coding and implementation patterns associated with smart contract search engines.

The Second State smart contract search engine has the components illustrated in Figure 11.1. You can get its complete source code and instructions from https://github.com/second-state/ smart-contract-search-engine.

- An Elasticsearch instance that indexes application binary interfaces (ABIs) and public data fields from contracts against contract addresses
- A full blockchain node that provides contract-related data as a standard JavaScript Object Notation–Remote Procedure Call (JSON-RPC) service

- A Python-based harvester script that extracts data from a blockchain node and then indexes and stores the data in Elasticsearch

- A Python-based web service that supports submitting contracts to index and Elasticsearch-like queries for real-time smart contract data

- A JavaScript library, es-ss.js, that enables client applications to interact with the web services

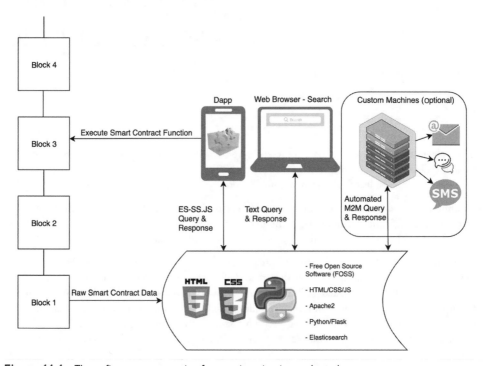

Figure 11.1   The software components of a smart contract search engine

It is easy to start a new smart contract search engine using Docker, but it requires a few hours to fully index a production blockchain and then keep all the indexed contracts updated with each new block. To make it easier for developers to get started, Second State and the community run a few search engine instances for public use.

- *Ethereum mainnet*: https://eth.search.secondstate.io/

- *Ethereum Classic (ETC) mainnet*: https://etc.search.secondstate.io/

- *CyberMiles mainnet*: https://cmt.search.secondstate.io/

- *Second State DevChain*: https://devchain.ss.search.secondstate.io/

You can load these URLs in a browser to see the current status of each of the public search engines. From there, you can search contract addresses that conform to specified contract interfaces (i.e., the ABI code) and then get up-to-date values in public fields for a contract address. For example, you could search all ERC20-compliant token contracts and see the symbol, supply, and values for each. You could also upload new ABIs to be indexed.

However, the most interesting use of a smart contract search engine is to serve as a data aggregator for new types of dapps. You can access the search engine functions programmatically from the es-ss.js library from your JavaScript application or web page. In the next section, we will look into a dapp that utilizes the search engine to interact with multiple smart contracts at the same time.

Getting Started with a Smart Contract Search Engine

The best way to get hands-on experience with a smart contract search engine and the es-ss.js library is through the BUIDL integrated development environment (IDE). See Chapter 3 for more on the BUIDL IDE tool. The simple dapp I will showcase here displays a number of AccountBalanceDemo contracts deployed on the blockchain. Each of these contracts stores a number that can be changed by the user. The search engine tracks and displays the tally of those numbers inside the contracts in real time. Figure 11.2 shows the dapp in action in a web browser.

The following code listing shows the smart contract. The contract simply stores a number that can be updated by the `setAccountBalance()` function call. You can copy and paste it into BUIDL's contract editor.

```
pragma solidity >=0.4.0 <0.6.0;

contract AccountBalanceDemo {

  string accountName;
  uint accountBalance;

  constructor(string _accountName) public {
    accountName = _accountName;
  }

  function setAccountBalance(uint _accountBalance) public {
    accountBalance = _accountBalance;
  }

  function getAccountName() public view returns(string) {
    return accountName;
  }

  function getAccountBalance() public view returns(uint) {
    return accountBalance;
  }
}
```

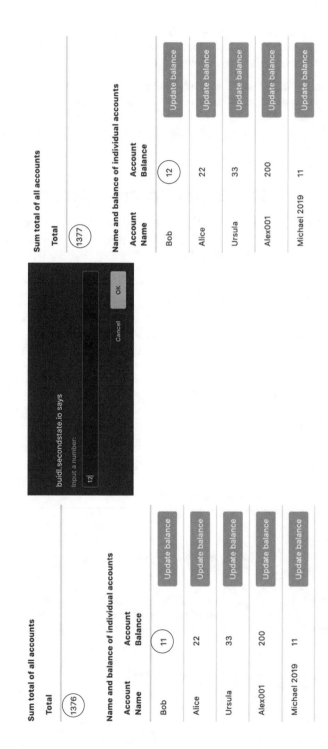

Figure 11.2   The AccountBalanceDemo dapp

Compile and deploy the smart contract by clicking the **Compile** and **Deploy to the chain** buttons. Make sure you give the account a name in the _accountName field before you click the **Deploy to the chain** button (see Figure 11.3).

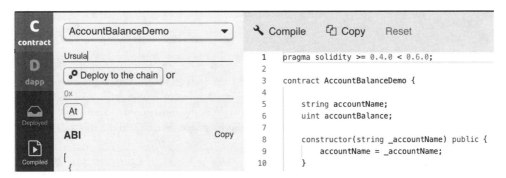

Figure 11.3   Deploying a new contract to be managed by the search-based dapp

Next, the following code listing shows the HTML code for the dapp. You can copy and paste it into BUIDL's dapp/HTML editor. It shows multiple AccountBalanceDemo contracts in a table and then the tally of their account balances in another table.

```
<!doctype html>
<html lang="en">
  <head>
    ... ...
    <title>Data Stores</title>
  </head>
  <body>
    <div class="container">
      <p>This page shows a list of individual accounts …</p>
      <p>Each account entity ...</p>
      <p>This page demonstrates ...</p>
      <b>Sum total of all accounts</b>
      <table class="table">
        <thead>
          <tr><th scope="col">Total</th></tr>
        </thead>
        <tbody id="totalBody"></tbody>
      </table>
      <p><b>Name and balance of individual accounts</b></p>
      <table class="table">
        <thead>
          <tr>
            <th scope="col">Account Name</th>
            <th scope="col">Account Balance</th>
            <th scope="col"></th>
```

```
          </tr>
        </thead>
        <tbody id="individualBody"></tbody>
      </table>
    </div>
  </body>
</html>
```

The HTML tables are rendered by JavaScript. As discussed earlier, the JavaScript application can use the web3.js library to communicate with a blockchain node. It could also use the es-ss.js library to communicate with the search engine. Both web3.js and es-ss.js are initialized and made available in the JavaScript by BUIDL. The following code listing shows the JavaScript application. You should copy and paste it into BUIDL's dapp/JavaScript editor. You should put the code outside of the /* Don't modify */ section.

```javascript
var abi_str = JSON.stringify(abi);
var sha = esss.shaAbi(abi_str).abiSha3;
reload();

function reload() {
  document.querySelector("#totalBody").innerHTML = "";
  document.querySelector("#individualBody").innerHTML = "";
  var tInner = "";
  var total = 0;
  esss.searchUsingAbi(sha).then((searchResult) => {
    var items = JSON.parse(searchResult);
    items.sort(compareItem);
    items.forEach(function(item) {
      tInner = tInner +
        "<tr id='" + item.contractAddress + "'><td>" +
        item.functionData.getAccountName +
        "</td><td>" + item.functionData.getAccountBalance +
        "</td><td><button class='btn btn-info' " +
        "onclick='setNumber(this)'>Update balance</button></td></tr>";
      total = total + parseInt(item.functionData.getAccountBalance);
}); // end of JSON iterator
    document.querySelector("#totalBody").innerHTML =
      "<tr id='total'><td>" + total + "</td></tr>";
    document.querySelector("#individualBody").innerHTML = tInner;
  }); // end of esss
}

function setNumber(element) {
    var tr = element.closest("tr");
    instance = contract.at(tr.id);
    var n = window.prompt("Input a number:");
    n && instance.setAccountBalance(n);
    setTimeout(function() {
```

```
      element.innerHTML = "Sending …";
      esss.updateStateOfContractAddress(
        abi_str, instance.address).then((c2i) => {
          reload();
      });
    }, 2 * 1000);
}

function compareItem(a, b) {
    let comparison = 0;
    if (a.blockNumber < b.blockNumber) {
        comparison = 1;
    } else if (a.blockNumber > b.blockNumber) {
        comparison = -1;
    }
    return comparison;
}
```

When the page loads, the `reload()` JavaScript function calls the Elasticsearch es-ss.js API to get all contracts with the AccountBalanceDemo type from the blockchain. It then computes the tally in the total variable. Notice that the current state, in other words, the account name and balance, of each contract is contained in the search result. We can simply display this information without having to interact with the slower blockchain nodes. The `reload()` function constructs HTML Document Object Model (DOM) elements to display those contract public data fields.

```
esss.searchUsingAbi(sha).then((searchResult) => {
  var items = JSON.parse(searchResult);
  items.forEach(function(item) {
    // Puts the items into the table
    total = total + parseInt(item.functionData.getAccountBalance);
  });
  // Displays the total
});
```

The Update balance buttons in the table trigger the `setNumber()` JavaScript function, which in turn calls the contract's `setAccountBalance()` function via web3. The JavaScript then calls the `esss.updateStateOfContractAddress()` function to explicitly inform the search engine that this contract has changed and calls the `reload()` function to refresh data from the search engine.

```
function setNumber(element) {
  ... ...
  instance.setAccountBalance(n);
  ... ...
  esss.updateStateOfContractAddress(
    abi_str, instance.address).then((c2i) => {
      reload();
  });
}
```

> ## Note
>
> Strictly speaking, the `updateStateOfContractAddress()` function call is not necessary, as the search engine works in near real time, and it automatically picks up the changes you just made in the `setAccountBalance()` function call via web3. But, as a best practice for improved stability, we recommend you explicitly inform the search engine of changes you make whenever you can.

Finally, you can hit the **Run** button to run the dapp in BUIDL and use the Publish button to publish it on a public web site (see Figure 11.2).

The FairPlay Dapp Example

FairPlay uses smart contracts to conduct automated prize draws that are fair and transparent. It allows anyone to create and participate in product giveaways and e-commerce marketing campaigns. It is a dapp running on the CyberMiles public blockchain, an Ethereum-compatible blockchain that features low-cost and fast consensus (learn more in Chapter 14).

The FairPlay dapp can be accessed from any web browser. The dapp runs web3.js and es-ss.js to fetch data from public blockchain nodes and search engine Elasticsearch nodes. The user does not need any special software (i.e., a crypto wallet) to view active and past giveaways. The FairPlay web app is simply a collection of HTML and JavaScript files (see Figure 11.4). Any user can start a web server on a computer and serve those files locally or publically. Hence, FairPlay is decentralized and resistant to censorship.

Figure 11.4 FairPlay is a web app that can be hosted by anyone and accessed on any web browser.

When the user needs to make a smart contract transaction, such as creating a new giveaway or participating in an existing giveaway, the web page directs the user to open the CyberMiles app to digitally sign and complete the operation (see Figure 11.5).

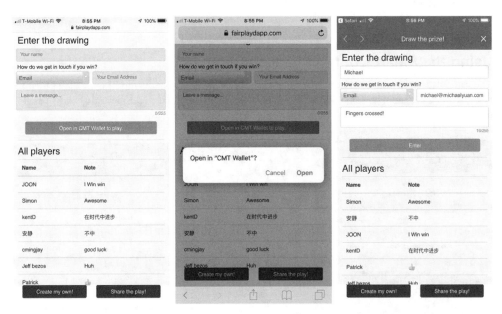

Figure 11.5   The FairPlay web app opens the CyberMiles app to send smart contract transactions.

FairPlay is a dapp in front of blockchain smart contracts. Under the hood, FairPlay has a modular architecture that is easy to develop and maintain. Key to this architecture is the smart contract search engine.

A Modular Architecture

Most of today's dapps rely on a single monolithic smart contract to serve as the "back end." The smart contract manages all application users and states. Even for systems that consist of multiple contracts, there is typically a registry or manager contract that provides aggregated information about the system.

However, a large smart contract is difficult to write and maintain. It tends to be error-prone and nearly impossible to fix when an error or issue is discovered, exacerbating the security problems that have plagued dapps today. The registry contract is also constrained by the limitations of today's smart contract programming languages and virtual machines. It cannot support complex data query operations.

The FairPlay dapp took a different approach. The dapp consists of many giveaway events, but each event is its own smart contract. When we create a new giveaway, we deploy a new instance of the FairPlay smart contract. When an event ends, its smart contract instance is discarded.

That allows us to continuously improve the FairPlay contract to add features and fix bugs, as each future giveaway event uses a new smart contract. However, a key challenge in this approach is how the dapp organizes all those smart contracts created by different addresses at different times and makes the information inside all those contracts available in a unified UI. Enter the search engine.

Using the Smart Contract Search Engine

The FairPlay dapp home screen displays results from the search engine (see Figure 11.6). It allows users to find giveaways containing specific keywords or tags, as well as giveaways the user previously participated in. The search engine indexes information from all FairPlay contracts deployed on the blockchain.

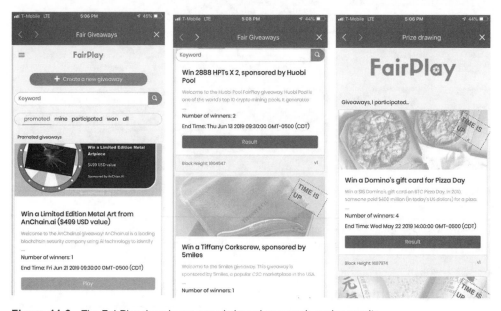

Figure 11.6   The FairPlay dapp home page is based on search engine results.

The smart contract search engine is also decentralized—anyone can create a search engine-based dapp in front of all FairPlay smart contracts. Each search engine-based dapp could use different algorithms and queries to surface and promote FairPlay giveaways tailored to its users and audience. This architecture is illustrated in Figure 11.7.

Each smart contract in the FairPlay dapp completes a limited set of specific business transactions. Smart contracts are small pieces of autonomous code that are designed to enforce simple business rules on the blockchain. All related smart contracts are aggregated in the search engine to provide a useful UI to users.

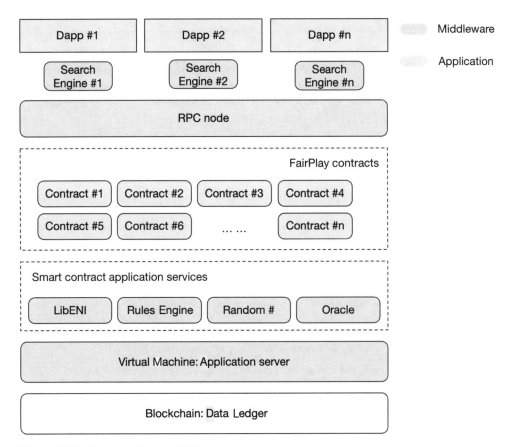

Figure 11.7   The decentralized FairPlay dapp

Use Cases

The FairPlay dapp is an example of how the smart contract engine supports data-intensive e-commerce dapps. The following sections present some more use cases.

Crypto Assets

Crypto assets are represented by a large number of standard contracts such as ERC20, ERC721, and even ERC1400. A search engine could provide an aggregated view of all account balances and transactions across those contracts.

Essentially, every ERC smart contract standard could benefit from a search engine that aggregates and displays information across all contracts of the same type.

DeFi

Decentralized crypto exchanges often have multiple asset pools each represented by a smart contract. A search engine can provide deep insights into the history and current state of those pools.

In general, decentralized finance (DeFi) solutions, such as algorithmic stable coins, crypto loans, and staking pools, all have asset pools held by smart contracts. A search engine could provide deep insights into those pools.

Gaming

Blockchains allow participants from anywhere in the world to play games against each other without the need for a central operator or a trusted setup. A decentralized game is run entirely in accordance with a smart contract's logic. The smart contract will not allow a player to perform an invalid move or participate out of turn. The smart contract ensures correctness and fairness, right from the initial rules of engagement through to the final payout or reward.

Dapps, which constitute the front end (a visually stimulating component of the game), obtain the real-time state of the game, programmatically, via the smart contract search engine API.

The entire ecosystem is safe and reliable. The following steps are repeated until a satisfactory outcome is achieved:

1. The dapp visually displays the current state of the game to the end users.
2. If it is their turn, each end user makes a choice by touching or swiping the screen.
3. The dapp submits that choice to the smart contract.
4. The smart contract validates the instruction set that the dapp sent.
5. The smart contract executes the instruction set if valid.
6. The smart contract's state is/isn't updated accordingly.
7. The dapp redisplays the current state of the game (via the API) to the end users.

Conclusion

In this chapter, I discussed how the smart contract search engine can provide rich and up-to-date blockchain data to enable complex dapps. For application developers, the search engine services (i.e., the es-ss.js library) can supplement web3 and support a modular architecture for dapps.

## 12

Smart Contract Security and Best Practices

By Victor Fang, PhD*

A smart contract, coined by American computer scientist Nick Szabo, is the revolutionary feature that defines blockchain 2.0, compared to the peer-to-peer decentralized transactions in the blockchain 1.0 era such as Bitcoin, Ripple, and so on.

As of 2019, Ethereum is the most widely adopted smart contract-enabled blockchain. An Ethereum smart contract is decentralized software that can be executed and verified on the Ethereum public blockchain.

Ethereum smart contracts are programmed in Solidity, a JavaScript-like programming language (ECMAScript syntax), and they run in the Ethereum Virtual Machine (EVM). You can learn more about Ethereum smart contracts in Chapter 6. Since Ethereum's launch in 2015, developers have witnessed a plethora of successful applications, as follows:

- Tokens, such as initial coin offerings (ICOs), security token offerings (STOs), and stable coins
- Dapps, such as FOMO3D and CryptoKitties
- Decentralized exchanges, such as the Decentralized Ethereum Asset Exchange (IDEX)

However, developers have also experienced major security vulnerabilities that caused billions of dollars in losses and concerns among the blockchain communities.

In this chapter, I will focus on the Ethereum smart contract and discuss the following:

- Major Ethereum smart contract hacks and vulnerabilities in history
- Best practices to secure smart contracts

---

* Victor Fang, PhD, is founder and CEO of AnChain.ai.

Major Ethereum Smart Contract Hacks and Vulnerabilities

Since the launch of Ethereum, the community witnessed major hacks that took over the headlines. In this chapter, I will review a few major hacks and illustrate the vulnerabilities behind those exploitations.

Decentralized Autonomous Organization Hack

The decentralized autonomous organization (DAO) hack is probably the most notorious hack in Ethereum history. A DAO is a decentralized autonomous organization. Its goal is to codify the rules and decision-making apparatus of an organization, eliminating the need for documents and people in governing and creating a structure with decentralized control.

In June 2016, an attacker drained 3.5 million ETH (about $50 million) from the DAO smart contract, after the ICO token sale had ended. It led to a hard fork of Ethereum. The technique the attackers used was reentrancy.

Reentrancy is also known as *recursive call vulnerability*. It occurs when external contract calls are allowed to make new calls to the calling contract before the initial execution is complete. For a function, this means that the contract state may change in the middle of its execution as a result of a call to an untrusted contract or the use of a low-level function with an external address. The minimal example for reentrancy is as follows:

```
function withdraw(uint _amount) {
    require(balances[msg.sender] >= _amount);
    msg.sender.call.value(_amount)();  // Reentrancy bug here.
    balances[msg.sender] -= _amount;
}
```

In this code example, `msg.sender.call.value` can be exploited by hackers. An attack contract could recursively call it until all gas is consumed.

In fact, reentrancy is quite common. In October 2018, SpankChain, a cryptocurrency project focused on the adult industry, suffered a breach that saw almost $40,000 in ETH stolen.

The AnChain.ai threat research team illustrated the recursive nature of reentrancy when SpankChain was attacked, as shown in Figure 12.1. Note that the hacker launched the attack contract that would cause SpankChain to recursively send ETH to the hacker's address, until all gas was consumed. Each `call_0`, `call_1_0`, and `call_1_1_0_0` is an EVM internal transaction indicating an external smart contract call. In this case, each internal call stole 0.5 ETH from the SpankChain smart contract!

BEC Token Hack

The Beauty Chain (BEC) token is particularly interesting because it shows how smart contract-based crypto assets can have a massive impact on a centralized crypto exchange (OK Exchange) in a subtle way, causing billions of dollars in losses.

Figure 12.1 The recursive nature of the reentrancy when the SpankChain smart contract was attacked

BEC was a high-profile cryptocurrency in China, and its stated goal was to be "a truly decentralized and beauty-themed ecosystem."

It started trading on OKEX on February 23, 2018. From its peak market cap of around $70 billion, it gradually came down to around $2 billion USD as of April 22, when its trading value suddenly dropped to zero. OKEX subsequently suspended trading of BECs.

The BEC token hack was because of an *integer overflow* vulnerability in its ERC20 smart contract. The annotated code line in the following listing multiplies two uint256 numbers and assigns the result to another uint256 variable, `amount`. Unfortunately, there is no overflow checking on that line. When a hacker passes a legitimate but large uint256 variable, it can cause the product to overflow. Figure 12.2 shows the transaction that exploits the integer overflow vulnerability.

```
function batchTransfer(address[] _receivers, uint256 _value)
                       public whenNotPaused returns (bool) {
  uint cnt = _receivers.length;
  uint256 amount = uint256(cnt) * _value; // Overflow
  require(cnt > 0 && cnt <= 20);
  require(_value > 0 && balances[msg.sender] >= amount);
```

```
balances[msg.sender] = balances[msg.sender].sub(amount);
for (uint i = 0; i < cnt; i++) {
  balances[_receivers[i]] = balances[_receivers[i]].add(_value);
  Transfer(msg.sender, _receivers[i], _value);
}
return true;
}
```

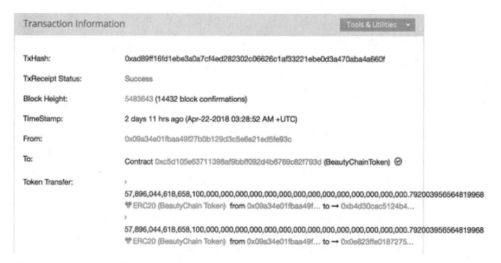

Figure 12.2   The exploited overflow vulnerability transaction of the BEC smart contract

The way to prevent this hack is to use SafeMath for all arithmetic. In fact, this smart contract used SafeMath in all except this particular function, and it caused catastrophic damage not only to BEC but also to all exchanges that traded it.

> **Note**
>
> There are ways to prevent integer overflows in smart contracts. The Lity language and virtual machine extensions to Ethereum check for integer overflow at compile time and then detect and abort the smart contract when there are integer overflows at runtime. See Chapter 14 for more.

The Parity Wallet Hack

The *Parity multisig bug* vulnerability showcases another way that a cryptographic smart contract design bug can damage part of the ecosystem: the wallet. The impacted Parity wallet is one popular wallet for Ethereum and tokens.

In fact, this bug is one of the common bugs in the top-ten list from Open Web Application Security Project (OWASP), categorized under access control. These issues are common in all programs, not just smart contracts.

The Parity multisig bug impacted all users with assets in a multisig wallet created in Parity wallet that was deployed after July 20, 2017, worth $155 million USD. This bug was patched immediately after the hack.

The attacker sent two transactions to each of the affected contracts.

Step 1: Obtain Exclusive Ownership of the Multisig

In the wallet contract, the `payable()` function contains a bug that causes all public functions from the library to be callable by anyone, including `initWallet`, which can change the contract's owners.

Unfortunately, `initWallet` has no checks to prevent an attacker from calling it after the contract was initialized. The attacker exploited this and simply changed the contract's owner state variable to the hacker's addresses. This modified the access control and persisted in the immutable Ethereum blockchain.

Step 2: Move All of Its Funds

After the hacker took over the ownership, it was just a matter of invoking the execute function to send all the funds to the hacker's account! This execution was automatically authorized since the attacker was then the only owner of the multisig, effectively draining the contract of all its funds.

FOMO3D and LastWinner Dapp Hack

Dapps are a dominant trend enabled by smart contracts. As of March 2019, there were 2,667 dapps running on public blockchains, and the number will likely grow tremendously. Please see Chapter 7 for more on Ethereum dapp development.

FOMO3D is a gambling dapp (Figure 12.3) that was so popular in July/August 2018 that it even congested the Ethereum blockchain. The FOMO3D game rules are simple and as follows:

- A user buys a key, in other words, a lottery ticket, to participate.
- When anyone buys a key, the countdown clock adds a few seconds, with 24 hours being the maximum.
- The final buyer when the clock hits 0 wins the jackpot!
- Each key buyer receives random airdrop bonuses.

In fact, FOMO3D is a typical Ponzi scheme that theoretically should never stop, because it is driven by human nature: greed.

Unfortunately, FOMO3D, and its copycat LastWinner, were both hacked in August 2018. Those hacks led to the discovery of *blockchain advanced persistent threats* (BAPTs). *Advanced persistent threat* (APT) is defined as stealthy and continuous computer hacking processes, often orchestrated by people targeting a specific entity. So, BAPTs are APTs applied to blockchains.

Figure 12.3   FOMO3D dapp, played by Victor Fang in July 2018

> **Note**
>
> According to *MIT Technology Review*, "In August 2018, AnChain.ai identified five Ethereum addresses behind an extremely sophisticated attack that exploited a contract flaw in a popular gambling game to steal $4 million." In response, the creators of FOMO3D, commented that everything worked as intended. "No rules we set in place were broken. Our experiments strive to find exploits where human nature and blockchain interact. We design our projects around fighting such threats, We were not a bank that was robbed. The very goal of our project was for someone to win it and run away with everything!"

Random number generation (RNG) is commonly used in dapps, just like all online Internet games. Think about an online poker game. The house will generate the hand based on a random number generator for every play.

A perfect random number should mathematically have high entropy and cannot be predicted. However, on-blockchain RNG turns out to be quite challenging because of the nature of the blockchain: immutable, decentralized, transparent.

Once the dapp has "bad randomness," it will be exploited by hackers who can predict the game play.

> **Note**
>
> The Lity language and virtual machine extend the Ethereum protocol to provide highly secure random number seeds for smart contracts when the underlying blockchain consensus is delegated proof of stake (DPoS). Please see Chapter 14 for more details.

The following is the code snippet of the FOMO3D `airdrop()` function that will generate a random number based on various sources such as `timestamp`, `block coinbase`, `sender`, and so on, yielding the result if the participant is the winner or not.

```
function airdrop() private view returns(bool) {
  uint256 seed = uint256(keccak256(abi.encodePacked(
  (block.timestamp).add
  (block.difficulty).add
  ((uint256(keccak256(abi.encodePacked(block.coinbase)))) / (now)).add
  (block.gaslimit).add
  ((uint256(keccak256(abi.encodePacked(msg.sender)))) / (now)).add
  (block.number)
  ))); // Random number generation

  if((seed - ((seed / 1000) * 1000)) < airDropTracker_)
    return(true);
  else
    return(false);
}
```

Technically, this `airdrop()` function is bug-free. However, in the context of a blockchain-based smart contract, this code is vulnerable, as explained here:

- The Ethereum blockchain takes seconds to reach the consensus.

- This code can be executed in milliseconds in a typical computer, which is 1,000 times faster than on the blockchain.

- This smart contract source code is transparent to everyone on the blockchain.

- All the random number seeds used are transparent to everyone on the blockchain; in other words, there's a lack of entropy.

Based on these facts, it is feasible for a hacker to design a malicious smart contract to exploit this bad randomness, by precomputing the `airdrop()` result, and participating in FOMO3D only when the result is known to be winning! Brilliant idea!

Figure 12.4 visualizes the entire hacking campaign. There were 2 million transactions involved over the course of 2 weeks, and there were 22,000+ Ethereum addresses involved. Most of them were malicious attack smart contracts, launched by the five wallet addresses!

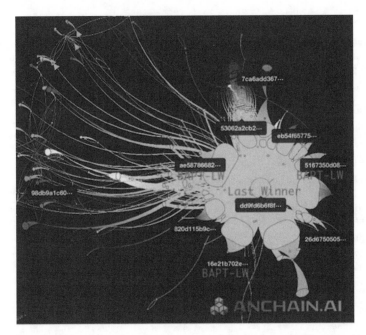

Figure 12.4   Visualization of the BAPT-LW hacker group (more than five ETH wallet addresses) attacking LastWinner, a FOMO3D copycat dapp, in August 2018

Unknowns and Beyond

Note that these reported vulnerabilities may be only the tip of the iceberg. There were more than 1 million smart contracts deployed on Ethereum at the end of 2018, while only 50,000 of them contained publicly accessible source code.

Based on research powered by the AnChain.ai smart contract auditing sandbox, more than 0.6 percent of the 50,000 mainnet-deployed smart contract source code is vulnerable to a reentrancy attack. There are 57,911 known vulnerabilities among all of them.

Even a known vulnerability can repeat history. On January 16, 2019, the Constantinople protocol upgrade was delayed, at the last minute, because of a security vulnerability enabled by EIP 1283. This vulnerability led to the possibility of a new reentrancy vector making previously known secure withdrawal patterns (`.send()` and `.transfer()`) unsafe in specific situations, where the attacker could hijack the control flow and use the remaining gas enabled by EIP 1283. The upgrade was hence delayed. Otherwise, another Ethereum catastrophe would happen.

On the other hand, there may be unknown vulnerabilities that already exist but have not yet been discovered, like zero-day bugs in the cybersecurity industry.

I will conclude this section with the Decentralized Application Security Project (DASP) top-ten vulnerabilities of 2018:

- Reentrancy
- Access control

- Arithmetic
- Unchecked low-level calls
- Denial of service
- Bad randomness
- Front running
- Time manipulation
- Short addresses
- Unknown unknowns

Best Practices for Securing Smart Contracts

As you can see from the previously mentioned major smart contract hacks, developing secure smart contracts can be quite challenging.

In fact, Steve McConnell's "Code Complete" shows the following statistics for the number of bugs per line of code:

- *Industry average*: About 15 to 50 errors per 1,000 lines of delivered code
- *Microsoft applications*: About 10 to 20 defects per 1,000 lines of code during in-house testing and 0.5 defect per 1,000 lines of code in released products

Another challenge for the Ethereum blockchain is that it's hard to change the smart contract code once it's deployed. Think about Microsoft Windows patches that arrive weekly to fix known vulnerabilities. There is no such mechanism on the blockchain. It's "code is law."

> **Note**
>
> The Lity project provides a mechanism to upgrade Ethereum-compatible smart contracts on Lity-based blockchains. The idea is to declare the contract interface at the contract address and then provide proxy implementations of all the functions.

Hence, it is critical to write secure code in the upcoming smart contract era. Fortunately, there are various projects and startups that aim to help developers secure their smart contracts by performing auditing to identify vulnerabilities.

The following are a few best practices.

Expert Manual Auditing

The widely adopted way to audit smart contracts, especially the ICO tokens, is called *expert manual auditing*. Solidity is new programing language and lacks security tools compared to the commercial tools in the well-established cybersecurity industry such as Coverity for enterprise C++/Java source code auditing. The experts are mostly computer language experts with experience to identify vulnerabilities manually.

Formal Verification

Formal verification (FV) is one of the promising fields for smart contract auditing that aims to mathematically prove the source code correctness. According to an EE Times article by Alok Sanghavi, "Formal verification is the act of proving or disproving the correctness of intended algorithms underlying a system with respect to a certain formal specification or property, using formal methods of mathematics." In fact, the formal method dates back 40 years ago, and there are various applications such as Windows leveraging formal verification to prove some of the critical kernel modules' source code correctness.

Sandbox

A *sandbox*, simply put, is a specially designed virtual machine that can automatically execute the opcode instructions in a restricted environment. It's a proven technology in cybersecurity; companies like FireEye and Palo Alto Network develop malware sandbox products that can detect the most sophisticated malware like APT32, and so on.

For example, modern advanced malware is polymorphic, which means it will modify its own bytes, while most antivirus (AV) software still relies on signature-based detection, which is a hash of the payload bytes. Hence, this polymorphic malware can bypass the AV detection since they have different hashes, even though they function similarly. Alternatively, the sandbox will analyze the code execution behaviors and look for suspicious patterns in a fully automated fashion.

Inspired by the proven success of the malware sandbox, AnChain.ai developed the world's first smart contract auditing sandbox and launched in February 2019. A good sandbox product should have built-in features such as static analysis, dynamic execution, statistical analysis, code similarity, and so on.

Tools

Based on these best practices, the following are popular open source tools that can get you started with secure smart contracts:

- *Mythril Classic*: This is an open source EVM bytecode security analysis tool. See https://github.com/ConsenSys/mythril-classic.

- *Oyente*: This is an alternative for static smart contract security analysis. See https://github.com/melonproject/oyente.

- *Slither*: This is a Solidity static analysis framework. See https://github.com/crytic/slither.

- *Adelaide*: This is the SECBIT static analysis extension to the Solidity compiler. See https://github.com/sec-bit/Adelaide.

> **Note**
>
> The Lity project (see https://www.litylang.org) provides Ethereum-compatible tools to perform static analysis at compile time, using tools like Oyente and ERC Checker. See Chapter 15 for more details.

Conclusion

In this chapter, I covered the major Ethereum smart contract hacks and vulnerabilities in its short history and discussed best practices for securing smart contracts.

Ethereum is still in its infancy. I consider it to be like 1990's Internet, slow and vulnerable. But it will soon become as mature as 2019's Internet. However, with data breaches and APT hacks occasionally making headlines, even Internet security still has a long way to go. Security is a collaborative effort that involves many specialized experts, teams, and tools. Are you ready to secure your smart contracts?

## 13

The Future of Ethereum

By Tim McCallum

The creator of Ethereum, Vitalik Buterin, defines *blockchain* as a decentralized system that contains shared memory, and as such, a good blockchain application is one that needs both a decentralized architecture and shared memory capabilities across the network's architecture. Ethereum's focus, to date, has been on decentralization (philosophically, decentralizing the Internet). The Internet, while possessing the design characteristics to be decentralized, has since its inception become increasingly centralized. The Ethereum network provides guaranteed decentralized computation on a global scale. In addition to this, the Ethereum network holds shared memory within the entire network, known as the *state*.

These attributes, in a technical sense, make Ethereum a "world computer." It has already proven that it can support next-generation decentralized applications (dapps) that facilitate customized online payments, authentication mechanisms, decentralized storage solutions (swarm), digital currencies, and much more.

In this chapter, I begin by covering the 2018 development of Ethereum. I will discuss how the Ethereum foundation's researchers and Ethereum developers are solving present-day challenges. I then step into the future by uncovering developments that are at the fringe; these are developments that could materialize as proof of concepts for early adoption around 2020. Before concluding the future of Ethereum, I look well into the future at the "hard-to-implement" paradigm shifts that, if realized, could propel Ethereum forward, beyond what is even imaginable today in terms of privacy, scalability, and security.

> **Note**
>
> Potential improvements to the Ethereum network go through the Ethereum Improvement Proposal (EIP) process before being implemented. The stages for EIPs are draft, accepted, final, and differed. Finalized EIPs are proposals that have been adopted. For a proposal to succeed, the issuer is required to provide detailed information including the motivation, specifications, rationale, and backward compatibility. The proposal may also provide code examples.

One of the most famous EIPs is EIP20, which defines the smart contracts for issuing ERC20 tokens on the Ethereum blockchain. You can read the EIP20 standard at `https://github.com/ethereum/EIPs/blob/master/EIPS/eip-20.md`. You can review all EIPs at `https://github.com/ethereum/EIPs`.

Ethereum 1.0

There were three main categories of challenges on the table for Ethereum in 2018. These are privacy, consensus, and scalability. The Ethereum Foundation's researchers and Ethereum developers have already made inroads into solving these problematic areas. As you will read shortly, Ethereum has already released its hybrid proof-of-work (PoW)/proof-of-stake (PoS) consensus mechanism known as Casper the Friendly Finality Gadget (FFG). The future Ethereum road map is very exciting and full of activity. To kick things off, let's take a look at the problems and solutions around privacy, consensus, and scalability in a bit more depth.

Privacy

The privacy paradox is such that while lots of nodes are verifying your data on the public ledger (providing security through collaborative consensus), having your data on the public ledger, in fact, compromises your privacy. Here is an example. If somebody knew the date, time, and amount particulars of a transaction that you sent or received, that person could inspect the public ledger and identify your account's address (public key). This issue is common to most public distributed ledgers (blockchains), not just Ethereum. What is important is, from that moment, that person could track your account balance, income, and spending via the public ledger. This is an invasion of your privacy. Inroads have been made into resolving the privacy problem at the base protocol level. The Byzantium fork released by Ethereum in October 2017 introduced new cryptographic algorithms (zero-knowledge proofs and ring signatures). These cryptographic tools and other enhancements to the Ethereum network such as the introduction of state channels are all going to help developers resolve these and other privacy problems.

Consensus

Chapter 2 discussed the PoW and PoS consensus mechanisms of blockchains. Ethereum, since its inception, has always been a PoW blockchain. However, with the next-generation Ethereum, it is moving toward PoS. The switch from PoW to PoS is perhaps the greatest challenge and opportunity facing the Ethereum community today.

The advent of the PoW protocol introduced one of the most revered blockchain attributes: immutability. More specifically, it is computationally impractical to reverse past transactions while computers (nodes on the peer-to-peer blockchain network) are competing to expend their computational energy, creating new blocks (mining the blockchain). Ethereum currently also uses the PoW consensus protocol, and just like with Bitcoin, the PoW consensus process on the Ethereum network thrives as computers all compete on the network, expending their computational energy, to create new blocks on top of the blockchain.

While PoW has many strengths, it is also criticized in relation to energy efficiency and potential centralization of the PoW mining process.

Proof of Stake

In October 2017, Ethereum's Vitalik Buterin and colleague Virgil Griffith released a publication called Casper the Friendly Finality Gadget. Casper FFG is a partial consensus mechanism that combines PoS algorithm research and Byzantine fault-tolerant consensus theory. Importantly, for implementation, Casper FFG was designed to overlay an existing operational PoW blockchain. Hence, Casper FFG is a hybrid PoW/PoS consensus solution. While a formal move to PoS will only happen on Ethereum 2.0, the PoS experimentation has already started on Ethereum 1.0.

There are more than three Ethereum testnets. These Ethereum testnets are sandboxes, used to simulate the Ethereum network and the Ethereum Virtual Machine (EVM). Ethereum's hybrid PoW/PoS implementation, Casper FFG, was launched in its own testnet (not in production) in January 2018. The following discussion is an early overview of the Casper FFG PoW/PoS hybrid consensus solution.

In PoW mining, a miner is given a challenge: finding a nonce. Finding the nonce is done by brute force and involves randomly guessing repeatedly until the nonce is discovered. This process is miners' proof that they have worked. That's why it's called *proof of work*. In PoS, the blocks are created by validators. Validators are allowed to participate in creating blocks only if they put skin in the game. This involves staking a large deposit (at this early stage believed to be around 1,500 ETH). That's why it's called *proof of stake*.

PoS validation is unlike PoW mining from a hardware perspective as there is no specialized competing hardware required. The validators are all virtual (software). The process of joining and leaving the role of being a validator in PoS is known as *bonding* and *unbonding*, respectively. So, how is the bonding and unbonding recorded? Casper FFG saves the bonding and unbonding activity in the blockchain state (along with account balances and so forth). Anyone can join the set of validators by sending an Ethereum transaction to the Casper contract (along with some parameters such as a withdrawal address and of course ETH for gas).

The basic premise behind PoS validation involves economic incentives. For example, a bonded validator who exerts clearly bad behavior (like creating two blocks at the same height) will be penalized economically. On the other hand, a bonded validator that does not deliberately attack the network will receive returns, or interest, on the deposit that they have staked. In the Casper FFG PoS implementation, the number of opportunities where manipulation is more profitable than the costs associated with performing the manipulation is small. Ideally, there would be close to zero (no) opportunities to manipulate (attack) the network without encountering a severe economic penalty. In a given PoW blockchain implementation (where all nodes are running the same PoW consensus mechanism), the chain with the most blocks (the longest chain) wins (see Figure 13.1). This is because it exhibits the most proof of work.

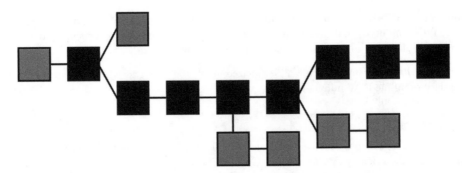

Figure 13.1   The PoW algorithm identifies the longest chain as the authoritative one.

In Casper FFG PoS, the chain with the most value at risk (VaR) supporting it wins. The general principle is that if you support a block that does not make it into the main chain, instead of being rewarded you get penalized. You lose an amount of ETH that is equal to the block reward. In practice, let's propose that there are two blocks available to support. The block on chain A has a 90 percent chance of succeeding. The block on chain B has a 10 percent chance of succeeding. If you support chain A, you will be rewarded. If you support chain B, you will be penalized. A potential economic conundrum comes into play if you start thinking that you could support both A and B for profit. Ethereum has a clever way of making this unappealing. In this case, where you have split your bet two ways, you will only be allowed to receive 50 percent of the reward from chain A (if it succeeds) and 50 percent of the reward from chain B (if it succeeds). This betting on both sides will always net a lesser result than just supporting chain A. This economic incentive results in convergence, and this is the desired path to ensure a single honest chain via PoS consensus. The following is a simple, albeit concrete, example for demonstration purposes.

Suppose the block reward is 10 ETH. Suppose you, as a validator, support a block on chain A and a block on chain B. In a scenario where chain A succeeds, you would receive 5 ETH (only 50 percent of the block reward) from your efforts on chain A, and you would lose 10 ETH (the entire block reward) for supporting a block on chain B. The net result for this scenario would be negative 5 ETH for your efforts.

In PoS, the validator needs to authenticate. It has been proposed that, instead of simply using a private key, a validator code function be created. This modular design would mean that the validator could choose alternative signatures when authenticating. For example, the validator could choose to use a Lamport signature as these are believed to be secure against quantum computer threats.

Scalability

Blockchain systems trade off against decentralization, scalability, and security. It is reasonably easy to solve any two out of these three issues at any one time. Vitalik Buterin quips that this is a blockchain "trillema," whereby you can easily solve two issues at the cost of the third, but you can't easily solve all three.

Plasma

Plasma is just one of the strategies that could address blockchain scalability. Plasma is different from sharding (covered later in the chapter). A successful plasma implementation would send transactions off-chain to improve scalability. In this regard, plasma is what is known as a second-layer solution. Second-layer solutions are implemented through code that is written outside of the base protocol layer (or, commonly known as the layer 1 protocol). More specifically, second-layer solutions have no effect on the base protocol layer's consensus mechanism. Just to clarify, plasma differs from sharding in that a successful sharding solution would be coded into the base protocol layer. Plasma is designed to be compatible with on-chain scaling solutions such as sharding and therefore not only can coexist but can even be complementary. In fact, on-chain scalability improvements will just further increase the scalability of the second-layer solution.

Plasma is a set of nested blockchains. These plasma blockchains are created using smart contracts on the main Ethereum network. Uploading your smart contract onto the public Ethereum blockchain allows you to launch your own specific applications. Applications can include decentralized exchanges, social networks, payment networks, and even your own private Ethereum blockchain implementation. These plasma blockchains (your applications) are all accountable to the public Ethereum blockchain.

The scalability is brought about by the fact that while processing an extremely high volume of transactions, the plasma blockchains do not submit their entire transaction volume to the public Ethereum blockchain. Instead, the plasma blockchains send only a small amount of data (block header hashes) about the plasma blockchains state. Plasma works on the premise that data being submitted to the main chain is free from fraudulent activity, while the public Ethereum blockchain is not required to perform computation in general. If anyone can publish a proof that fraudulent activity took place (a dispute), the public Ethereum blockchain performs computation, resolving the dispute and punishing the offending participant.

State Channels

State channels are a mechanism that allow two participants to sign promises, at given points in time. These time-based off-chain signed promises provide proof of activity. State channels provide an opportunity for decentralized applications to interact with other parties (customers) off-chain. This provides a cheap and fast user experience, which would not be possible on-chain. State channels are smart contracts. State channels are also a second-layer solution to the Ethereum scalability problem. From a usability perspective (dapp development), having a high volume of off-chain activity means low to negligible gas fees. As such, dapps that employ state channels as part of their solution not only offer near real-time activity but also the ability for customers to send and receive micro-payments. A use case for this could be a gambling application that allows a high volume of micro-betting, in real time, for entertainment purposes.

Raiden

The Raiden network leverages off-chain state channels. The Raiden network offers micro payments of ERC20-compliant tokens while taking negligible fees and providing responses to transactions in near real time. The difference between state channels and the Raiden network is that rather than creating a new state channel for every new interaction between two parties,

Raiden creates a network of channels whereby all participants are transitively connected via a web of ERC20 token–complaint payment channels, making use of natural network topology architecture.

Token Improvements

The ERC20 tokens have proven to be a great success. ERC20 has found one of the first killer applications for Ethereum, as an initial coin offering (ICO) token sale platform. The Ethereum community is working on further improving tokens issued from the Ethereum smart contracts.

One of the more interesting ideas is nonfungible tokens (NFTs). A key characteristic of money is fungible, meaning that a dollar bill is completely interchangeable with another dollar bill. That is the case for blockchain tokens as well. While you can trace the use of each token in the ledger, no two tokens are different. But with NFTs, a token is truly unique. The famous Ethereum game CryptoKitties is a good example of how NFTs can be applied, as each "cat" is completely unique. The ERC721 proposes an NFT standard that is compatible with ERC20. Such NFTs could enable many token applications ranging from collectibles trading to real estate transactions. To participate in this EIP, please refer to https://github.com/ethereum/eips/issues/721.

Beyond Ethereum 1.0

Ethereum has had plans for some time to create a blockchain to surpass the current second-layer solutions on offer. The overall vision has primarily been to create a blockchain solution that is capable of scaling to thousands of on-chain transactions per second, with the most promising of the proposed solutions being sharding.

Sharding

The original idea for sharding was that the main Ethereum blockchain would publish what is known as a *validator manager contract*. In this scenario, the validator manager contract would simply be a single smart contract on the Ethereum 1.0 blockchain. It was decided (in July 2017) shortly after disparate development processes in the areas of both Casper (PoS) and sharding that this architecture would change. The most significant change to the original idea was to make the core component of the sharding system not just a smart contract but instead a complete PoS chain. This shift from a PoW smart contract to a self-sufficient PoS chain would remove the need for gas, reduce transaction times, and reduce dependency on the underlying EVM.

The "Ethereum 2.0" section explains this new sharding architecture, namely, the introduction of the beacon chain.

Zero-Knowledge Proofs

This section explains the basic premise of the zero-knowledge proofs. In a given binary situation (where there are only two outcomes available, either yes or no), a "prover" with the secret weapon to discern a binary statement from the situation must convince a skeptical "verifier" that the binary statement is correct, while not revealing the secret. In 2003 a Weizmann Institute of Science faculty member, Oded Goldreich, introduced a novel zero-knowledge proof involving a color-blind validator. In this scenario, the validator possessed two cards, one red and the other green. To the color-blind validator, the cards looked the same, other than the fact that the word *red* was written on the back of the red card, and the word *green* was written on the back of the other. Let's play out this scenario and assume that the validator is skeptical about the prover's claim to be able to discern the cards without seeing the words on the back. To move this experiment forward, the validator would repeatedly show the prover the front side of each card, in a random fashion. Each time, the validator would ask the prover what color he sees. After some time, the verifier would eventually be convinced that the prover is capable of discerning the colors of the two individual cards. This is mostly because the verifier performed this over many rounds and the validator randomly switched the cards behind his back during each round.

The following are the three properties that a zero-knowledge proof must satisfy:

- *Completeness*: This is when the honest verifier is convinced that the honest prover returned the correct answer in the binary statement.

- *Zero knowledge*: This is where the verifier has no knowledge of how the prover came up with the binary statement and learns nothing from the process other than that the binary statement provided by the prover is correct.

- *Soundness*: This is where a prover (even a dishonest one who is just guessing the answer of the binary statement) is able to convince an honest verifier that the answer is correct.

While the first two properties can be quite easily satisfied during one round of an interactive zero-knowledge proof exercise, there is statistically only a 50 percent chance of achieving soundness. Put simply, a dishonest prover could just take a 50/50 guess to the binary situation and get it right 50 percent of the time.

With this in mind, it is important to remember that zero-knowledge proofs are probabilistic. They are not deterministic. They rely on randomness to succeed.

This information describes a specific type of zero-knowledge protocol known as *interactive*. In an interactive zero-knowledge protocol, the verifier and the prover must repeat each round until the verifier is convinced, without any reasonable doubt, that the prover knows the secret.

A noninteractive zero-knowledge protocol is different because it requires only a single round. A noninteractive zero-knowledge proof, however, requires a "trusted setup." One advantage of the noninteractive zero-knowledge protocol is that it allows many verifiers to all independently query the ability of the prover. Think of this as a one-to-many relationship between the prover and verifier entities, as opposed to the interactive zero-knowledge protocol's one-to-one relationship.

ZK-SNARKs

Zero-Knowledge Succinct Non-interactive ARguments of Knowledge (ZK-SNARKs) are able to be satisfied through computer code, and as such zero-knowledge proof implementations have tremendous potential in the online space. Just one example of ZK-SNARKs' potential is the creation of a decentralized, anonymous, sealed-bid auction. In this case, while the logic of determining the winner would execute successfully, the winner's identity and the winning bid amount could both remain confidential.

You can think of ZK-SNARKs in the following way. ZK-SNARKs are for arbitrary computations, just as hashing algorithms are for arbitrary data. Put simply, you can turn an arbitrary computation into a ZK-SNARK, and since verifying arbitrary computations is at the core of the Ethereum blockchain, ZK-SNARKs are of course relevant to Ethereum. If implemented in Ethereum, ZK-SNARKs would not be limited to a single computational problem. Enabling ZK-SNARKs for Ethereum would, among other things, reduce the gas costs for certain pairing functions and elliptic curve operations. Overall, the biggest payoff for enabling ZK-SNARKs would be improved (guaranteed) performance of the EVM. Unfortunately, an implementation of this magnitude would be extremely difficult to complete and as such might take many years to move from proof of concept to early adoption. This may be something that will be implemented in the future of Ethereum. Let's now compare ZK-STARKs.

ZK-STARKs

The confidentiality of a zero-knowledge proof is already being used to enhance privacy in cryptocurrencies. For example, Zcash already uses the ZK-SNARKs protocol. I just mentioned the possibility of an Ethereum implementation of ZK-SNARKs and the associated advantages. However, a shinier new cousin, Zero Knowledge Succinct Transparent ARguments of Knowledge (ZK-STARKs), looks to resolve one of the primary weaknesses of ZK-SNARKs: the reliance on a trusted setup. Interestingly, ZK-STARKs have also arrived with much simpler cryptographic assumptions. You may recall that ZK-SNARKs were promising advantages in relation to pairing functions and elliptical curve operations. Well, ZK-STARKs avoid the need for elliptic curves, pairings, and the knowledge-of-exponent assumption; instead, ZK-STARKs rely purely on hashes and information theory.

This means that while ZK-STARKs bring about efficiency gains and more, they are also secure against attackers with quantum computers. Looking toward the future, ZK-STARKs could replace ZK-SNARKs, providing superior scalability and privacy, specifically to decentralized public ledgers like Ethereum. It is also important to note that these advantages all come at a cost. In other words, the size of a proof goes up from 288 bytes to a few hundred kilobytes. Further research is required in relation to shortening proof length or the aggregation and compression of several ZK-STARK proofs.

In the context of public blockchain applications, there is a high need for trust minimization, possibilities that elliptic curves could break, and a seemingly real possibility of quantum computers coming around. Given all of these points, implementing ZK-STARKs in decentralized public ledgers seems worth it, even if there are costs involved.

Ethereum 2.0

Ethereum 2.0 comprises many separate components. Casper PoS, sharding, and Ethereum-flavored WebAssembly (eWASM) have been on the minds of Ethereum developers for quite some time. For example, Vitalik Buterin has been writing about PoS implementation ideas since as far back as 2014. This blend of technologies somehow resulted in Ethereum 2.0 adopting the unfortunate name of Shasper, a combination of sharding and Casper PoW. Thankfully, most of the time nowadays you will see it referred to as either Serenity or simply Ethereum 2.0.

After years of research and development, these Ethereum 2.0 ideas are making their way into the code repositories of many Ethereum developers throughout the community. For example, there are many individual implementations of the Ethereum 2.0 specification, such as a Rust implementation of the Ethereum 2.0 beacon chain and a Java implementation of the Ethereum 2.0 beacon chain. The official Ethereum reference implementation, which these other repositories are modeling, is a Python implementation of the Ethereum 2.0 beacon chain.

The Ethereum 2.0 specification documents indicate that Ethereum 2.0 can initially be implemented without any consensus changes to Ethereum 1.0. This means that at this early stage, the Ethereum 1.0 base layer will not undergo a fork or chain split while moving these exciting ideas forward into production. As I will discuss shortly, a contract (the gateway to the Ethereum 2.0) will be added to Ethereum 1.0, and deposits into this contract will allow users to become validators on the Ethereum 2.0 beacon chain.

The Beacon Chain

One of the core components, mentioned in the Ethereum 2.0 specifications, is the beacon chain. The *beacon chain* is the central PoS chain that underpins the sharding system. The beacon chain stores and maintains a registry of validators.

Validators

The beacon chain invites new validators to join Ethereum 2.0. As previously mentioned, validators join the beacon chain by simply depositing ether into the appropriate Ethereum 1.0 contract. An actively participating validator is able to propose blocks on the beacon chain. A validator who creates an Ethereum 2.0 beacon chain block is also known as a *proposer*. In addition to proposing blocks, validators are also able to sign off on beacon chain blocks. However, to do so, the validator has to be part of a committee. Validators cannot self-select to be part of a committee. Instead, committees of independent validators are assembled in a random fashion. Randomness is generated by the beacon chain itself. A validator can exit the beacon chain voluntarily or be forced to exit in the event that the validator attacks the chain.

Shard Chain

There are many shard chains. Shard chains are where end-user transactions take place and where transaction information is stored. When signing off (attesting to) a block, the committee of validators create what is known as a *crosslink*. A crosslink is essentially a set of validator signatures, attesting to a block in a shard chain that is then confirmed into the beacon chain. A crosslink allows updates in a shard chain to be communicated with the beacon chain; in other words, crosslinks are used to determine the finality of shards.

Note

A very interesting implication of sharding is that today's Ethereum-compatible blockchains such as Ethereum Classic and CyberMiles can now interoperate within the new Ethereum 2.0

ecosystem. For example, Ethereum Classic and its established miner community will stay as a PoW chain within the ecosystem. Its native cryptocurrency, the ETC, will become the PoW store-of-value coin in the ecosystem.

One of the design goals of Ethereum 2.0 is to allow for a typical consumer laptop to process (validate) shards, including any system-level validation such as the beacon chain. This is made possible because the sharding architecture now uses its own PoS chain as opposed to the original idea, mentioned earlier, where the old sharding architecture used to consist of a single smart contract on the PoW chain.

You may have already realized by now that Ethereum 2.0/Serenity is a new blockchain, albeit it's one that links to the existing Ethereum 1.0 PoW chain (i.e., the new PoS chain is aware of the block hashes of the PoW chain, and so forth). The goal for this architecture will allow ether to be moved between the original PoW chain and the PoS chain. In addition, the long-term vision would be to allow applications from the current blockchain to be redeployed on a shard of the Ethereum 2.0 system. This would be implemented via a new EVM interpreter written in eWASM.

eWASM

Currently there are separate compilers for each of the smart contract programming languages. You can build and install either the Solidity or Vyper compiler software and run it on local disk. Alternatively, you can use the free online code editors for both Solidity and Vyper.

The job of a compiler is to convert your high-level smart contract code into bytecode and application binary interface (ABI). Once your code is compiled, it can be executed by the EVM.

eWASM is Ethereum's own implementation of WebAssembly. WebAssembly is currently being designed as an open standard by a W3C Community Group.

eWASM is being developed to replace the EVM. Once eWASM is implemented, developers will be able to write smart contracts in other languages such as Rust and C/C++ as opposed to just Solidity and Vyper. It is important to note that eWASM will be completely backward compatible with the current EVM. This means smart contracts that are currently written in Solidity or Vyper will still be able to execute in the new environment.

Delivery Phases of Ethereum 2.0

The delivery phases of Ethereum 2.0 should run something like the following.

Phase 0

Ethereum 2.0 is expected to be implemented as follows. Phase 0, which I have briefly covered, involves the introduction of the beacon chain, so essentially Phase 0 is the beginning of the new PoS chain. More specifically, it's a PoS beacon chain without shards.

Phase 1

The next phase, Phase 1, will implement shards as data chains. Phase 1 will provide the foundations to create decentralized data applications; however, to fully implement any of these types of applications, the benefits of Phase 2 will be required. Put simply, Phase 1 is implementing basic sharding without an EVM.

Phase 2

EVM state transition functionality will be introduced in Phase 2. Phase 2 will introduce functionality to create and manage accounts and contracts as well as transfer funds between shards and so forth.

The subsequent phases 3, 4, 5, and 6 have plans to introduce the following:

- A light-client state protocol
- Cross-shard transactions
- Tight coupling with main chain security
- Super-quadratic or exponential sharding

It is hoped that state transition changes and transaction executions will improve significantly because of the implementation of eWASM. There is a comprehensive Ethereum 2.0 road map that details each proposed phase. Please keep in mind that these specifications do change frequently and that the proof-of-concept algorithms and code repositories are under heavy construction.

Post–Ethereum 2.0 Innovation

I mentioned ZK-STARKs previously in this chapter. The main difference between SNARKs and STARKs is transparency. More specifically, there is no "trusted setup" in ZK-STARKs (no secrets in the setup of the system). This is an interesting area of research, and there is a chance that Ethereum will eventually upgrade to the use of STARKs to perform tasks such as data availability checks, state execution correctness checks, and improved base-layer cross-shard transactions, to name a few.

Conclusion

In this chapter, I discussed the future direction of the Ethereum blockchain. Ethereum is not only a decentralized blockchain but also a decentralized developer community. It has a robust and democratic upgrade process known as the EIP. We are optimistic that Ethereum will remain one of the most widely used and technically advanced blockchains in the future.

Part IV

Building Application Protocols

While the original vision of Ethereum was a single public blockchain to serve as a "world computer," the reality is much more nuanced. It is now clear that a single public blockchain cannot scale to the capacity needed for mass consumer applications. Ethereum itself is moving toward the direction of multiple interconnected blockchains for sharding and state channels (for more about side chains, see Chapter 13). In fact, a compelling idea for sharding is to divide computing load onto various blockchains according to business application. For example, there could be a blockchain specializing in e-commerce, another specializing in gambling games, and yet another one specializing in payments and stable coins. These specialized blockchains are called *application protocol* blockchains.

I envision a world with many interconnected application protocol blockchains, each with a specially optimized virtual machine to efficiently handle one type of application. The Ethereum protocol will thrive by providing an interoperability layer for all those specialized and optimized blockchains.

Indeed, in the history of enterprise software engineering, successful products are always optimized for their specific application use cases. One size fits all does not work. In this part of the book, I will discuss how to develop optimized blockchains for specific application protocols. In this book, we will use open source software developed by Second State to customize and optimize the Ethereum platform, including the Lity language extension to Solidity (www.LityLang.org). We will also use the CyberMiles public blockchain (www.CyberMiles.io) as a case study. The CyberMiles public blockchain is fully compatible with Ethereum but optimized for e-commerce applications.

## 14

Extending the Ethereum Protocol

In the previous chapters of this book, you learned about the power and also the limitations of Ethereum. Ethereum is one of the first and certainly the most popular blockchain smart contract platform. It is a protocol with multiple open source implementations from the community and has a robust software upgrade process known as Ethereum Improvement Proposals (EIPs). However, as a big organization with many stakeholders, Ethereum improvement is a slow process. As a "world computer," Ethereum is also unlikely to optimize for specific applications.

I believe there are opportunities for many different public blockchains. Each of them will optimize Ethereum for specific application protocols. However, all of them will need to fix at least a few of Ethereum's most glaring problems, as described here:

- The Ethereum Virtual Machine (EVM) has many limitations. While the EVM is Turing complete, it is inefficient to implement many algorithms. For example, it is currently impossible to implement public-private key applications on Ethereum because a single public key infrastructure (PKI) encryption operation will consume Ethereum gas fees worth hundreds of dollars. Even basic string operations are slow and expensive with the standard EVM.

- Ethereum is too slow. At about 20 transactions per second (fewer for smart contract transactions), Ethereum is not suitable for most application use cases.

- It does not yet scale. With the Ethereum public blockchain in 2019, the more people who use it, the worse the user experience gets.

- It could be unsafe, especially for beginners. It is easy to send Ethereum assets to the wrong address or lose assets because of poorly written smart contracts.

- Smart contract programming is hard. Code audits have shown that Ethereum smart contracts average about 100 obvious bugs per 1,000 lines of code. That is an astonishing number for applications managing financial assets. In contrast, Microsoft business applications, which are a lot less mission critical, average about 15 bugs per 1,000 lines of code.

In this chapter, I provide an overview of the technical approaches that could potentially alleviate these Ethereum shortcomings.

Fully Compatible, Yet Faster

Second State creates Ethereum-compatible virtual machines that can run on a variety of underlying consensus mechanisms. This allows developers to choose the most suitable blockchain to deploy their applications. For example, the virtual machine can run as a Tendermint application (see Chapter 20) to take advantage of the Byzantine fault tolerant (BFT) Tendermint consensus engine, as well as the various delegated proof-of-stake (DPoS) mechanisms that can be implemented on top of Tendermint (e.g., the CyberMiles public blockchain).

The performance impediment of Ethereum is primarily a result of its proof-of-work (PoW) consensus mechanism. A huge amount of meaningless computation must be performed for each block of data that can be added to the blockchain. An Ethereum-compatible blockchain can easily achieve 100× performance gain by simply replacing the PoW module with a DPoS or delegated Byzantine fault tolerance (DBFT) module. For example, on the CyberMiles blockchain, consensus is reached by 19 validator nodes (i.e., super nodes) before a new block is created. The validators are elected by CyberMiles token holders and are required to run high-performance hardware in tier 1 data centers.

> **Note**
>
> Being Ethereum-compatible, all Ethereum scalability solutions are also available on EVM-based blockchains. This allows users to take advantage of extensive research conducted by the Ethereum community and contribute improvements back to the Ethereum community. A great example here is the Plasma protocol, which aims to build layer 2 networks to scale Ethereum to millions of transactions per second.

Furthermore, as we will discuss in the next section, the virtual machine can offload complex computational tasks to native library functions. That allows for vastly improved smart contract execution speed and much lower gas costs for such tasks. For many operations, the native functions could represent four to six orders of magnitudes in terms of performance gains (see Chapter 18 for more).

Smart Enhancements to the EVM

Lity is a new programming language extension to Solidity, with support for its features in an extended EVM version. Here are some of Lity's features:

- Lity provides a new language keyword to call native library functions written in C or C++. This is known as the libENI framework. Through libENI, each Lity-based blockchain can be customized and optimized for address-specific application scenarios. I will discuss libENI in Chapter 18.

- Lity supports fixed-point math and sophisticated math operations. It provides deterministic results for fractional number operations, which was a key limitation in Ethereum.

- Lity supports timer-based operations scheduled for a future time. The scheduled execution is crucial for many classes of use cases, such as interest and dividends payment, trust and will, delivery confirmations, and so on. This is also called *long-running contracts*.

- Lity supports "trusted" operations that can be invoked only by current validators or super nodes of the underlying blockchain. This allows for trusted smart contracts on the blockchain that can provide a first-class substitute for community-based oracles, which connect the blockchain to the outside world.

- Lity supports secure random numbers generated by validators or super nodes of the underlying blockchain.

- Lity supports alternative mechanisms for paying for gas fees in blockchains that require gas for executing smart contracts.

- Lity supports a new type of "upgradeable" smart contract. Those contracts only expose the function interfaces to the world at the contract address. The actual implementation of those functions are proxy contracts deployed at other addresses on the blockchain. Lity supports virtual machine operations to change the smart contract's proxy implementation. That allows developers to upgrade or fix critical bugs on smart contracts.

- Lity supports new language constructs such as rule expressions so that application developers can build business rules directly into the smart contract (see Chapter 17). Those are commonly known as *domain-specific language* (DSL) features.

Next, let's look into some concrete examples from this list.

Trusted Oracles

One of the most important services on blockchains is the oracle service. An *oracle* is typically a smart contract that makes external data (i.e., off-chain, real-world, or cross-chain data) deterministically available on the blockchain. It provides a single source of truth for off-chain states and hence allows blockchain nodes to reach consensus.

The traditional oracle is highly centralized and goes against the spirit of the decentralized blockchain. For example, Fedex might establish a delivery service oracle that provides delivery status of packages. A weather station might establish a weather oracle. To use those oracles, blockchain users and dapps must trust the entities behind those oracles.

A second approach for oracles is to create a community-based cryptoeconomic game for members of the community to compete and provide the truth in a smart contract. Examples of such oracles include the BTC Relay to provide information about the Bitcoin blockchain, and the Ethereum Alarm Clock to provide time.

Lity, however, takes a different approach to create trusted smart contracts and make oracles first-class citizens. This approach works on DPoS blockchains. In a DPoS blockchain, the validators (super nodes) are trusted entities. They must stake a large number of tokens from their own account and from their supporters/community. Those tokens are subject to slashing and confiscation if the validator misbehaves. So, if a smart contract can be updated only by current validators, data from this contract should have a high level of trust on the DPoS blockchain.

In the Lity language, a built-in function called `isValidator` checks whether the current transaction sender/function caller is a validator. It works on any Lity-based DPoS blockchain.

```
// isValidator is a built-in function provided by Lity.
// isValidator only takes one parameter, an address,
// to check this address is a validator or not.
isValidator(<address>) returns (bool returnValue);
```

Then with the `ValidatorOnly` modifier, we can construct smart contracts that act as trusted oracles on the blockchain.

```
contract BTCRelay {
  uint[] BTCHeaders;
  modifier ValidatorOnly() {
      require(isValidator(msg.sender));
      _;
  }

  function saveBTCHeader(uint blockHash) ValidatorOnly {
    BTCHeaders.append(headerHash);
  }

  function getBTCHeader(uint blockNum) pure public returns (uint) {
    return BTCHeaders[blockNum];
  }
}
```

Secure Random Numbers

Getting secure random numbers is a significant challenge for blockchain smart contracts. Lity pioneered an approach to access a random number series from a seed in the current block header. The random seed is based on the hashes of all transactions in the current block, and it is extremely difficult to manipulate even for the validator node that builds and proposes the block.

Inside the smart contract, you can access the random number series by simply calling the built-in function `rand()`. The following is an example:

```
pragma lity >=1.2.6;

contract RandDemo {
  uint x;
  function getRand () public returns (uint) {
    x = rand();
    return x;
  }
}
```

You should not call `rand()` in a `view` or `pure` function. If the random number does not need to be recorded on the blockchain (i.e., outside of a transaction in a `view` function executed on a single node), it does not need to be generated by the blockchain. The calling application should simply generate a random number locally, which is much cheaper in terms of resource consumption.

Alternative Gas Fees

One of the major hurdles of blockchain application adoption is that end users are asked to pay a gas fee to perform certain functions on the blockchain. The gas mechanism is crucial for the blockchain's security, as it prevents DoS attackers from overwhelming the blockchain nodes with computationally intensive requests. However, the gas requirement also means that new end users must be taught to purchase cryptocurrencies and manage private keys before they can even start to use decentralized applications.

Lity provides an alternative approach to onboard new users to blockchain applications. Through the `freegas` keyword, the smart contract owner can designate a contract function that should have gas fees paid by the owner herself. When the user calls those functions, she would indicate that she is not paying gas by setting `gasPrice` to 0.

- If the `gasPrice=0` transaction calls a function that is *not* `freegas`, the transaction will fail.
- If the `gasPrice=0` transaction calls a `freegas` function in a contract that does not have a balance, the transaction will fail.

Of course, the caller can specify a regular `gasPrice` (e.g., 2Gwei), and in that case, the caller pays for gas even if the contract function is `freegas`.

If the `gasPrice=0` transaction calls a `freegas` function in a contract that has a sufficient balance, then the function executes, and the gas fee is deducted from the contract address. The caller pays nothing, and the contract pays gas at the system's standard gas price.

Note

There is a configurable rate limit for making gasPrice=0 transactions. The blockchain node software can prevent users from exploiting the system by sending a lot of free transactions.

The following is an example. On the CyberMiles blockchain, if an end user calls the test function with `gasPrice=0` and the contract address has a CMT balance, the transaction's gas fee will come out of the contract address.

```
pragma lity >= 1.2.7;

contract FreeGasDemo {
  int a;
  function test (int input) public freegas returns (int) {
    a = input;
    return a;
  }

  function () public payable {}
}
```

The `payable` function is important as it allows the contract to receive funds that will later be used as gas. Figure 14.1 shows the `freegas` transaction in action on the CyberMiles public blockchain.

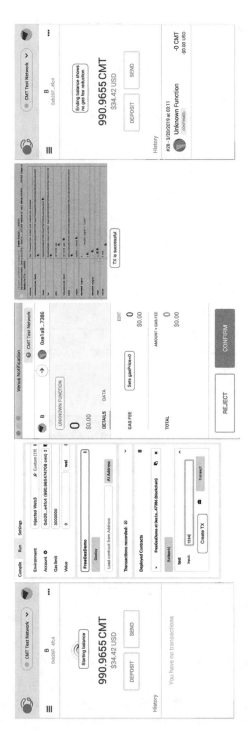

Figure 14.1   The caller makes a `freegas` transaction by setting `gasPrice` to zero.

Safety First

Through language and virtual machine enhancements in Lity, we can proactively prevent many classes of security problems. The following are some examples:

- The Lity compiler automatically checks the structural signature of the smart contracts it compiles. If it detects the smart contract is likely to be one of the popular types (e.g., an ERC20 or ERC721 token contract), it will check that all required methods are implemented and the contract is free of common errors. The Lity compiler throws errors if it sees a noncompliant ERC20 contract (learn more in Chapter 15).

- The Lity compiler checks for known code issues and bug patterns, such as the ERC20 contract's compliance to the ERC223 safety standard. It throws warnings and can attempt to automatically fix some most serious issues.

- The Lity language provides access to secure random numbers generated by blockchain validators, when the consensus mechanism allows.

- The Lity virtual machine automatically checks for unsafe operations at runtime, such as integer overflow, which is a common ERC20 issue that had resulted in billions of dollars of value destruction. When a contract encounters an integer overflow in Lity runtime, it will stop execution with an error instead of proceeding with the overflowed buffer, as Ethereum does today. This eliminates a whole class of errors.

As an open source collaborative effort, the Lity project aims to continuously bring updates to those security features, such as support for new ERCs and new code vulnerability patterns, to the community.

Conclusion

In this chapter, I discussed how the Lity project extends the Ethereum protocol both at the consensus layer and at the virtual machine layer to create Ethereum-compatible blockchains that support much needed performance/security/usability enhancements as well as experimental features. In the next several chapters, we will look into application design and development on the Lity language and virtual machine.

15

Extending Ethereum Tools

In the previous chapter, you saw how the Lity language and virtual machine extends and improves on the Ethereum protocol. The open source Ethereum ecosystem also encourages such platforms to extend and fork existing tools to incorporate new features.

Lity tools include wallets, block explorers, and coding/deployment tools. These tools are customized and configured for each blockchain and are supported by commercial providers, such as Second State (www.SecondState.io).

In this chapter, I will cover Lity-customized tools for the CyberMiles public blockchain. They include the following:

- The Venus chrome extension is CyberMiles' extension of the Metamask wallet for Ethereum.
- The Europa integrated development environment (IDE) is Lity and CyberMiles' fork of the Remix IDE for Ethereum.
- The web3-cmt.js library is the customized web3 library that supports the CMT cryptocurrency on the CyberMiles blockchain. It can be customized to any Lity-based blockchain.
- The CyberMiles App (aka the CMT wallet) is a mobile wallet application that runs CyberMiles dapps inside the wallet.
- The `lityc` project provides tools to analyze and secure Lity smart contract source code.
- A blockchain explorer web service provides a query and search interface for blockchain data on a Lity-based blockchain. On CyberMiles, this data service is available at www. CMTTracking.io.

> **Note**
> With Second State's BUIDL online IDE (http://buidl.secondstate.io), you can experiment with the latest Lity features on a live blockchain. There is no need to deal with cryptocurrencies or gas fees or event wallets, just Lity contracts and web3 JavaScript applications. Learn more in Chapter 3.

Smart Contract Tools

In this section, I will review how to develop and deploy smart contracts on the CyberMiles blockchain using the Europa online IDE together with the Venus wallet.

Venus Wallet

The Venus wallet (Figure 15.1) is a Chrome browser extension to manage your CyberMiles blockchain accounts. It is based on the open source Metamask software. It stores and manages your private keys to those accounts on your computer (i.e., a wallet for private keys and, by extension, cryptocurrency stored in those accounts). For developers, Venus is a great tool since it integrates with other development tools and allows you to interact with CyberMiles accounts.

First, make sure you have the latest Google Chrome browser installed. You can get it at https://www.google.com/chrome/.

Next, follow the instructions on the CyberMiles web site to install Venus on your Chrome browser: https://cybermiles.io/venus.

Now, you should see the Venus icon on your Chrome toolbar. Click it to bring up its user interface (UI). You should create a password for your Venus wallet. This is important since your password protects your account private keys stored on this computer. Once you create the password, Venus will give you a 12-word recovery phrase. That is the only way for you to recover the password, so keep it safe!

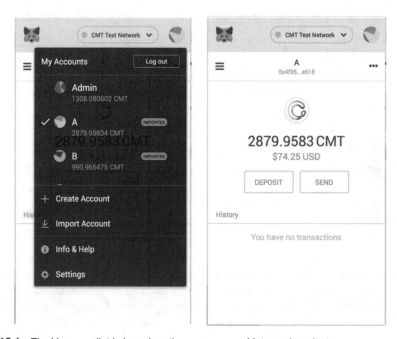

Figure 15.1   The Venus wallet is based on the open source Metamask project.

For development purposes, select the top-left drop-down list from the Venus UI, and select CyberMiles Testnet, which is a CyberMiles public blockchain maintained for testing purposes.

You will also need to create an account on the testnet to store your testnet CMTs there. Select the icon at the top right of the Venus UI, and click **Create Account**. Venus will create an account address and its associated private key for you. You can name this account so that you can access it in the Venus UI later. You can also use Venus to manage mainnet CMTs, which can be traded on exchanges for U.S. dollars. But to do that, you should make sure that your computer is physically secure since real money will be at stake.

Of course, you still need to fund your account with some testnet CMTs to use it. Go to the public CyberMiles testnet faucet at https://travis-faucet.cybermiles.io/ and request 1,000 testnet CMTs for your address! The testnet CMTs can be used only on the testnet. They are not traded on any exchanges and can disappear at any time when the testnet is retired. Unlike the mainnet CMTs, testnet CMTs have zero monetary value.

Now you have set up Venus and are ready to interact with your first smart contract on the CyberMiles testnet!

Europa IDE

The Europa IDE is based on Remix on the Ethereum blockchain but customized for CyberMiles. Europa is completely web-based. Just go to its web site to load the web app: http://europa.cybermiles.io/.

In the code editor to the right, let's enter a simple smart contract. What follows is an example of the `HelloWorld` smart contract. It is written in Solidity/Lity.

```
pragma solidity ^0.4.17;

contract HelloWorld  {

    string helloMessage;
    address public owner;

    constructor () public {
        helloMessage = "Hello, World!";
        owner = msg.sender;
    }

    function updateMessage (string _new_msg) public {
        helloMessage = _new_msg;
    }

    function sayHello () public constant returns (string) {
        return helloMessage;
    }
```

```
    function kill() public {
        if (msg.sender == owner) selfdestruct(owner);
    }
}
```

The HelloWorld smart contract has two key methods.

- The sayHello() method returns a greeting to its caller. The greeting is initially set to "Hello, World!" when the smart contract is deployed.

- The updateMessage() method allows the method caller to change the greeting from "Hello, World!" to another message.

Hit the **Start to compile** button in the right panel (Figure 15.2) to compile this contract. This will generate the bytecode and application binary interface (ABI) to be used later. When you click the ABI or Bytecode button, the ABI or bytecode will be copied to the computer's clipboard, and you can paste them into other files or applications later.

Figure 15.2   Compiling a CyberMiles smart contract on Europa

Next, on the Run tab of Europa, you can connect Europa to your Venus account via the Injected Web3 drop-down box. Europa will automatically detect your currently selected Venus account.

You should now see options to deploy the smart contract to the blockchain. Click the **Deploy** button to deploy the contract to the blockchain. The contract will be deployed on the CyberMiles testnet. At this time, Europa will pop up and ask you to send the "gas fee" from your account address (Figure 15.3). The gas fee is required by the CyberMiles blockchain to pay for the network service required to deploy your contract.

After you submit the request, wait for a few minutes for the CyberMiles network to confirm the deployment of your contract. The contract deployment address will be shown in the confirmation (Figure 15.4), and the deployed contract and its available methods will be available on the Europa Run tab as well.

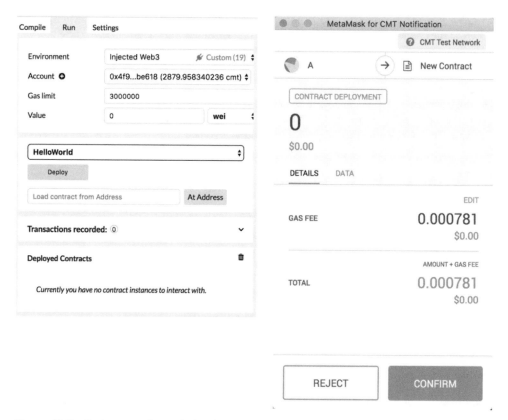

Figure 15.3   Paying a gas fee to deploy the contract

Figure 15.4   The contract is now deployed, and the available methods are shown.

If you have already deployed the smart contract on the testnet, you already know the deployed address of the contract. You can simply enter the contract address on the box next to the At Address button and then click the button. This will configure Europa to use an already-deployed contract. No gas fee is needed in this case.

Once Europa is connected to your deployed contract, it shows the contract methods on the Run tab. You can enter a new greeting next to the updateMessage button and click the button to update the message (Figure 15.5). Since blockchain storage is required to store the updated message, you will again be prompted to pay a gas fee through Venus.

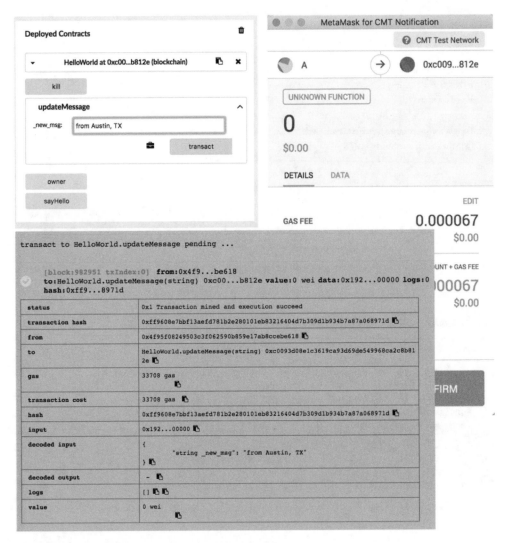

Figure 15.5   Calling the updateMessage() method

Once the network confirms the message update, you will again see a confirmation message. After the `updateMessage()` is confirmed, you can call `sayHello()` from Europa (Figure 15.6), and you will see the updated message.

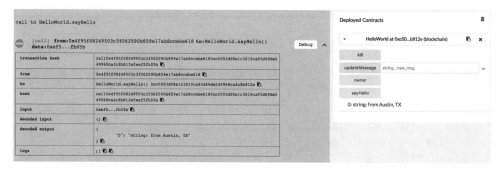

Figure 15.6   Calling the `sayHello()` method

The Europa IDE is easy to use. It is an excellent choice for beginners. You can also interact with the blockchain through command-line tools on each node. The node software provides more capabilities, and we will discuss it later in this chapter.

The `lityc` Compiler and Analysis Tool

The `lityc` software extends the Ethereum `solc` to provide a compiler for the Lity language. It compiles the Lity smart contract into ABI and bytecode. You can then use the Travis node console or web3-cmt.js to deploy the ABI and bytecode to the CyberMiles public blockchain as smart contracts. Please see Appendix A for more details.

While compiling and deploying can also be done in tools like Europa, a more interesting feature of the command-line `lityc` is its source code static analyzer. For example, the `lityc` compiler can check the contract's compliance to specified ERC specification. Let's consider the following contract. The `totalSupply()` function does not conform to the ERC20 specification.

```
pragma lity ^1.2.4;

contract ERC20Interface {
  // mutability should be view, not pure
  function totalSupply() public pure returns (uint);
  function balanceOf(address owner) public view returns (uint);
  function allowance(address owner, address spender)
                          public view returns (uint);
  function transfer(address to, uint tokens) public returns (bool);
  function approve(address spender, uint tokens) public returns (bool);
  function transferFrom(address from, address to,
    uint tokens) public returns (bool);
```

```
   event Transfer(address indexed from, address indexed to, uint tokens);
   event Approval(address indexed owner, address indexed spender, uint tokens);
}
```

Running lityc to compile it will yield the following error message:

```
$ lityc --contract-standard ERC20 wrong_mutability.sol

wrong_mutability.sol:3:1: Info: Missing 'totalSupply' with
type signature 'function () view external returns
(uint256)'. ERC20Interface is not compatible to ERC20.
contract ERC20Interface {
^ (Relevant source part starts here and spans across multiple lines).
```

At the time of this writing, lityc supports the following ERC specifications, and more are being added on a regular basis:

- ERC20

- ERC223

- ERC721

- ERC827

- ERC884

Furthermore, if you have the Oyente static analysis tool installed on your computer, lityc can automatically run Oyente when compiling. See the following code for an example:

```
$ lityc --abi StringReverse.sol

======= StringReverse.sol:StringReverse =======
Contract JSON ABI
[…]

INFO:root:contract StringReverse.sol:StringReverse:
INFO:oyente.symExec:    ============ Results ===========
INFO:oyente.symExec:      EVM Code Coverage:                     29.8%
INFO:oyente.symExec:      Parity Multisig Bug 2:                 False
INFO:oyente.symExec:      Callstack Depth Attack Vulnerability:  False
INFO:oyente.symExec:      Transaction-Ordering Dependence (TOD): False
INFO:oyente.symExec:      Timestamp Dependency:                  False
INFO:oyente.symExec:      Re-Entrancy Vulnerability:             False
INFO:oyente.symExec:    ====== Analysis Completed ======
```

Oyente is an open source project that is actively developed and updated to detect even more problem patterns with smart contract source code. Oyente integration with lityc will likely drive adoption of static analyzer tools in blockchain applications.

Dapp Tools

While Europa is a great tool, it is too hard for regular people. To make your smart contracts available to the general public, you typically need to build a web-based UI. For that, you need the web3-cmt.js JavaScript library to interact with the CyberMiles blockchain.

From this point on, I presume you have successfully deployed the previous HelloWorld contract to the CyberMiles mainnet and recorded its deployed contract address. The reason is that production version of the CyberMiles App (CMT wallet) works only with CyberMiles mainnet contracts (see the "CyberMiles App" section).

web3-cmt

Once Europa is installed, it automatically injects a custom instance of the web3 object (or web3.cmt object) into the page's JavaScript context. Method calls that require private keys will automatically prompt the user to select an account, and Metamask will use the selected private key to sign the transaction before sending it to the Ethereum network. In addition, all web3 API calls must be asynchronous. So, we use the web3 callback API to handle the return values. The source code for the helloworld_europa.html file follows:

```
<!DOCTYPE html>
<html lang="en">
  <head>
    <script>
      window.addEventListener('load', function() {
        var hello = web3.cmt.contract(...).at("...");

        var new_mesg = location.search.split('new_mesg=')[1];
        if (new_mesg === undefined || new_mesg == null) {
        } else {
          new_mesg = decodeURIComponent(new_mesg.replace(/\+/g, '%20'));

          web3.cmt.getAccounts(function (error, address) {
            if(!error) {
              hello.updateMessage(new_mesg, {
                  from: address.toString()
              }, function(e, r){
                if(!e)
                  document.getElementById("status").innerHTML =
                    "<b>Submitted to blockchain</b>. " +
                    "New message will take a few seconds to show up! " +
                    "<a href=\"helloworld_europa.html\">Reload page.</a>";
              });
            }
          });
        }
```

```
        hello.sayHello(function(error, result){
          if(!error)
            document.getElementById("mesg").innerHTML = result;
        });
      })
    </script>
  </head>

  <body>
  <h2>Hello World</h2>
    <form method=GET>
      New message:<br/><br/>
      <input type="text" name="new_mesg"/><br/><br/>
      <input type="submit"/>
      <p id="status"/>
    </form>
    <p>The current message is: <span id="mesg"/></p>
  </body>
</html>
```

The `web3.cmt.contract(...).at("...")` function takes the contract's deployment address on the blockchain as a parameter. You can find it on the Run tab in Europa. The `contract` function takes a JSON structure known as the contract's ABI, which you can copy from Europa, as shown in Figure 15.2.

The web application now allows users to interact with the `HelloWorld` smart contract directly from the Web (Figure 15.7). The "submit new message" action requires Europa to send gas fees since it invokes the `updateMessage()` method on the contract. Notice that all web3 functions are nested and invoked asynchronously.

Using Europa together with `web3-cmt` is one of the best ways to get started with CyberMiles application development. But for the average user, the process of installing and using Europa is a significant barrier of entry. Next, let's explore how to run dapps inside the CyberMiles App (CMT wallet) mobile application.

CyberMiles App

The CyberMiles App is a consumer-grade mobile wallet application that requires no complicated installs. You can get the CyberMiles App at http://app.cybermiles.io/.

To run a dapp from the CyberMiles App, the easiest approach is to create a QR code from the dapp's URL and then use the wallet application to scan the URL. You can create a QR code for any URL at www.qr-code-generator.com/. Figure 15.8 shows the entire process.

Alternatively, the dapp could be on a regular web site and redirect to the CyberMiles App when it needs to send transactions to the blockchain. The FairPlay dapp discussed in Chapter 11 is a good example of this. Figure 15.9 shows another, simpler example.

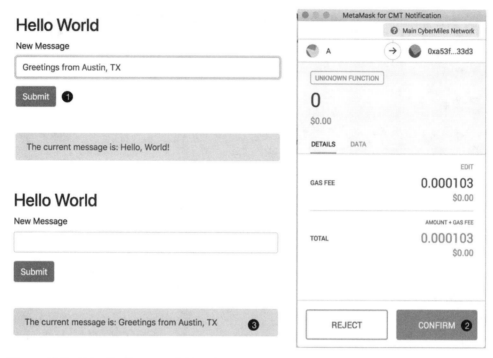

Figure 15.7   Using the Europa wallet to write to a contract

Figure 15.8   Scanning a bar code to load a dapp in the CyberMiles App

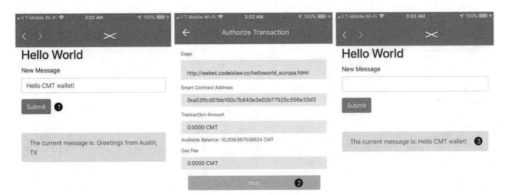

Figure 15.9   Using the CyberMiles App to run the dapp and pay for gas fees

Dapp user experience in the CyberMiles App is one of the advantages CyberMiles has over Ethereum.

Conclusion

In this chapter, I reviewed tools for the Ethereum-compatible CyberMiles blockchain. I reviewed the available wallets, web3 library, and development/deployment tools for CyberMiles. In the next chapter, we will put these together and see a few complete example dapps that were developed using Lity and have been deployed on the CyberMiles public blockchain.

## 16

Example Dapps

In the previous two chapters, I discussed how to extend the Ethereum protocol and related development tools. But how do those extensions and improvements translate into real-world applications? In this chapter, I will discuss a few complete dapps deployed on CyberMiles to illustrate how Ethereum extensions make it possible for developers to create interactive dapps for the blockchain.

Everything discussed in this chapter is compatible with Ethereum. But as discussed, CyberMiles offers some important advantages as an Ethereum-compatible development and deployment platform.

- CyberMiles has a much faster transaction confirmation time than Ethereum. That is important for interactive dapp user experience (UX) since it reduces the time needed for operations to be confirmed and recorded on the blockchain.

- CyberMiles has a mobile wallet application that can run web3-based JavaScript applications in an embedded mode. The CMT wallet is available in all iOS and Android app stores, and you can load the dapp by scanning a bar code pointing to the JavaScript code.

- The CyberMiles blockchain uses the CMT token to pay for gas fees. As the CMT price is much lower ETH, it can accomplish much more with the same amount of money.

Next, let's get started.

Case Study 1: Valentines

The Valentines dapp is for people to declare and record their love permanently on the blockchain. Through the CyberMiles App (CMT wallet), anyone can create a love declaration and share the QR code (see Figure 16.1).

The recipient of the declaration uses her CyberMiles App to scan the QR code and open the dapp. From there, she can reply to the declaration. Once she replies, she can share the QR code to the world so that anyone can open the dapp and witness the declaration and reply recorded on the blockchain (Figure 16.2).

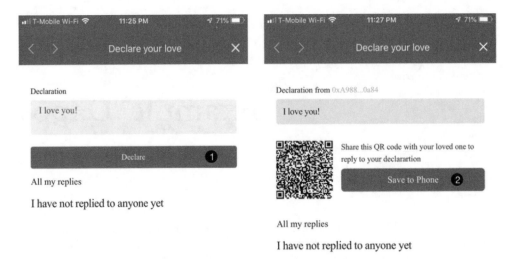

Figure 16.1   Declaring your love

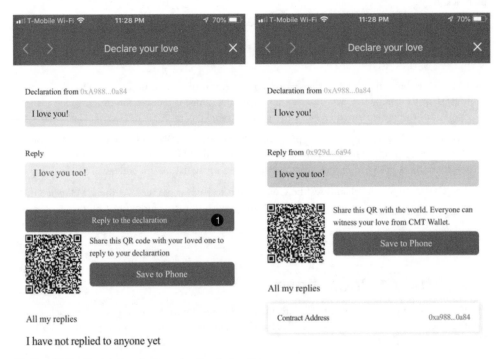

Figure 16.2   Replying and witnessing the declaration

Next, let's review the smart contract code behind the Valentines contract and then the JavaScript dapp to interact with the Valentines contract.

The Valentines Smart Contract

The Valentines smart contract contains all the declarations and replies (each of them is a valentine) submitted from the dapp. It has two main functions: `declare()` to create a new declaration and `reply()` to reply to an existing declaration. It also has two informational functions (`view` functions), `getDeclaration()` and `getReplies()`, to help dapps retrieve information from the blockchain.

```
contract Valentines {
    struct Declaration {
        string stmt;
        address reply_from;
        string reply_stmt;
    }
    mapping(address => Declaration) declarations;
    mapping(address => address[]) replies;

    function declare (string _stmt) public {
        Declaration memory d = Declaration(_stmt, 0, "");
        declarations[msg.sender] = d;
    }

    function reply (address _from, string _stmt) public {
        declarations[_from].reply_from = msg.sender;
        declarations[_from].reply_stmt = _stmt;
        replies[msg.sender].push(_from);
    }

    function getDeclaration (address _from) public view returns (string,
        address, string) {
        return (declarations[_from].stmt, declarations[_from].reply_from,
            declarations[_from].reply_stmt);
    }

    function getReplies (address _from) public view returns (address[]) {
        return (replies[_from]);
    }
}
```

The contract's four functions are self-explanatory. The `Declaration` struct contains a declaration and its reply. The declaration is mapped to its creator in the `declarations` mapping array. The `replies` array maps each address to the declarations it replied to. Note that each address can make one declaration but can reply to multiple declarations.

Next, you can deploy the contract to the CyberMiles blockchain and record the deployed contract address. The easiest approach is probably to use the CyberMiles Europa tool or the Second State BUIDL tool configured for CyberMiles. The JavaScript dapp accesses this deployed contract.

The JavaScript Dapp

The dapp is written in JavaScript and runs in the client browser in conjunction with a wallet application. The getDeclaration() function in the declare.js file calls the smart contract's getDeclaration() function and then uses the results to update the HTML user interface (UI) in the declare.html file. The following code snippet shows the getDeclaration() function in the JavaScript dapp. Notice that all web3-related operations are done asynchronously since many are remote calls, and we have to guarantee the correct order to execution. The contract_address value is the previously mentioned contract address after successful deployment. It is hard-coded into the dapp. The targetAddress value is the address from which this declaration was made. The userAddress value is the current user's CMT address.

```
var getDeclaration = function () {
    web3.cmt.getAccounts(function (e, address) {
        if (e) {
            // ...
        } else {
            userAddress = address.toString();
            if (!targetAddress) {
                targetAddress = userAddress;
            }

            contract = web3.cmt.contract(abi);
            instance = contract.at(contract_address);
            instance.getDeclaration (targetAddress, function (e, r) {
                if (e) {
                    // ...
                } else {
                    stmt = r[0];
                    reply_from = r[1];
                    reply_stmt = r[2];
                    // show the UI based on the state
                    // of this targetAddress's declaration
                }
            });

            instance.getReplies (userAddress, function (e, r) {
                if (e) {
                    // ...
                } else {
                    // show replies on UI
                }
            });
        }
    });
}
```

When the user makes a declaration, the contract's `declare()` function is called. Notice that we have to pay a small gas fee to invoke this function since it saves data on the blockchain. Upon successful return of the contract function call, the JavaScript waits for the transaction to be confirmed on the blockchain (when the block is produced and accepted by the validators) and then reloads the `getDeclaration()` function to update the UI.

```
var declare = function () {
    var v = $("#declaration-field").val();
    if (v == null || v == '') {
        // ...
    }
    $(".main-button").css("background-color", "#696969");
    $('#declaration-submit').text(lgb.wait);
    $('#declaration-submit').removeAttr('onclick');

    instance.declare(v, {
        gas: '200000',
        gasPrice: 2000000000
    }, function (e, result) {
        if (e) {
            // ...
        } else {
            setTimeout(function () {
                getDeclaration();
            }, 20 * 1000);
        }
    });
}
```

When a second user replies to the declaration, the dapp calls the `reply()` function on the contract and updates the UI after the transaction is confirmed on the blockchain.

```
var reply = function () {
    var v = $("#reply-field").val();
    if (v == null || v == '') {
        // ...
    }
    $(".main-button").css("background-color", "#696969");
    $('#reply-submit').text(lgb.wait);
    $('#reply-submit').removeAttr('onclick');

    instance.reply(targetAddress, v, {
        gas: '200000',
        gasPrice: 2000000000
    }, function (e, result) {
        if (e) {
            // ...
```

```
        } else {
            setTimeout(function () {
                getDeclaration();
            }, 20 * 1000);
        }
    });
}
```

So far, we have reviewed the core logic of the Valentines dapp and how it interacts with data and functions on the blockchain via web3. The dapp uses open source libraries to perform other important tasks. For example, it uses the `qrcode.js` script to generate QR codes on the fly. It uses the `IUToast` script to create messages and alerts for users.

The Valentines dapp has only a single web page and a single JavaScript control file. It interacts with an already deployed smart contract. In the next section, we will study a more complex dapp called WeBet.

Case Study 2: WeBet

The WeBet dapp is a peer-to-peer betting application. It allows anyone to create a bet contract inside the CyberMiles App (Figure 16.3) and share the bet (Figure 16.4). The bet is a multiple-choice question.

Other people can then use their own CyberMiles Apps to place bets (Figure 16.5). They get to the bet by simply scanning the QR code shared by the bet contract's creator. They each select a choice and send CMTs to the contract as the bet on that choice.

The creator can declare a winning choice after the bets are placed (Figure 16.6). There could be multiple winners since several people could select the same choice.

The winners use their CMT wallets to claim winnings from the bet (Figure 16.7).

Another use case of the WeBet dapp is to create "commitment contracts." That is, someone can create a personal goal (e.g., to lose 10 pounds in a month) and bet on the goal outcome with a large amount of CMTs (e.g., 10,000 CMTs) as a commitment. Then, friends and family will each bet a small amount (e.g., 1 CMT) on the opposite outcome. If the creator achieves his goal, he will get the commitment CMTs back. If not, friends and family will share the commitment CMTs.

This type of personal betting application is well suited for the public blockchain. The blockchain dapp could potentially provide a much better user experience than a traditional web application.

- The smart contracts on the public blockchain guarantee that the application developer or host cannot cheat by changing the betting records, or even running away with the funds. Similarly, it is difficult for governments or other entities to shut down these contracts.

- It is much easier to transfer "value" on the blockchain. To bet with small amounts of fiat money, you still need the whole banking infrastructure and its high fees. On an established public chain like CyberMiles or Ethereum, the tokens have an established exchange rate with U.S. dollars and are much easier and cheaper to use as payments.

Figure 16.3   Creating a new WeBet contract

Figure 16.4   Sharing a WeBet contract

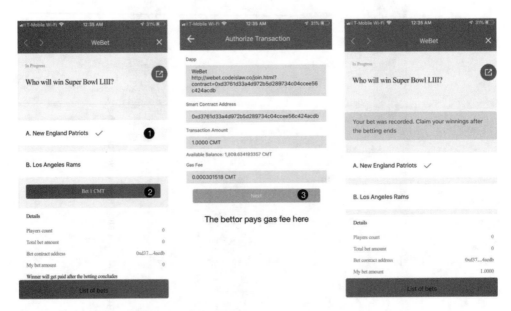

Figure 16.5   Placing a bet on a WeBet contract

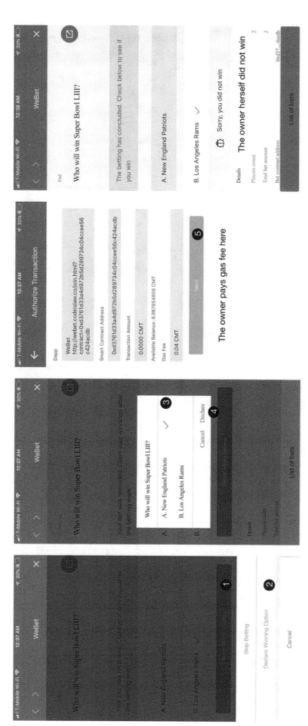

Figure 16.6   Declaring a winner choice

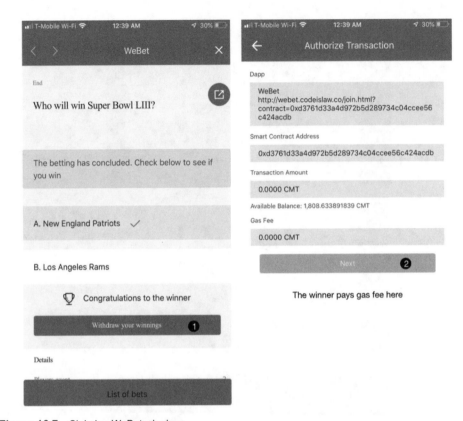

Figure 16.7   Claiming WeBet winnings

Next, let's review the smart contract code behind the WeBet contract and then the JavaScript dapp to interact with WeBet contracts.

> **Note**
>
> You have probably noticed that the WeBet contract owner must declare the winning choice for the bet. Can the contract owner cheat here? Yes, mapping real-world off-chain information (i.e., whether he lost 10 pounds) onto the blockchain is always a challenge. However, it is also important to note that everything related to the WeBet contract, including the declaration and all the bets, are recorded on the blockchain for everyone to see. If a contract owner does cheat, he forever damages his reputation.
>
> We could also modify the product to require multiple known "arbiters" to verify the contract owner declaration before it takes effect. However, that makes the product more complex to use.

WeBet Smart Contract

The overall structure of the WeBet smart contract written in Solidity is as follows. As discussed, the dapp creates a new instance of the WeBet contract for every new betting contract.

```
contract BettingGame {

    address public owner;

    struct Bet {
        int8 choice;
        uint256 amount;
        bool paid;
        bool initialized;
    }
    mapping(address => Bet) bets;

    string public game_desc;
    int8 public number_of_choices;
    uint256 public min_bet_amount;
    bool public allow_user_bet_amount;
    uint256 total_bet_amount;
    int8 public total_bet_count;

    mapping(int8 => uint256) choice_bet_amounts;

    int8 public correct_choice;
    string public correct_choice_txt;

    int8 public game_status; // 0 not started; 1 running;
                             //2 stopped; 3 ended; 4 cancelled

    modifier onlyOwner() {
        assert(msg.sender == owner);
        _;
    }

    constructor (string _game_desc, int8 _number_of_choices,
        uint256 _min_bet_amount, bool _allow_user_bet_amount) public {
        require(_number_of_choices > 0);
        require(_min_bet_amount > 0);

        owner = msg.sender;
        game_status = 1;
        game_desc = _game_desc;
        number_of_choices = _number_of_choices;
        min_bet_amount = _min_bet_amount;
        allow_user_bet_amount = _allow_user_bet_amount;

        total_bet_count = 0;
        total_bet_amount = 0;
        correct_choice = -1;
        correct_choice_txt = "";
    }
```

```
function placeBet (int8 _choice) public payable {
    // see later
}

function stopGame() external onlyOwner {
    require (game_status == 1);
    game_status = 2;
}

function resumeGame() external onlyOwner {
    require (game_status == 2);
    game_status = 1;
}

function endGame(int8 _correct_choice, string _correct_choice_txt)
        external onlyOwner {
    correct_choice = _correct_choice;
    correct_choice_txt = _correct_choice_txt;
    game_status = 3;
}

function cancelGame() public {
    require (msg.sender == owner || isValidator(msg.sender));
    game_status = 4;
}

function payMe () public {
    // See later
}

function checkStatus (address _addr) public view returns (int8,
        string, int8, uint256, uint256, bool, int8) {
    // see later
}

function getBetInfo()public view returns(int8,string,int8,int8,uint256,bool){
    return (game_status, game_desc, correct_choice, total_bet_count,
        total_bet_amount, allow_user_bet_amount);
}

function getAnswer() public view returns (int8, string) {
    return (correct_choice, correct_choice_txt);
}

function terminate() external onlyOwner {
    selfdestruct(owner);
}
}
```

The constructor method creates the contract with all the information needed to set up the betting.

- The `game_desc` string contains the bet's title, description, and all the choices. They are constructed in a single string with the ; symbol to delimit various components. For example, the `game_desc` string could be as follows: `bet title;choice 1;choice 2;choice 3`. We are not passing and storing choices in string arrays because of Solidity's limitations on string arrays. The parsing work is left for JavaScript in the dapp as it is not core to the transaction logic of the contract.

- The `number_of_choices` value specifies the number choices contained in the `game_desc` string. In our example, it would be 3. This helps the dapp JavaScript parse the information components.

- The `min_bet_amount` value is the minimum amount each user must bet to participate in the game. It is in the unit of CMTs.

- The `allow_user_bet_amount` value is a `boolean` variable that specifies whether a user can bet in an amount greater than `min_bet_amount`.

Once the contract is created, the `game_status` variable defaults to 1, which means the betting has started. Through methods such as `stopGame()`, `resumeGame()`, `endGame()`, and `cancelGame()`, you can change the game status. That allows the contractor owner to stop voting before declaring a winner. For example, a sports bet should stop once the game starts in the real world, and the winner will be declared when the real-world game ends. The `getBetInfo()` function returns the basic information and status of the bet.

The `bets` array in the contract maps an address to `Bet`. Each `Bet` struct in the array is created by a bet. It contains the better's choice, the amount she bets, and whether this user has claimed her winnings if she wins. The better's address is the key in the `bets` array.

The `choice_bet_amounts` array in the contract maps each choice to its aggregated bet amounts (in the unit of CMTs). It allows easy computation of the winning for each betting address. The `checkStatus()` function is called by the dapp to check the bet status and winning of the current user address.

```
function checkStatus (address _addr) public view returns (int8, string,
      int8, uint256, uint256, bool, int8) {

    safeuint payout = 0;
    if (game_status == 3 && bets[_addr].choice == correct_choice) {
        payout = bets[_addr].amount * total_bet_amount /
choice_bet_amounts[correct_choice];
    } else if (game_status == 4) {
        payout = bets[_addr].amount;
    }

    return (game_status, game_desc, bets[_addr].choice,
      uint256(bets[_addr].amount), uint256(payout),
      bets[_addr].paid, correct_choice);
}
```

Now the key function in the entire contract is the `placeBet()` function. It is called by any users who want to place a bet on a choice in this contract. The function is `payable`, meaning that the user can attach a payment to its call. The payment is the bet placed on the choice. It should at least meet the `min_bet_amount`. Once a bet is made, the contract's `bets` and `choice_bet_amounts` arrays are both updated.

```
function placeBet (int8 _choice) public payable {
    require (game_status == 1); // game is running
    require (_choice <= number_of_choices); // Valid choice
    require (msg.value >= min_bet_amount); // Meet min bet amount
    require (bets[msg.sender].initialized == false); // Only bet once

    Bet memory newBet = Bet(_choice, msg.value, false, true);
    bets[msg.sender] = newBet;

    choice_bet_amounts[_choice] = choice_bet_amounts[_choice] + msg.value;
    total_bet_amount = total_bet_amount + msg.value;
    total_bet_count += 1;
}
```

A user checks her winnings by calling the `checkStatus()` function from her betting address. If the user wins, she can get paid from the contract by calling the `payMe()` function. Notice that if the `game_status` indicates that the owner has canceled the bet, every better is refunded.

```
function payMe () public {
    require (bets[msg.sender].initialized); // Must have a bet
    require (bets[msg.sender].amount > 0); // More than zero
    require (bets[msg.sender].paid == false); // chose correctly

    if (game_status == 3) {
        // game ended normally
        require (bets[msg.sender].choice == correct_choice);
        uint256 payout = bets[msg.sender].amount * total_bet_amount /
          choice_bet_amounts[correct_choice];
        if (payout > 0) {
            msg.sender.transfer(uint256(payout));
            bets[msg.sender].paid = true; // cannot claim twice
        }
    } else if (game_status == 4) {
        // Just refund the bet
        msg.sender.transfer(uint256(bets[msg.sender].amount));
        bets[msg.sender].paid = true; // cannot claim twice
    } else {
        require (false); // Just fail
    }
}
```

The Solidity smart contract is deliberately simple. It mostly deals with important application states and automatic transfer of "money" (i.e., CMTs in this case). It is a back-end service for the JavaScript dapp.

WeBet JavaScript Application

The WeBet dapp is a JavaScript application that can be executed inside the CyberMiles App or in a Chrome browser with the CyberMiles Venus (Metamask for CMT) extension enabled. In the `browser.js` file, we test if the `web3.cmt` object is `nil`. If it is, the user will be directed to install the CMT wallet on mobile devices or Venus Chrome extension on PCs and then restart the dapp.

Since the dapp is just a collection of static JavaScript and HTML files, the files can be served from any anonymous web server or even be bundled inside the device client. There is no need for a central server to manage the application state. In our example, the dapp files are served from http://webet.codeislaw.co/.

Create a New WeBet Contract

The `start.html` and `start.js` files in the dapp work in tandem to support the creation and deployment of a new WeBet contract. The HTML file captures the user input about the contract details (e.g., title, choices, minimum bet amount), and the JS file creates the contract on the blockchain. The following is the initialization code for the `start.js` script:

```
$(function () {
    webBrowser.openBrowser();
    getAbi();
    getBin();
    initLanguage();
    initUserAddress();
    // ...
});

var initUserAddress = function () {
    var interval = setInterval(function () {
        web3.cmt.getAccounts(function (e, address) {
            if (address) {
                userAddress = address.toString();
                $("#userAddress").val(address);
                userAddress = address;
                tip.closeLoad();
                clearInterval(interval);
            }
        });
    }, 300);
}
```

Notice that every blockchain-related operation is done asynchronously. The app shows a spinner and asks the user to wait while it discovers the user's current account address from the wallet. The `startGame()` JavaScript function is mapped to the click event when the user hits the Submit button to create a WeBet contract.

```
var startGame = function () {
    var inputs = document.getElementsByName("choice");
```

```
        var numChoices = 0;
        var gameDesc = '';

        for (var i = 0; i < inputs.length; i++) {
            if (inputs[i].value != null && inputs[i].value != '') {
                var inputValue = inputs[i].value
                gameDesc += inputValue.trim() + ";";
                numChoices++;
            }
        }
        var title = $("#title").val();
        var betMinAmount = $("#betMinAmount").val();
        var allowUserBet = $("#allowUserBetCheckbox").val();
        var allowUserBetAmount = false;
        var minBetAmount = web3.toWei(betMinAmount, "cmt");
    gameDesc = gameDesc.replace(/(^;)|(;$)/g, "");
        // deploy and start the game
        var contract = web3.cmt.contract(betAbi);
        var feeDate = '0x' + contract.new.getData(gameDesc, numChoices - 1,
          minBetAmount, allowUserBetAmount, {data: betBin.object});
        web3.cmt.estimateGas({data: feeDate}, function (e, returnGas) {
            var gas = '1700000';
            if (!e) {
                gas = Number(returnGas * 2);
            }
            contract.new([gameDesc, numChoices - 1, minBetAmount,
                    allowUserBetAmount], {
                from: userAddress.toString(),
                data: feeDate,
                gas: gas,
                gasPrice: '2000000000'
            }, function (e, instance) {
                if (e) {
                    tip.close();
                    tip.error(lang.tip.createFailed);
                } else {
                    contract_address = instance.address;
                    // ...
                    setTheContractAddressAndTurn(instance);
                }
            });
        });
    };
```

Aside from the regular input validation and processing code, the main part of the function is nested in two asynchronous blocks. The estimateGas() function asks a connected blockchain node to estimate the amount of gas fee needed to create this contract. We multiply the gas by 2 since the estimate is sometimes conservative. Notice that this is the *gas limit*, or the maximum amount gas the user authorizes to use. The user will be charged only for the actual gas used when creating the contract. Then, the `contract.new()` function passes information to the contract's `constructor()` function and asynchronously returns the newly created contract's address.

The dapp UI displays a spinner until the contract address is successfully created and returned. It then calls the `setTheContractAddressAndTurn()` function to navigate to the betting screen.

```
var setTheContractAddressAndTurn = function (result) {
    if (result != null && (result.contractAddress != 'undefined'
            || result.address != 'undefined')) {
        tip.right(lang.bet.betCreated);
        setTimeout(function () {
            var turnAddress = result.contractAddress;
            if (turnAddress == 'undefined') {
                turnAddress = result.address
                saveLocalStorageBet(turnAddress);
            }
            console.log(turnAddress);
            window.location.href = './join.html?contract=' + turnAddress;
        }, 2000);
    }
};
```

The dapp now navigates to the `join.html` screen. The URL with the contract address is how other people access this bet from their CyberMiles App (CMT wallets). The `join.html` screen can create a QR bar code to be shared with friends and potential betters.

Bet on a Choice

The `join.html` and `bet.js` files work in tandem to present the betting UI. The `getGameStatus()` function retrieves information from the contract's `checkStatus()` function. It is a **pure view** function and hence requires no gas to operate. Once the JavaScript `getGameStatus()` function receives the result, it parses the title, choices, the current choice, the current bet, and the user's award status, and then displays those information items on the `join.html` screen. I will not repeat that code in this book as it is lengthy, but you can see it in the source code listing.

The `confirmOptionSubmit()` function is called when the user submits her bet. It calls the contract's `placeBet()` function asynchronously after estimating gas. The bet is sent to the contract as a value for the payable `placeBet()` function.

```
var confirmOptionSubmit = function () {
    var amount = $("#minBetAmount").val();
    var selectedValue = $("#selectedValue").val();
    // ... validate game status ...
    var allowBet = $("#allowUserBetAmount").val();
    if (allowBet == 'true') {
        var betAmount = $("#SubmitValue").val();
        betAmount = onlyNumber(betAmount);
        if (betAmount <= 0 || betAmount < amount) {
```

```
                tip.error(lgb.tip.moreThanZero);
                return;
            }
            amount = betAmount;
        }


    // change the submit button color and event

        var feeData = instance.placeBet.getData(selectedValue + "");
        var amountStr = String(web3.toWei(amount, "cmt"));
        web3.cmt.estimateGas({
            data: feeData,
            to: contract_address,
            value: amountStr
        }, function (error, gas) {
            var virtualGas = '20000000';
            if (error) {
                console.log("error estimating gas");
            } else {
                virtualGas = gas;
            }
            instance.placeBet(selectedValue, {
                value: web3.toWei(amount, "cmt"),
                gas: virtualGas,
                gasPrice: 2000000000
            }, function (e, result) {
                if (e) {
                    // ...
                } else {
                    showUserChoice(gameStatus, userChoice, correctChoice);
                    $("#msg").html(lgb.bet.pendingBet);
                    $('#msg').css('display', 'block');
                    getGameStatus('bet');
                }
            });
        });
    }
```

Once the placeBet() function call returns, the dapp does not wait for the transaction to be
confirmed. It just goes ahead and updates the UI to show the current selected choice and a
message showing that the bet is submitted. The getGameStatus() function refreshes the page
every ten seconds to get the latest from the blockchain. Once the transaction is confirmed on the
blockchain, the message changes to say that the bet is recorded.

Declare the Winning Choice

When the bet.js script displays information retrieved from the WeBet smart contract, it
determines whether to display the owner's control options, such as the options to stop the bet or
to declare a winning option.

```
web3.cmt.getAccounts(function (e, address) {
    // ...
    contract = web3.cmt.contract(betAbi, contract_address);
    instance = contract.at(contract_address);
instance.checkStatus(userAddress, function (gameError, result) {
// ...
        instance.owner(function (e, owner) {
            if (owner && owner.toLowerCase()==userAddress.toLowerCase()) {
                if (gameStatus != 3) {
                    showBetSetting(contentId, afterBtnName,
                        lgb.bet.setting, betSetting);
                }
            }
        });
    });
});

var showBetSetting = function (btnId, afterBtnName, buttonName, betFun) {
    var showColor = "#1976d2";
    if (!document.getElementById(btnId)) {
        fun.addButton(btnId, afterBtnName, buttonName, showColor, betFun);
    }
}
```

When the user touches the owner button, she sees a dialog box to declare a winning option. The action is mapped to the declareBetGame() function.

```
var declareBetGame = function () {
    var choiceValue = $("#declareValue").val();
    var dateTime = new Date();
    var desc = "This Bet Game stop at the Time : " +
        dateTime + "and the correct choice is" +
        fun.getLetterByNum(choiceValue);
    if (choiceValue <= 0) {
        tip.error(lgb.tip.selectOption);
        return;
    }
    var feeData = instance.endGame.getData(choiceValue, desc);

    web3.cmt.estimateGas({
        data: feeData,
        to: contract_address
    }, function (error, gas) {
        var virtualGas = '20000000';
        if (error) {
            console.log("error getting gas");
        } else {
            virtualGas = gas;
        }
```

```
            instance.endGame(Number(choiceValue), desc, {
                gas: virtualGas,
                gasPrice: 2000000000
            }, function (e, result) {
                if (e) {
                    // ...
                } else {
                    getGameStatus('declare');
                }
            });
        });
    }
```

The contract's endGame() function is called. This allows the contract to compute winnings for
each bet participant. After the remote function call returns, the WeBet UI refreshes.

Claim Your Winnings

When the user loads the dapp again after the winning choice is declared, she sees whether her bet
choice is the winning one. And if she wins, she sees an option to get the reward into her current
account address.

```
var showRightChoice = function (contentId, userChoice, correctChoice,
        afterBtnName, withdrawButtonName, statusPaid, payoutAmount) {
    if (userChoice > 0) {
        if (correctChoice == userChoice) {
            if (statusPaid) {
                showWithdrawSuccess(contentId, payoutAmount);
            } else {
                showWithdraw(contentId, afterBtnName,
                    withdrawButtonName, withdraw);
            }
        } else {
            showFailed(contentId);
        }
    } else {
        showNotJoin(contentId);
    }
}

var showWithdraw = function (contentId, afterBtnName, buttonName, betFun) {
    var id = "winner-div";
    var showColor = "#1976d2";
    if (!document.getElementById(id)) {
        fun.addButton(contentId, afterBtnName, buttonName, showColor, betFun);
    }
    var content = '<div class="winner-show">...</div>';
    fun.addDivInnerhtml(domType[0], [attrType[0]], appendType[1],
      content, [id], contentId);
}
```

When the user clicks the button to claim her winnings, the contract's **payMe()** function is called.

```
var withdraw = function () {
    instance.payMe(function (e, result) {
        if (e != null) {
            if (e.code == '1001') {
                tip.error(lgb.withdraw.info + lgb.cancelled)
            } else {
                tip.error(lgb.withdraw.info + lgb.error)
            }
        } else {
            console.log(result);
            $("#msg").html(lgb.bet.pendingWithdraw);
            $('#msg').css('display', 'block');
            document.getElementById(contentId).style.display = 'none';
            getGameStatus('withdraw');
        }
    });
}
```

This design requires the user to come back to her bet and pay the gas fee to claim her winnings. Another option is to automate the contract so that the owner pays the gas fee at **endGame()** and the contract automatically distributes the winnings.

With the current WeBet design, the dapp user needs to access her past bets. In our setup, we use data stored locally or on replaceable servers to achieve decentralization. That is the topic of the next section.

Dapp Off-Chain Operations

The WeBet dapp illustrates how to store nonessential application data in off-chain services. The off-chain data is not stored in a central server like with typical web apps. The data belongs to each WeBet dapp user.

The JavaScript Local Storage

The WeBet dapp uses JavaScript's **localStorage** API for storing data related to the current user. For example, in the **start.js** file, we use the local storage to save the user's current address and the newly created contract address. They are needed for the next web page, **join.html**, which can be shared with other betting participants.

```
var saveLocalStorageBet = function (contractAddress) {
    if (window.localStorage) {
        var storage = window.localStorage;
        var item = {"userAddress": userAddress,
                    "contractAddress": contractAddress};
        storage.setItem("bets", item);
    }
}
```

The local storage can be used to store data that is private to the current user. It is stored on the device that runs the wallet. Only people who have access to the device can get this data.

Replaceable Third-Party Services

The my.html and my.js files work together to display a list of WeBet contracts the current user has participated in. The Ethereum protocol does not provide a way to query the blockchain nodes for this type of information. For the WeBet dapp, we build an online service that ingests the blocks from a CyberMiles node, builds a relational database for the data in the blocks (e.g., contracts, owners, and bets), and then provides an API to query the database.

This database is decentralized because it can be deployed by anyone using open source software. So, the dapp has many potential choices for this data source. There is no single power of failure or control. The following is the relevant code in my.js:

```
var requestListInfo = function (pageNo) {
    var methodId = 'de2fd8ab,83bd72ba,3cc4c6ce,9c16667c,340190ec';
    var url = 'https://api.cmttracking.io/api/v3/contractsByType?funcIds='
      + methodId + "&limit=" + pageSize + "&page=" + pageNo
    $.ajax({
        url: url,
        dataType: 'json',
        type: 'GET',
        async: true,
        success: function (result) {
            if (result && result.data && result.data.objects) {
                $("#totalCount").val(result.data.meta.total);
                var totalPage = parseInt(
                    result.data.meta.total / pageSize) + 1;
                $("#totalPage").val(totalPage);
                var lastCount = result.data.meta.total % pageSize;
                if (pageNo < totalPage) {
                    lastCount = pageSize;
                }
                var id = "listContent";
                divCount = 0;
                if (result.data.objects.length <= 0) {
                    tip.closeLoad();
                    return;
                }
                console.log(result.data.objects);
                for (var i = 0; i < result.data.objects.length; i++) {
                    var obj = result.data.objects[i];
                    appendChildList(obj.address, id,
                                    lastCount, userAddress);
                }
            }
        },
```

```
        error: function (e) {
            console.log("Get user contract address failed" + e)
        }
    });
}
```

In this case, the service is deployed at `api.cmttracking.io` and allows searching for smart contract addresses via their bytecode signatures.

Conclusion

In this chapter, using the Valentines and WeBet dapps as examples, I showed how to create complete dapps on the CyberMiles public blockchain.

17

Business Rules and Contracts

The blockchain virtual machine is essentially a state machine that reacts to state changes in the accounts (i.e., the transactions). Of course, as part of the reaction, the virtual machine can also cause additional state changes. In many cases, such state changes can be defined and described by sets of formal rules ("If this, then that," or ITTT). In fact, in modern computer systems, most machine-to-machine interactions are defined by such rules.

However, when we have multiple interacting systems, explicitly coding and executing rules using a general programming language becomes impossible even for seasoned computer programmers. For example, in a typical airline mileage program, the points a person earns depend on complex rules for her account status, account history, the ticket purchased, and the flight taken. Each of those systems has its own rules, and the final execution outcome (the points awarded after this flight) is a "join" operation for all of those rules. Furthermore, those rules should not be programmed or maintained by computer programmers, as they are often changing depending on business requirements. A business analyst must be able to create, validate, and maintain those rules. That had given rise to the business rules engine (BRE).

A typical BRE consists of a specialized computer programming language (formal rules language), runtime to execute rules, and optional visual tools to create and manage rules. BREs are available in almost any programming language and are widely available from commercial and open source providers. Examples of well-known BREs include Drools, Jess, Pega, ILOG, and InRule. Lity, the programming language and virtual machine, is the first blockchain-based BRE.

Supporting the rules language and tools in blockchain smart contracts could help bring a large number of business analysts/programmers and their existing rules applications into the blockchain ecosystem. A BRE allows people to build decentralized financial, e-commerce, and other applications using familiar tools. On the other hand, the blockchain provides a secure and verifiable platform to execute business rules and could bring a new level of trust to a BRE.

In this chapter, we will explore how the Lity smart contract language and the CyberMiles public blockchain support formal business rules in the smart contract itself.

An Example

The Lity rules definition is simple. The overall approach is to first define when the rule should be triggered and then define the triggered actions.

Let's examine a rule that will give retirees their stipend when there is available budget. The BRE has a "working memory" space to store personal profiles, as well as the budget. When the rule is fired, the execution engine in the Lity virtual machine goes through all the objects in the working memory and identifies the combinations that meet the when clause. It executes the then clause and updates the state of the objects in the working memory. The virtual machine executes this rule over all objects in the working memory until the when clause can match no object in the working memory anymore.

```
rule "payPension" when {
  p: Person(age >= 65, eligible == true);
  b: Budget(amount >= 10);
} then {
  p.addr.transfer(10);
  p.eligible = false;
  b.amount -= 10;
}
```

In the previous code snippet, the Lity virtual machine matches a person who is older than 60 and is eligible for the stipend. It then checks whether the budget is still available. If both conditions are met, the when clause finds a match, and the then clause is triggered. The then clause sends the fund to the person and reduces the budget. One of the then actions is to change the person's eligible attribute to false so that this person will not be matched by the when clause again because, as described, the rules engine runs the rule over and over again until no more match can be found.

Now, how do we get the Person objects and the Budget object into the working memory of the Lity rules engine? This is done via the factInsert and factDelete statements in Lity. The following code listing shows the contract in its entirety. The Budget object is inserted into the working memory when the contract is created. The addPerson() function adds a Person object to the working memory. It keeps a reference to the person in the ps array so that the person can be removed from the working memory later if needed. The pay() function fires the rule against all objects in the working memory.

```
contract AgePension {
    struct Person {
        int age;
        bool eligible;
```

```
        address addr;
    }

    struct Budget {
        int amount;
    }

    mapping (address => uint256) addr2idx;
    Person[] ps;
    Budget;

    constructor () public {
        factInsert budget;
        budget.amount = 100;
    }

    function addPerson(int age) public {
        ps.push(Person(age, true, msg.sender));
        addr2idx[msg.sender] = factInsert ps[ps.length-1];
    }

    function deletePerson() public {
        factDelete addr2idx[msg.sender];
    }

    function pay() public {
        fireAllRules;
    }

    function () public payable { }

    rule "payPension" when {
        p: Person(age >= 65, eligible == true);
        b: Budget(amount >= 10);
    } then {
        p.addr.transfer(10);
        p.eligible = false;
        b.amount -= 10;
    }
}
```

You can type this contract into CyberMiles' Europa online integrated development environment (IDE) and deploy it to the live CyberMiles public blockchain network (Figure 17.1). You can use the Europa UI to directly interact with contract methods such as addPerson() and pay() to see the rules execution in action.

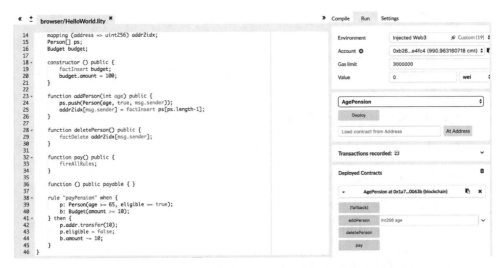

Figure 17.1 Deploying the rules contract via Europa on the CyberMiles public blockchain

---

Note

The BUIDL IDE can also compile and deploy Lity smart contracts with embedded rules. Try it!

Now you have seen a simple example of the Lity rules smart contract. In this example, the functionality can be easily implemented using regular if-then statements. In the next sections, let's look into the rules language and more common rules use cases.

Rules Language

Modern BREs including Lity use the Rete algorithm to construct, evaluate, and then execute a network of interfering rules.

All rules can be sequenced into a series of nesting if-then statements. However, when the rules are complex, the if-then structure could become complicated. Consider the following simple rules for airline rewards:

- The customer is given silver status when the number of award miles reaches 25,000 miles.

- The customer is given gold status when the number of award miles reaches 50,000 miles.

- Silver customers get a 10 percent bonus of award miles from any flight.

- Gold customers get a 20 percent bonus of award miles from any flight.

This example involves only two sets of simple inferencing rules, the customer status and the flight awards. Now, consider the rules to compute awards for all customers on a flight. Some customers might reach the silver or gold status on the flight. So, the if-then sequence will need to first compute award miles, then update the status, and then recompute the award miles for some customers again.

If the rules are more complex and include a few more inferencing rule sets, the if-then sequence could be exponentially more complex. Each rule set will need to be evaluated and executed again and again inside every combination of other rule sets. The deeply nested sequence cannot be built by hand and is impossible to test and validate. Furthermore, if the rules are changed by business requirements, the entire sequence of evaluation, revaluation, and execution would need to be rebuilt.

Rete Algorithm

The Rete algorithm, invented by Dr. Charles Forgy, solves this problem elegantly. Without going into details of the algorithm, it allows us to declare individual rules as nodes in a network (known as the Rete network) and connect the nodes via inference relationships between rules. Once a Rete network is defined, the algorithm automatically applies to a collection of objects in working memory (i.e., the customer and flight objects in the airline example). The Rete algorithm efficiently evaluates and re-evaluates the objects by traversing the network nodes and then executes the rules.

For developers and business analysts, we can simply declare the rules and place objects into the working memory. We no longer need to build the highly nested if-then sequence and can now rely on computers to execute the Rete algorithm on the rules and objects.

The Lity rules engine implements the Rete algorithm. The overall syntax of the Lity rules is as follows:

```
contract C {
    rule "ruleName"
    // Rule attributes
    when {
        // Filter Statements
    } then {
        // Action Statements
    }
}
```

Next, let's look into the structure of the rules.

Rule Attribute

A rule can have the following attributes.

The salience attribute indicates the activation priority of a rule. A contract can have multiple rules, and they are ordered by salience. The higher salience rules are evaluated and executed first. It defaults to integer value 0. In the following example, the second rule is evaluated first.

```
rule "test1" salience 20 when {
  p: Person(val >= 10);
} then {
  p.addr.send(1);
  p.val--;
  update p;
}

rule "test2" salience 30 when {
  p: Person(val >= 20);
} then {
  p.addr.send(2);
  p.val--;
  update p;
}
```

When true, the `no_loop` attribute forbids a rule to activate itself with the same set of facts. This is for the purpose of preventing an infinite loop. It defaults to `false`. In the following example, the rule is fired only once for every `Person` in working memory.

```
rule "test" no_loop true when {
  p: Person(age >= 20);
} then {
  p.age++;
  p.addr.send(1);
  update p;
}
```

When true, the `lock_on_active` attribute forbids a rule to be activated more than once with the same set of facts. This is stronger than `no_loop` because it also prevents the reactivation of the rule even if it is caused by another rule's actions.

Rule Filters

The filter statements specify how to match the facts (struts and objects) against the rule. It is a series of statements joined by **AND**, meaning that all of them must be satisfied for a combination of objects to be matched and filtered.

Each statement specifies an object type and filter criteria for its attributes. It starts with pattern binding, which specifies the fact identifier referred to in this rule scope. After binding, the pattern type specifies the type of the fact object. Then, a set of constraints describes conditions of this fact. The constraints must be `boolean` expressions.

```
rule "test" when {
  p: Person(age >= 65, eligible == true);
} then {
  ... ...
}
```

The previous pattern describes a fact **p** with the **Person** type; its constraints are that the **age** must be greater or equal to **65** and that **eligible** must be **true**.

Rule Actions

The action statements specify the functions to be called on the filtered facts. For example, the following code in the action block calls **transfer()** and then updates the person's eligibility:

```
rule "test" when {
  p: Person(age >= 65, eligible == true);
} then {
  p.addr.transfer(10);
  p.eligible = false;
  update p;
}
```

The **update** keyword in the actions block is a special keyword for the rules language. The update object statement informs the rule engine that this object may be modified and the rules may need to be reevaluated.

Rule Inheritance

Rules can be inherited. Sometimes constraints of a rule are based on constraints of another rule. In this case, this rule can extend another rule.

For example, a department store wants to give elder customers a 10 percent discount and their cars free parking. The discount rule is described as follows:

```
rule "test1"
when {
    customer : Customer( age > 60 );
} then {
    customer.discount = 10;
}
```

The free parking rule can extend the constraint of elder customers (older than 60). Then this rule can be written as follows:

```
rule "test2"
    extends "test1"
when {
    car : Car ( ownerID == customer.id );
} then {
    car.freeParking = true ;
}
```

The inheritance allows developers and analysts to build on complex libraries of rules based on past work.

Working Memory

As we have seen in the example, the `factInsert` and `factDelete` statements are used to manage facts in the working memory for rules to filter and act on.

The `factInsert` operator takes an object with a storage data location and evaluates to a fact handle, which has type `uint256`. Insert the reference to the storage object into working memory. An example is as follows:

```
contract C {
  struct fact { int x; }
  fact[] facts;
  constructor() public {
    facts.push(fact(0));
    // insert the fact into working memory
    factInsert facts[facts.length-1];
  }
}
```

Note that `factInsert fact(0);` cannot be compiled. The reason is that `fact(0)` is a reference with memory data location, which is not persistent and thus cannot be inserted into working memory.

The `factDelete` operator takes a fact handle (a `uint256`) and evaluates to `void`. It removes the reference of the fact from working memory.

Finally, `fireAllRules` is a special statement that launches the Lity rule engine execution.

More Business Examples

There are many applications for rules in smart contracts. You have already seen a simple example of an airline points program. In general, public blockchains are great platforms for such points programs since they provide transparency in the supply, issuance, and use of such points, and they could allow the points from different merchants to be exchanged and traded. In this section, I will go over a few more simplified examples to give you some ideas of real-world application use cases for rules.

Insurance Claim

Consider a travel insurance company that provides a claim for flight delays as follows:

- If the flight is delayed for more than four hours, everyone receives at least $100.
- If the flight is delayed for more than six hours, everyone receives up to $300 in accountable expenses.

The first rule (four hours or more) is represented as follows:

```
rule "four hour fix amount" when {
    p: Person()
```

```
    f: Flight(delay >= 4, id == p.flightID)
} then {
    p.claimAmount = max(100, p.claimAmount);
}
```

For the second rule (six hours or more), $100 in compensation is implied in the first rule, so we need to consider only the limited expense here.

```
rule "six hour limited amount" when {
    p: Person()
    f: Flight(delay >= 6, id == p.flightID)
} then {
    p.claimAmount = max(min(p.delayExpense, 300), p.claimAmount);
}
```

The rules engine can be useful in evaluation insurance claims as the payouts are all the rules written into the insurance contracts.

Taxes

This example illustrates how to calculate taxes using a rule engine. In most countries, tax rates are divided into brackets. That is, certain income ranges are taxed at corresponding rates. Often, more income indicates higher tax rates. For example, in the 2018 U.S. federal tax system, single filers pay the following rates based on their income:

- *$0 to $9,525*: 10 percent

- *$9,526 to $38,700*: 12 percent

- *$38,701 to $82,500*: 22 percent

- *$82,501 to $157,500*: 24 percent

- *$157,501 to $200,000*: 32 percent

- *$200,001 to $500,000*: 35 percent

- *$500,001 or more*: 37 percent

The rates are marginal rates, meaning that the tax payer pays that rate only on the amount of her income that falls into the specified range. For example, if you have $10,000 in taxable income, the first $9,525 is subject to the 10 percent rate, and the remaining $475 is subject to the tax rate of the next bracket, which is 12 percent. Now, let's look at the rules. For the first tax bracket, the net income from $0 to $9,525 is taxed at 10 percent.

```
rule "first bracket" when{
    p: Person(income > 0)
} then {
    p.tax += min(9525, p.income) * 10 / 100;
}
```

Similarly, the net income from \$9,526 to \$38,700 is taxed at 12 percent in the second tax bracket. Note that \$9,525 of income has already been taxed in the first tax bracket, so \$9,525 should be subtracted from the amount taxed here.

```
rule "second bracket" when{
    p: Person(income > 9525)
} then {
    p.tax += (min(38700, p.income) - 9525) * 12 / 100;
}
```

In the same way, the rest of the brackets are represented as follows:

```
rule "third bracket" when{
    p: Person(income > 38700)
} then {
    p.tax += (min(82500, p.income) - 38700) * 22 / 100;
}

rule "fourth bracket" when{
    p: Person(income > 82500)
} then {
    p.tax += (min(157500, p.income) - 82500) * 24 / 100;
}

rule "fifth bracket" when{
    p: Person(income > 157500)
} then {
    p.tax += (min(200000, p.income) - 157500) * 32 / 100;
}

rule "sixth bracket" when{
    p: Person(income > 200000)
} then {
    p.tax += (min(500000, p.income) - 200000) * 35 / 100;
}

rule "seventh bracket" when{
    p: Person(income > 500000)
} then {
    p.tax += (p.income - 500000) * 37 / 100;
}
```

Of course, the tax code has many other rules to adjust a person's taxable income, categorize income into additional rate brackets (e.g., all capital gains are taxed at 10 percent), and refund some taxes when certain rules are met. The tax code is a compelling use case for rules engine!

Product Combos

Finally, let's look at an example of commerce applications. It's common practice for online and offline stores to offer discounts when a customer orders multiple products at the same time. Consider restaurants, for example; a hamburger costs $11 and a drink costs $3, and these sum up to $14. This summation rule could be simply represented as follows:

```
rule "Burger"
  salience 10
  lock_on_active
when{
    b: Burger();
    bl: Bill();
} then {
    bl.amount += 11;
}

rule "Drink"
  salience 10
  lock_on_active
when{
    d: Drink();
    bl: Bill();
} then {
    bl.amount += 3;
}
```

However, many restaurants offer a meal combo discount. For example, a drink with a hamburger is discounted by $2. With a rules engine, this discount rule can be automatically applied as follows:

```
rule "Combo" when{
    b: Burger(combo==-1);
    d: Drink(combo==-1);
    bl: Bill();
} then {
    b.combo = bl.nCombo;
    d.combo = bl.nCombo;
    bl.nCombo++;
    bl.amount -= 2;
    update b;
    update d;
}
```

nCombo is the number of combos in a bill, and the combo value of a burger/drink denotes the combo number (-1 denotes no combo) that the burger/drink belongs to. Each burger or drink belongs to at most one combo to prevent duplicate discounts.

Conclusion

Blockchain smart contracts are a natural fit for formal rules. Smart contracts are just sets of rules executed by computers without human intervention when certain conditions are met. Conversely, the blockchain guarantees the correct execution of the rules.

In this chapter, I discussed the Lity rules language and engine. It enables formal business rules to be constructed and executed in blockchain smart contracts. Note that many examples in this chapter originally appeared in the Lity documentation.

18

Building an Application-Specific EVM

One of the key features of Lity is the libENI facility. It allows developers to add native C/C++ functions to the Lity virtual machine. While Solidity and Lity are both Turing complete languages, they are inefficient. And that translates to slow performance and high gas costs for many common computer operations on the blockchain, such as string manipulation and encryption/decryption. The libENI native functions allow developers to support those operations in blockchain smart contracts in a highly efficient manner. The importance of libENI is twofold.

- If you are building your own blockchain, you can customize it for specific application use cases by bundling a selected library of libENI functions. For example, if you are building a blockchain specifically for the exchange of privacy data, you could bundle libENI functions commonly used for data encryption. Commercial providers, such as the Second State, provide tools for you to create custom libENI bundles for your own blockchains.

- If you are developing smart contracts on a Lity-enabled public blockchain, such as the CyberMiles public blockchain, you could add new system-wide functions via libENI. On the CyberMiles blockchain, the libENI modules and functions can be developed by anyone and added to the blockchain virtual machine via the consensus of the validators. It is the most democratic way to extend the blockchain virtual machine.

Note

The Ethereum road map also calls for native and precompiled contracts. These contracts are developed by Ethereum core developers and deployed with Ethereum software updates. The libENI extensions for public blockchains, on the other hand, can be developed by anyone and need to be approved only by the underlying blockchain's consensus.

For example, on the CyberMiles blockchain, anyone can propose to add a libENI function to the blockchain through a governance TX. The CyberMiles validators or super nodes vote on the governance TX to approve or reject it. That enables dynamic and democratic extension to the virtual machine outside of the software development cycle and outside of the "core" developer community. The community-developed libENI functions can be added to virtual machines without stopping, forking, or restarting the blockchain.

In this chapter, I will explain how to use, develop, and deploy libENI functions. We will use CyberMiles as an example to demonstrate how libENI on-chain governance works. The Lity team is adding to libENI implementations on a regular basis. It is developing complete sets of string libraries, encryption libraries, JSON libraries, and other common utilities as highly efficient and optional libENI functions to the Lity virtual machine.

Using libENI Functions

The CyberMiles blockchain software comes with a few simple libENI functions already pre-installed. They allow us to experiment with libENI functions in our smart contracts immediately. But first, you will need to install the `lityc` compiler to build smart contracts written in the Lity programming language.

You can choose to build the `lityc` compiler from source or directly download a binary build for one of its supported OS platforms. The binary distribution page is on GitHub at https://github.com/CyberMiles/lity/releases. But if you are inclined to build your own, use the following:

```
$ git clone https://github.com/second-state/lity.git
$ cd lity
$ mkdir build
$ cd build
$ sudo apt-get install cmake libblkid-dev e2fslibs-dev
    libboost-all-dev libaudit-dev
$ cmake ..
$ make
... ...
$ ./lityc/lityc --help
```

Now that you have `lityc` installed, we will go through a couple of examples to see how libENI functions are used in smart contracts.

The String Reversing Example

This example shows a rather trivial libENI function that reverses any string it receives. The following is an example contract. As you can see, it is similar to a regular Solidity contract. However, the keyword `eni` is not available in Solidity, and it will not compile using a regular Solidity compiler.

```
pragma solidity ^0.4.23;

contract ReverseContract {
  function reverse(string input) public returns(string) {
    string memory output = eni("reverse", input);
    return output;
  }
}
```

The keyword eni is followed by two parameters. reverse is the name of the libENI function. Each libENI function added to the virtual machine must have a unique name. The string parameter input is the parameter passed into the reverse libENI function. You can pass any number of parameters into your libENI functions.

Let's save the code in a file named Reverse.lity. You must use the lityc compiler to compile the source to generate the bytecode and application binary interface (ABI) definition.

```
$ ./lityc/lityc --bin Reverse.lity
======= ./Reverse.lity:ReverseContract =======
Binary:
608060405234...


$ ./lityc/lityc --abi Reverse.lity
======= ./Reverse.lity:ReverseContract =======
Contract JSON ABI
[{"constant":false,"inputs":[{"name":"input","type":"string"}],
"name":"reverse","outputs":[{"name":"","type":"string"}],
"payable":false,"stateMutability":"nonpayable","type":"function"}]
```

On the travis client's web3-cmt console (similar to the GETH console on Ethereum), you can now deploy the contract bytecode and ABI to the CyberMiles node you run.

```
> personal.unlockAccount(cmt.accounts[0],'1234');
> bytecode="0x608060..."
> abi = [{"constant":false,"inputs":[{"name":"input",
"type":"string"}],"name":"reverse","outputs":[{"name":"","type":"string"}],
"payable":false,"stateMutability":"nonpayable","type":"function"}]
> contract = web3.cmt.contract(abi);
> contractInstance = contract.new(
  {
    from: web3.cmt.accounts[0],
    data: bytecode,
    gas: "4700000"
  },
  function(e, contract) {
    console.log("contract address: " + contract.address);
    console.log("transactionHash: " + contract.transactionHash);
  }
);
```

Once the contract is deployed with a confirmation from the blockchain, you will see its contract address printed on the console. You can call its reverse method.

```
> contractInstance.reverse.call("hello", {from: cmt.accounts[0]})
olleh
```

Since most libENI functions require the blockchain nodes to perform work, they typically require gas fees. That is why we have a from account to pay gas fees for this libENI function call.

The RSA Example

The RSA example shows how to use a pair of RSA public and private keys to encrypt and decrypt data inside a smart contract. Such functions enable blockchain accounts to exchange private information via smart contracts. They are crucial building blocks for a wide range of applications including data marketplaces and content distribution.

> **Note**
>
> An interesting RSA application is a data marketplace. Let's use a marketplace for medical records to illustrate how an RSA re-encryption scheme works in this context. Patients own their own medical records, and they authorize Bob (the data broker or the hospital) to aggregate and sell the medical records on their behalf. Alice (the data user or researcher) buys the patients' data from Bob. And Bob distributes the profit back to the patients. How do we automate and record the whole process on-chain?
>
> Bob sets up three RSA keys (a public encryption key 1, a public re-encryption key 2, and a private decryption key 3) and sets up a smart contract for the transaction. The smart contract contains both public keys 1 and 2.
>
> An individual patient authorizes Bob to sell her records by encrypting the records using key 1 and uploading the encrypted data to the contract. Alice agrees to buy the data from Bob and makes a payment to the smart contract. The smart contract re-encrypts all the records using key 2 and makes them publically available. Bob then sends private key 3 directly to Alice off-chain, which allows Alice to decrypt all the records held in the contract. Alice acknowledges receiving the private key 3 to the contract, and the contract automatically distributes the payments to patients and Bob.
>
> In this process, Alice and Bob are the only ones who can decrypt the whole data set. All patients know their own data. The public can verify the transaction, including all the monetary payments, but cannot see any data.

The following code illustrates a simple contract that encrypts a plaintext string using an RSA public key and then decrypts it using an RSA private key:

```
pragma solidity ^0.4.0;

contract RSACrypto {
    function encrypt(string pubkey, string plaintext)
                        public pure returns (string) {
        string memory ret;
        ret = eni("rsa_encrypt", pubkey, plaintext);
        return ret;
    }

    function decrypt(string prikey, string ciphertext)
                        public pure returns (string) {
        string memory ret;
```

```
        ret = eni("rsa_decrypt", prikey, ciphertext);
        return ret;
    }
}
```

In this example, you can see that the libENI functions rsa_encrypt and rsa_decrypt take multiple input parameters. In this section, I will show you how to use lityc to generate the bytecode and ABI interface in one go.

```
$ ./lityc/lityc --abi --bin -o output RSACrypto.lity
$ cat output/RSACrypto.abi
[{"constant":true,"inputs":...}]
$ cat output/RSACrypto.bin
608060405234801...
```

Next, deploy the bytecode and ABI to a local or testnet CyberMiles blockchain and receive a contract address upon successful deployment.

```
> personal.unlockAccount(cmt.accounts[0],'1234');
> bytecode="0x608060..."
> abi = [{"constant":false,"inputs":...}]
> contract = web3.cmt.contract(abi);
> c = contract.new(
  {
    from: web3.cmt.accounts[0],
    data: bytecode,
    gas: "4700000"
  },
  function(e, contract) {
    console.log("contract address: " + contract.address);
    console.log("transactionHash: " + contract.transactionHash);
  }
);
```

To use the RSA functions, you call the smart contract methods and pass in the key and data.

```
prikey = "-----BEGIN RSA PRIVATE KEY-----\nMIIEowIBAA...";
pubkey = "-----BEGIN PUBLIC KEY-----\ +X\nlNlozUy...";

# Encrypt
> ciphertext = c.encrypt.call(pubkey, 'Hello World!',
                              {from: cmt.accounts[0]})
"49d511a44a3d2a24...b258e70282a"

# Decrypt
> c.decrypt.call(prikey, ciphertext, {from: cmt.accounts[0]})
"Hello World!"
```

Of course, in the real world, we cannot call smart contract methods using the private key since all such transactions are public records. This example is for illustration only.

The Scrypt Example

This scrypt example is to verify Dogecoin blockchain headers in a Lity smart contract. Why would anyone do this? The reason is that Dogecoin is a clone of the Bitcoin blockchain. Verifying a Dogecoin block header allows the smart contract to further verify the transactions inside that block. By extending this computation to the Bitcoin, we can develop Ethereum smart contracts that can automatically verify and respond to Bitcoin transactions, making cross-chain asset exchanges a possibility.

Yet, the verification of a Dogecoin header requires the smart contract to perform a scrypt operation, which is computationally expensive for Solidity and the EVM. Vitalik Buterin estimates that it requires 390 million units of Ethereum gas to perform and far exceeds the block gas limit of Ethereum. To address this problem, there is a bounty of $250,000 set up by the Ethereum and Dogecoin communities to award the first viable solution to perform a scrypt operation on Ethereum to verify a Dogecoin block. In this section, we will show that libENI provides such a solution at a low cost on a fully Ethereum-compatible blockchain virtual machine.

> **Note**
>
> BTCRely is a community service to verify Bitcoin transactions on Ethereum. It is set up as an Ethereum smart contract, which allows other contracts to request verification and pay a fee. The fee is used to incentivize a community of off-chain workers to perform the verification on their own computers and submit the results. The Truebit project has a similar approach for off-chain verification. However, in the end, those off-chain schemes are cryptoeconomic games that rely on incentives for "good behavior." They are expensive, slow, tedious, and not reliable.

The full source code of the scrypt example is available on the Lity documentation site at http://lity.readthedocs.io/en/latest/verify-dogecoin-block-on-travis.html. Here, you can see the key part of the smart contract that calls the libENI function `scrypt` to perform the work:

```
pragma solidity ^0.4.23;

contract DogecoinVerifier {

  ...

  function verifyBlock(uint version, string prev_block,
        string merkle_root, uint timestamp, string bits, uint nonce)
        pure public returns (bool) {
    DogecoinBlockHeader memory block_header =
        DogecoinBlockHeader(version, prev_block, merkle_root,
                            timestamp, bits, nonce);
    string memory block_header_hex = generateBlockHeader(block_header);
    string memory pow_hash = reverseHex(eni("scrypt", block_header_hex));
```

```
    uint256 target = bitsToTarget(bits);
    if (hexToUint(pow_hash) > target) {
      return false;
    }
    return true;
  }


  ...

}
```

Again, we use lityc to generate the bytecode and ABI interface in one go.

```
$ ./lityc/lityc --abi --bin -o output DogecoinVerifier.lity
$ cat output/DogecoinVerifier.abi
[{"constant":true,"inputs":...}]
$ cat output/DogecoinVerifier.bin
6080604052348015610010576000080fd5b506111d5...
```

We can now deploy the bytecode and ABI to the blockchain and receive a contract address upon successful deployment.

```
> personal.unlockAccount(cmt.accounts[0],'1234');
> bytecode="0x608060...."
> abi = [{"constant":false,"inputs":...}]
> contract = web3.cmt.contract(abi);
> contractInstance = contract.new(
  {
    from: web3.cmt.accounts[0],
    data: bytecode,
    gas: "4700000"
  },
  function(e, contract) {
    console.log("contract address: " + contract.address);
    console.log("transactionHash: " + contract.transactionHash);
  }
);
```

To call the contract and verify a Dogecoin block header, we need the following pieces of information. They are algorithmically linked together to form a valid blockchain header. All of them are public information readily available from the Dogecoin blockchain explorer. In the following example, we use block 2 from the Dogecoin blockchain.

- Version: 1
- Previous block hash:
  82bc68038f6034c0596b6e313729793a887fded6e92a31fbdf70863f89d9bea2
- Transaction Merkle root hash:
  3b14b76d22a3f2859d73316002bc1b9bfc7f37e2c3393be9b722b62bbd786983

- Timestamp: 1386474933 (converted from 2013-12-07 19:55:33 -0800)

- Difficulty (bits): 1e0ffff0

- Nonce: 3404207872

We can now call the verifyBlock method on the contract using the previous data.

```
# Block #2 of dogecoin
> c.verifyBlock.call(1, "82...", "3b...", 1386474933, "1e0ffff0",
                            3404207872, {from: cmt.accounts[0]})
true

# 1-bit of nonce changed
> c.verifyBlock.call(1, "82...", "3b...", 1386474933, "1e0ffff0",
                              3404207871, {from: cmt.accounts[0]})
false
```

While it is beyond the scope of this book, the native scrypt function lays the foundation for decentralized cross-chain operations with the Bitcoin blockchain.

Writing a libENI Function

Now we have seen how to use the libENI functions. In this section, I will discuss how to program your own libENI functions that can be dynamically deployed to the CyberMiles blockchain as virtual machine extensions. Let's use the simple reverse libENI function as an example. The entire example is available in CyberMiles' libENI public GitHub repository.

The libENI functions are written in C++ as OS native library functions. You need to use #include <eni.h>, create a subclass of eni::EniBase, and implement the following functions:

- A constructor that takes a string as its parameter. Remember to pass the string to the constructor of the superclass, eni::EniBase, which will convert the raw string into a json::Array containing the arguments for your ENI operation.

- A destructor.

- The parse virtual function to parse the arguments.

- The gas virtual function to calculate gas consumption from the arguments.

- The run virtual function to execute your ENI operation with the arguments.

The skeleton code for the reverse function is as follows:

```
#include <eni.h>
class Reverse : public eni::EniBase {
public:
  Reverse(const std::string& pArgStr)
    : eni::EniBase(pArgStr) { ... }
```

```
  ~Reverse() { ... }

private:
  bool parse(const json::Array& pArgs) override { ... }
  eni::Gas gas() const override { ... }

  bool run(json::Array& pRetVal) override { ... }
};
```

Next, let's look into the implementation of these three virtual functions.

Parsing Arguments

The parse function takes a json::Array containing the arguments given to your libENI operation. To ensure the other two functions, gas and run, process the arguments in the same way, please validate, preprocess, and store the arguments into member variables in the parse function.

The parse function should return true when all arguments are good and return false otherwise (e.g., lacking arguments, or the wrong type).

In this example, the json::Array constructed by eni::EniBase contains only the argument string for the libENI operation reverse. The following is the implementation of parse:

```
class Reverse : public eni::EniBase {
  ...
private:
  bool parse(const json::Array& pArgs) override {
    m_Str = pArgs[0].toString();
    return true;
  }

  std::string m_Str;
};
```

Estimating Gas

Before your libENI function can run, you need to estimate how much gas it will cost. Override the virtual function gas and return your estimated gas cost. In this example, we use the string length as its gas consumption.

```
class Reverse : public eni::EniBase {
  ...
private:
  eni::Gas gas() const override {
    return m_Str.length();
  }
};
```

You can return 0 for gas calculation errors. The virtual machine will not execute the libENI function if `gas` returns 0.

Executing the Function

Override the virtual function `run` and push the result of your libENI function back into the `json::Array` as the return value.

```
class Reverse : public eni::EniBase {
  ...
private:
  bool run(json::Array& pRetVal) override {
    std::string ret(m_Str.rbegin(), m_Str.rend());
    pRetVal.emplace_back(ret);
    return true;
  }
};
```

Mapping to libENI Function Name

Finally, we need to map the reverse C++ class to the reverse libENI function name. To do that, we export a C interface with `ENI_C_INTERFACE(OP, CLASS)`, where `OP` is your libENI function name (i.e., `reverse` in this example), and `CLASS` is the name of implemented class (i.e., `Reverse` in this example).

```
  ENI_C_INTERFACE(reverse, Reverse)
```

That's it. You have written a C++ program for the libENI function. In the next section, we will review how to build the function into a shared library file and deploy the file to a running blockchain.

Deploying the libENI Function

We use the GCC to build libENI classes into binary library files. You can look into the `Makefile` in the `examples/eni/reverse` directory in libENI public GitHub repository. Here are the key compiler settings:

```
CPPFLAGS=-I${LIBENI_PATH}/include
CXXFLAGS=-std=c++11 -fPIC
LDFLAGS=-L${LIBENI_PATH}/lib
LDADD=-leni

all:
  g++ ${CPPFLAGS} ${CXXFLAGS} ${LDFLAGS} -shared -oeni_reverse.so
    eni_reverse.cpp ${LDADD}
```

${LIBENI_PATH} is the path to locate libENI support libraries on your development machine. See the details in the GitHub documentation. Once you run make all, you should have the reverse.so library file built for your OS.

CyberMiles Governance

To deploy the reverse libENI function to a running CyberMiles blockchain, we will use the CyberMiles governance transactions. First, you need to set up a CyberMiles blockchain node and then connect to it using the travis client (see Appendix A for details).

From the travis client console, you have access to the web3-cmt JavaScript module. You can now create a new transaction to propose a new libENI function. The transaction includes a brief description of the library function and the location to download the library binary files for people to try. It also includes the MD5 hash of those files. Here is an example:

```
> personal.unlockAccount(cmt.accounts[0],'1234');
> var payload = {
  from: cmt.accounts[0],
  name: "reverse",
  version: "v1.0.0",
  fileUrl:
    '{"ubuntu":"http://host/eni_reverse_ubuntu16.04.so",
      "centos":"http://host/eni_reverse_centos7.so"}',
  md5:
    '{"ubuntu":"b44...906d", "centos":"04a...851"}'
}
> web3.cmt.governance.proposeDeployLibEni(payload, (err, res) => {
  if (!err) {
    console.log(res)
  } else {
    console.log(err)
  }
})
```

Once the proposeDeployLibEni transaction is processed, all nodes on the CyberMiles block-chain will download and cache the library files and start a seven-day voting period. The voting period can be customized by the expireBlockHeight or expireTimestamp parameter in the proposeDeployLibEni transaction. During the voting period, all validator nodes can vote on the proposal. proposalId is the result value from the proposeDeployLibEni transaction.

```
> personal.unlockAccount(cmt.accounts[0],'1234');
> var payload = {
  from: "0x7eff122b94897ea5b0e2a9abf47b86337fafebdc",
  proposalId: "JTUx+ODHO/OSdgfCOSn66qjn2tX8LfvbiwnArzNpIus=",
  answer: "Y"
}
> web3.cmt.governance.vote(payload, (err, res) => {
  if (!err) {
```

```
      console.log(res)
   } else {
      console.log(err)
   }
})
```

If at least two-thirds voting power voted yes for `proposalId`, all nodes will deploy the new libENI function and make it available at the seven-day mark or at the specified `expireBlockHeight` or `expireTimestamp`.

Conclusion

In this chapter, we discussed how to create and deploy new libENI functions to extend the Etheruem Virtual Machine (EVM). It allows developers or even the public chain community to dynamically extend the virtual machines with new functionalities without stopping or forking the blockchain.

Part V

Building Your Own Blockchain

In this part of the book, I go beyond Ethereum and discuss how to build your own blockchains. This enables developers to bypass the virtual machine and bake application logic directly into the blockchain itself for maximum efficiency. But of course, this type of application blockchain is also much less flexible and adaptable than smart contract-based blockchains.

Using the open source Tendermint framework, I illustrate how to build application blockchains, as well as user-facing applications for those blockchains.

19

Getting Started with Tendermint

Tendermint provides infrastructure software that allows developers to build their own blockchain solutions. The Tendermint approach has two unique characteristics.

- Tendermint utilizes a Byzantine fault tolerant (BFT) algorithm that allows for up to one-third of nodes failing or behaving maliciously.

- Tendermint consensus is reached by designated validator nodes. There are only a limited number of validators on the network.

At its core, Tendermint is a high-performance and scalable consensus engine. As a trade-off, it is also a weakly centralized solution; it is not completely decentralized like Bitcoin, as it requires designated validators and is somewhat less fault tolerant (Bitcoin allows 49 percent of nodes to fail while Tendermint allows one-third).

Because Tendermint is designed as a consensus engine, it attempts to separate the "application logic" and "consensus logic" of blockchain applications. That separation allows Tendermint software to be embedded in any other blockchains as a drop-in consensus engine replacement; the host blockchain just needs to implement the Tendermint API, known as the Application BlockChain Interface (ABCI), to use Tendermint's delegated proof-of-style (DPoS) consensus.

The clean separation between application and consensus logic in Tendermint makes it possible to build custom logic into blockchain applications. Those applications go far beyond the traditional smart contracts. They can utilize full stacks of enterprise software to handle complex application scenarios.

> **Note**
>
> The Substrate framework from Parity and Polkadot is similar to Tendermint and Cosmos SDK (see next chapter) in function.

How It Works

Every node of a Tendermint blockchain needs to run two pieces of software: the consensus engine known as Tendermint Core and an ABCI application specifically written for the blockchain (see Figure 19.1).

- The Tendermint Core software is responsible for building and synchronizing the blockchain across the network.

- The ABCI application is responsible for processing and validating all transactions that get stored in the blockchain. Each blockchain could have a different ABCI application for a different application scenario or logic. For example, a blockchain that records cryptocurrency transactions will have a very different ABCI application than one that records real estate deeds.

> **Note**
>
> The ABCI application can be arbitrarily complex and written in any language on any software stack. In fact, it can have its own database to store and manage its state. In a broad sense, it is a smart contract on steroids.

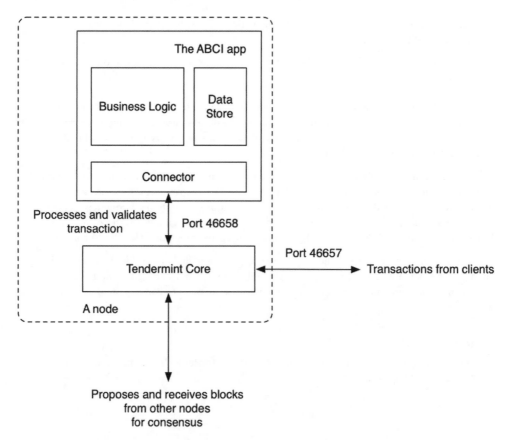

Figure 19.1 A Tendermint blockchain node

It Works as Follows

An external application sends a transaction request to any node on the network. The request is received by the Tendermint Core software. Notice that here we do not define what exactly is a transaction, as there are many different blockchain applications, and they have different definitions for transactions. For instance, some applications might define transactions as straight token exchanges, while others would consider recording a real-world event as a transaction. For our purposes, a transaction is simply a series of bytes to be recorded on the blockchain.

Upon receiving the request, the Tendermint Core software immediately forwards the transaction request to the ABCI application running on the same node. The ABCI application parses the transaction data and makes a preliminary determination on whether it is a validate transaction. At this stage, the transaction will not result in any state change (i.e., nothing gets written to the database managed by the ABCI application).

If the ABCI application's preliminary determination is valid, the Tendermint Core software will broadcast and synchronize the transaction to all nodes on the network.

At a fixed time interval, the network creates a new block with all the transactions that are validated during this time interval. Validator nodes will vote on the new block, and if at least two-thirds of validator nodes agree, the new block will be appended to the blockchain and broadcast to all nodes on the network.

Once a new block is added to the blockchain, each node will again rerun all the transactions included in the block to the node's local ABCI application for processing. At this time, the ABCI application can update its database to store the application state changes caused by those transactions.

Figure 19.2 summarizes the workflow described.

> **Note**
>
> After a block is added to the blockchain, all nodes run the same transactions in the same order. Hence, after a block is added, the ABCI application instances on all nodes have the same persistent state stored in their databases. For example, the ABCI application could update the user accounts database if the transactions move tokens/funds between users.

In the next section, let's go through the exercise to set up a single Tendermint node to see how the Tendermint Core software and ABCI app work together.

Set Up a Node

Let's download the precompiled Tendermint binary applications from the following web page: https://tendermint.com/downloads.

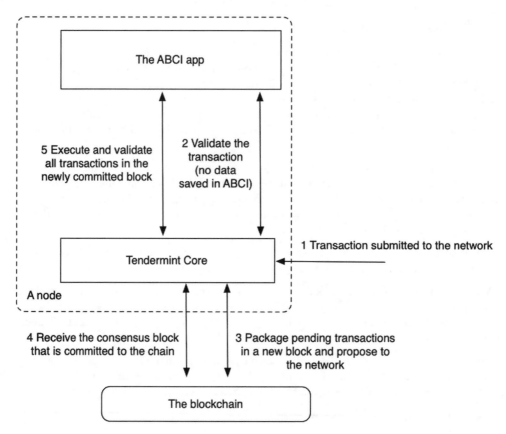

Figure 19.2 The workflow

You will need the `tendermint` and `abci` binaries for this step. Unpack the downloaded zip packages, and you will get the following executable binary files:

```
tendermint
dummy
counter
abci-cli
```

Move the binary files to the `$HOME/bin` directory so that they are accessible from the command line. You can now run them to check their versions.

```
$ tendermint version
0.10.3-'8d76408
```

The `dummy` program is a simple ABCI application. Once running, it listens for transactions from Tendermint Core on TCP port 46658. Being a "dummy" program, it will simply approve and validate all transactions. You can run the dummy program in a command-line window.

```
$ dummy
Starting ABCIServer
Waiting for new connection...
```

Next, in another command-line window, initialize the Tendermint Core software on this machine. The init command creates the configuration files for a network made up of a single validator node.

```
tendermint init
```

If you have initialized Tendermint Core on this computer before, you could either delete the $HOME/.tendermint directory and init again or use the following command:

```
tendermint unsafe_reset_all
```

> **Note**
>
> If you encounter an error during Tendermint node startup, make sure you kill all Tendermint-related processes on your computer.

Now, you can start the Tendermint node. The node immediately connects to the dummy ABCI app through port 46658 and starts to create blocks.

```
$ tendermint node
Executed block module=state height=1 validTxs=0 invalidTxs=0
Committed state module=state height=1 txs=0 hash=
Executed block module=state height=2 validTxs=0 invalidTxs=0
Committed state module=state height=2 txs=0 hash=
```

The following is the output from the dummy window, showing that a Tendermint node is connected:

```
$ dummy
Starting ABCIServer
Waiting for new connection...
Accepted a new connection
```

The Tendermint node listens on port 46657 for new transactions. So, let's now send a transaction to the network.

```
curl -s 'localhost:46657/broadcast_tx_commit?tx="hello"'
{
  "jsonrpc": "2.0",
  "id": "",
  "result": {
    "check_tx": {
      "code": 0,
      "data": "",
      "log": ""
    },
```

```
    "deliver_tx": {
      "code": 0,
      "data": "",
      "log": ""
    },
    "hash": "995DE4D6FA43728945C235642E5DCCB64C08B4A2",
    "height": 30
  },
  "error": ""
}
```

The transaction is received by Tendermint Core at port 46657, forwarded to the dummy ABCI app at port 46658, validated by dummy, and then recorded in the blockchain by Tendermint Core. The dummy application stores the key-value pair in the transaction in its own database. The Tendermint console shows the following:

```
$ tendermint node
... ...
Executed block module=state height=30 validTxs=1 invalidTxs=0
Committed state module=state height=30 txs=1 hash=EA4...934
... ...
```

> **Note**
>
> The broadcast_tx_commit message sends the transaction (in the tx parameter) to the network node and waits until the transaction is committed in a new block on the blockchain. There are other messages that can send the transaction without waiting for confirmation. You will see them in the next chapter.

Finally, we can query the blockchain for the transaction we just sent. The query is passed to the dummy ABCI application. Since the dummy application saves the value in all transactions it validates, it will be able to interpret and respond to the query and pass the results via Tendermint Core.

```
curl -s 'localhost:46657/abci_query?data="hello"'
{
  "jsonrpc": "2.0",
  "id": "",
  "result": {
    "response": {
      "code": 0,
      "index": 0,
      "key": "",
      "value": "68656C6C6F",
      "proof": "",
      "height": 0,
```

```
      "log": "exists"
    }
  },
  "error": ""
}
```

Set Up a Network

Of course, most blockchain networks have more than one node! To set up a network with multiple nodes, you can do the following.

First, run the `tendermint init` commands on all node computers on the network. In the `$HOME/.tendermint` directory, you will see the `genesis.json` file, which contains this node's public key. The node's private key is in the `priv_validator.json` file and should never be shared with anyone.

```
{
   "genesis_time":"0001-01-01T00:00:00Z",
   "chain_id":"test-chain-dmpZNA",
   "validators":[
     {
       "pub_key":
       {
         "type":"ed25519",
         "data":"F8...DC47D"
       },
       "amount":10,"name":""
     }
   ],
   "app_hash":""
}
```

Second, edit the `genesis.json` file on each node to add all peer nodes' public key into the `validators` array. Those nodes are known as *initial validators* for a network. The network can add or remove validators dynamically once it is running.

Finally, on each node computer, you can start `tendermint node` and the ABCI application (e.g., dummy). The nodes will discover each other by their public keys and then form a network. Notice that nodes on a network must run the same ABCI app since all nodes must process and validate transactions the same way.

Now you have a private Tendermint blockchain network. You can make it validate and record any transaction you like by writing your own ABCI applications, which you will see in Chapter 20. The Cosmos foundation also runs public test networks for developers and validators. For now, let's review how the Tendermint blockchain network works.

- A new transaction is received and preliminarily validated on a single node.
- At a fixed time interval, validator nodes package all transactions since the last block and propose a new block.
- Once validators agree on a new block, it is broadcast to all nodes.
- All nodes process all transactions in the same order when a new block is added to the blockchain.

As a result, the application state of the blockchain (databases managed by the ABCI application) on all nodes are in sync.

Conclusion

In this chapter, I discussed how the Tendermint blockchain works by separating the consensus logic and application logic. The application logic, encapsulated in an ABCI application, allows developers to write versatile blockchain applications. I also demonstrated how to set up a Tendermint node and a network with a simple ABCI application.

## 20

The Business Logic

In the previous chapter, I explained that the business logic of a Tendermint blockchain network is encapsulated in an Application BlockChain Interface (ABCI) application. So, as a developer, you just need to write an application to control how the network processes and validates transactions. Each ABCI application is a blockchain. Here are some examples:

- The Binance decentralized exchange is an application blockchain designed for crypto exchange operations. It is built on top of Tendermint.

- The `basecoin` application creates a blockchain network with a native cryptocurrency. You can extend the token to support your own cryptocurrency features by forking the project. See https://github.com/tendermint/basecoin.

- The `ETGate` application is built on `basecoin` and enables token exchanges between Ethereum and Tendermint blockchains. See https://github.com/mossid/etgate.

- The `ethermint` application allows you to run the Ethereum Virtual Machine (EVM) as an ABCI application on top of a Tendermint blockchain. This creates an Ethereum blockchain but with Tendermint's Byzantine fault tolerant (BFT) validators as opposed to PoW miners. See https://github.com/tendermint/ethermint.

- The Plasma Cash is a layer 2 network implementation for Ethereum based on the Tendermint engine. It is a blockchain that connects to the Ethereum network via smart contracts. The Plasma Cash side chain allows for high-speed transactions that are impossible on Ethereum.

- The `merkleeyes` application creates a blockchain network that records transactions on a Merkle tree. It simulates a journaled data store. The insert/remove operations on the tree are recorded as transactions on the blockchain, and the current data on the tree can be queried from the blockchain's query application programming interface (API) as well. See https://github.com/tendermint/merkleeyes.

- The CyberMiles application is a fully fledged ABCI application that incorporates delegated proof of stake (DPoS), on-chain governance, security features, and an enhanced EVM into a single ABCI application.

In this chapter, we explore the ABCI protocol and create a simple ABCI application. We will also discuss application frameworks that are built on top of the ABCI, such as the Cosmos software development kit (SDK).

The Protocol

You already learned how a Tendermint network works at a high level. In this section, we will look into the detailed mechanism, including the message exchange between Tendermint Core, which manages the blockchain, and the ABCI application, which manages the application-specific logic.

The ABCI protocol specifies the request/response communication between the Tendermint Core software and the ABCI application. By default, the ABCI application listens on TCP port 46658. Tendermint Core sends messages to the ABCI application and acts on the responses (Figure 20.1). The protocol defines several kinds of messages. They follow the Tendermint Core and ABCI application interaction flow outlined in the previous chapter.

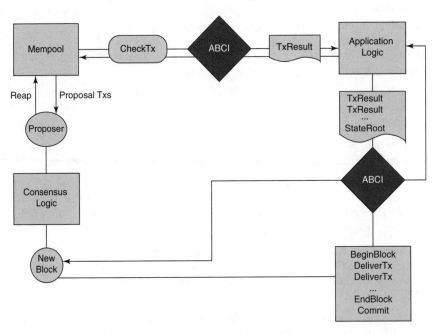

Figure 20.1   Tendermint ABCI messages in the consensus flow

Consensus on the Block

The first type of message is the CheckTx message. When the node receives a transaction request (via port 46657, which Tendermint Core listens on by default), it forwards the transaction to the ABCI application in a CheckTx message for preliminary validation. The ABCI application has its own logic to parse, process, and validate the transaction and then return a result. If the CheckTx result is okay, the Tendermint node will broadcast and synchronize the transaction to all nodes in the blockchain network.

It is important to note that every Tendermint node keeps its own pool of transactions that successfully passed the node's CheckTx. It is known as the node's *mempool*. The nodes on the network could each have a different set of transactions in the mempool. When a node proposes a new block, it packages together transactions in its own mempool. When the block is accepted by the network (i.e., consensus), all transactions in the block will be removed from all node mempools in the network. Figure 20.2 outlines the consensus flow of the new block.

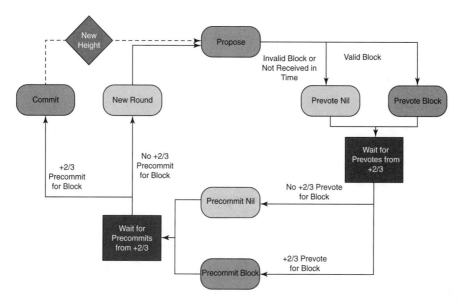

Figure 20.2   Tendermint consensus for each block

When a Tendermint network reaches consensus on a new block, the nodes are only agreeing on the block's structure and its cryptographic validity with regard to the previous blocks on the blockchain. The nodes actually have no idea about the validity of the transactions inside the block. To reach consensus on the results of the transactions inside the block, we will need the app hash from the commit message, which we will see next.

Consensus on the Transactions

The second, and most important type of message, is the DeliverTx message. At fixed-time intervals, all validator nodes in the network will reach consensus and determine the next block to be added to the blockchain. This new block contains all valid transactions submitted to the network during the time interval, and it is broadcast to all nodes on the network. Each node will run all the transactions in the block to the node's local ABCI application instance. Each transaction is embedded in a `DeliverTx` message. The block starts with a `StartBlock` message to the ABCI, followed by a series of `DeliverTx` messages for all transactions in the block, and ends with an `EndBlock` message.

The ABCI application processes the `DeliverTx` messages in the order they are received. The ABCI application maintains its own database and updates the database as it processes the transactions (e.g., the database could be a ledger for user accounts, and each transaction moves funds between accounts). Since all nodes process the same set of transactions in the same order, once they are done, the ABCI applications on all nodes should have the same persistent state (i.e., their database content should be synchronized).

> **Note**
>
> It is possible that the `DeliverTx` message to the ABCI application could return a failure result. Since the network validators have already reached consensus on the block, the blockchain will annotate the failed transaction in this block in the block header.

A critical requirement of the ABCI application is that it must be deterministic. When it processes a set of transactions, it must reach the same results, in terms of the success/failure of each transaction and the overall application state, every time regardless of which node did the processing. That means the ACBI application logic should not have any dependency on random numbers, timestamps, and so on.

The ABCI application does not save to a database after each `DeliverTx` message. Instead, it processes the entire block of transactions and saves only at the end when it sees a `Commit` message. The `Commit` message should return the current state of the node, such as the node's database hash, known as the *app hash*. The blockchain will stop working altogether if two-thirds of the validator nodes cannot agree on an app hash at the `Commit` of any block. If a node returns an app hash that is different than most nodes, this node is deemed corrupt and will not be able to participate in future consensus voting.

Getting Information

Finally, the ABCI protocol supports a third type of message, the `Query` message, which allows the Tendermint Core node to query the persistent state of the ABCI application. As mentioned, the ABCI application could maintain its own database, and the data stored in the database (i.e., its state) is determined by the history of transactions validated by the ABCI application. The blockchain node could query this database by issuing a query message.

A Sample Application

In the next sections, let's get into the details by building an ABCI application. The application keeps track of a series of facts by their sources and stores the tallies in a database. The facts are submitted by external applications to any node on the blockchain. If a fact is accepted by the application, it will be recorded in the blockchain as a transaction. We will implement this application in the Java and GO languages.

Once the blockchain (Tendermint Core) and the facts ABCI application are running, you can send a series of facts as transactions to the blockchain. Each fact contains a source and a statement. Recall that Tendermint Core listens at port 46657 for transactions submitted to the blockchain.

```
curl -s 'localhost:46657/broadcast_tx_commit?tx="Michael:True%20fact"'
{
  "jsonrpc": "2.0",
  "id": "",
  "result": {
    "check_tx": {
      "code": 0,
      "data": "",
      "log": ""
    },
    "deliver_tx": {
      "code": 0,
      "data": "",
      "log": ""
    },
    "hash": "2A02B575181CEB71F03AF9715B236472D75025C2",
    "height": 18
  },
  "error": ""
}
```

As mentioned in the previous chapter, there are several ways to send the transaction data (it could be any byte array in the `tx` parameter field).

- `/broadcast_tx_commit`: This is the message we used. It waits until the blockchain has validated the transaction and is added into a new block. When this message returns, you will be able to see both `CheckTx` and `DeliverTx` results.

- `/broadcast_tx_async`: This message sends the transaction data to a blockchain node and does not wait for the blockchain's response.

- `/broadcast_tx_sync`: This message sends the transaction data to a blockchain node and waits for the `CheckTx` to run. This message returns the `CheckTx` result.

On the facts application console, you can see the transactions are processed and validated. Notice that there are both `CheckTx` and `DeliverTx` messages on all nodes. While the transaction is sent to only one node, the node broadcasts the transaction to all nodes once it passes the `CheckTx` message. So, each node will see this transaction, check it, save it to the mempool, and process it again when the new consensus block containing this transaction is received.

```
Commit 0 items
Check tx : Michael:True fact
The source is : Michael
The statement is : True fact
```

```
The fact is in the right format!
Deliver tx : Michael:True fact
The source is : Michael
The statement is : True fact
The count in this block is : 1
The fact is validated by this node!
Commit 1 items
```

You can also query the blockchain for the current application state. The ABCI application returns a tally of facts by sources. Notice that the actual fact statements are stored in the blockchain as transactions, and the ABCI application stores only the tally in its data store. The `value` field in the response is a Base64-encoded string of the response text in the `log` field.

```
curl -s 'localhost:46657/abci_query?data="all"'
{
  "jsonrpc": "2.0",
  "id": "",
  "result": {
    "response": {
      "code": 0,
      "index": 0,
      "key": "",
      "value": "4A696D3A312C4D69636861656C3A32",
      "proof": "",
      "height": 0,
      "log": "Jim:1,Michael:2"
    }
  },
  "error": ""
}
```

Next, let's look into how to implement this simple facts ABCI application. We will discuss both Java and GO language implementations. You can just choose a language you are most comfortable with.

Java Implementation

The Java application is built on the jTendermint library. When the application starts up, it listens on ABCI's default TCP port 46658 to receive transactions from the Tendermint Core software running on the same node.

For the sake of simplicity, we will not use an external relational database to store the application state. Instead, we instantiate a global hash table in the application as the data store. The hash table key is a unique source of the facts, and the value is the number of facts associated with this source. The downside, of course, is that the application state is lost if the application crashes. When the application starts, it starts a socket server to listen for messages from the blockchain.

```java
public final class FactsApp
        implements IDeliverTx, ICheckTx, ICommit, IQuery {

    public static Hashtable<String, Integer> db;
    public static Hashtable<String, Integer> cache;

    private TSocket socket;

    public static void main(String[] args) throws Exception {
        new FactsApp ();
    }

    public FactsApp () throws InterruptedException {
        socket = new TSocket();
        socket.registerListener(this);

        // Init the database
        db = new Hashtable <String, Integer> ();
        cache = new Hashtable <String, Integer> ();

        Thread t = new Thread(socket::start);
        t.setName("Facts App Thread");
        t.start();
        while (true) {
            Thread.sleep(1000L);
        }
    }
    ... ...
}
```

The `ResponseCheckTx` method handles the `CheckTx` messages from Tendermint Core. As you probably recall, the `CheckTx` message is sent when the blockchain node receives a transaction request. The ABCI application simply parses the fact from the message into a source element and a statement element. If the message parses successfully, the ABCI application returns `ok`, and the transaction is broadcast and synchronized to all nodes on the network. For brevity, I removed the statements to log messages to the facts application console, which you saw in the previous section.

```java
public ResponseCheckTx requestCheckTx (RequestCheckTx req) {
    ByteString tx = req.getTx();
    String payload = tx.toStringUtf8();
    if (payload == null || payload.isEmpty()) {
        return ResponseCheckTx.newBuilder()
            .setCode(CodeType.BAD)
            .setLog("payload is empty").build();
    }
```

```
    String [] parts = payload.split(":", 2);
    String source = "";
    String statement = "";
    try {
        source = parts[0].trim();
        statement = parts[1].trim();
        if (source.isEmpty() || statement.isEmpty()) {
            throw new Exception("Payload parsing error");
        }
    } catch (Exception e) {
        return ResponseCheckTx.newBuilder()
            .setCode(CodeType.BAD)
            .setLog(e.getMessage()).build();
    }

    return ResponseCheckTx.newBuilder().setCode(CodeType.OK).build();
}
```

Note

The CheckTx message in this example is simplistic. In most applications, the CheckTx
message handler method will use the application's current database state to check the
transaction. The application state (i.e., the app hash) is updated by the last block's Commit
message. The CheckTx method should never modify the application state.

Next, after the network reaches consensus on the next block, each node will send transactions
in this block as a series of DeliverTx messages to the ABCI application. The ResponseDeliverTx
method handles the DeliverTx messages. It again parses the fact in the message and then
tallies by the source in a temporary cache. Since all nodes will see the same set of DeliverTx
messages in the same order, they should update the application's database in sequence. That
is, a second DeliverTx is working off the database after changes have been made by the first
DeliverTx. However, the DeliverTx itself should update only a temporary (often in-memory)
replicate of the database, and the changes are flushed to the permanent (often on-disk) database
at Commit. This is not only efficient but also ensures the application's database state is always
set at the Commit state of the last block. In this simple example, however, our application
database is in memory and the DeliverTx processing does not depend on the current state of
the database.

```
public ResponseDeliverTx receivedDeliverTx (RequestDeliverTx req) {
    ByteString tx = req.getTx();
    String payload = tx.toStringUtf8();
    if (payload == null || payload.isEmpty()) {
        return ResponseDeliverTx.newBuilder()
            .setCode(CodeType.BAD)
            .setLog("payload is empty").build();
    }
```

```
        String [] parts = payload.split(":", 2);
        String source = "";
        String statement = "";
        try {
            source = parts[0].trim();
            statement = parts[1].trim();
            if (source.isEmpty() || statement.isEmpty()) {
                throw new Exception("Payload parsing error");
            }
        } catch (Exception e) {
            return ResponseDeliverTx.newBuilder()
                .setCode(CodeType.BAD)
                .setLog(e.getMessage()).build();
        }

        // In the delivertx message handler,
        // we will only count facts in this block.
        if (cache.containsKey(source)) {
            int count = cache.get(source);
            cache.put(source, count++);
        } else {
            cache.put(source, 1);
        }

        return ResponseDeliverTx.newBuilder().setCode(CodeType.OK).build();
    }
```

When the ABCI application sees the `Commit` message, it saves all the temporary tallies to the `Hashtable`-based data store. It returns the hash code of the data store as the app hash. All nodes have to agree on the app hash after committing this block. If a node returns a different app hash than other nodes, it is deemed corrupt and will not be allowed to participate in the future consensus.

```
    public ResponseCommit requestCommit (RequestCommit requestCommit) {
        Set<String> keys = cache.keySet();
        for (String source: keys) {
            if (db.containsKey(source)) {
                db.put(source, cache.get(source) + db.get(source));
            } else {
                db.put(source, cache.get(source));
            }
        }
        cache.clear();

        return ResponseCommit.newBuilder()
          .setData(ByteString.copyFromUtf8(
          String.valueOf(db.hashCode()))).build();
    }
```

Finally, an external application can query the blockchain for the application state. In this case, a `Query` message will be passed from Tendermint Core to the application. The `ResponseQuery` method handles this message and returns the tallies for all sources from the data store.

```java
public ResponseQuery requestQuery (RequestQuery req) {
  String query = req.getData().toStringUtf8();

  if (query.equalsIgnoreCase("all")) {
    StringBuffer buf = new StringBuffer ();
    String prefix = "";
    Set<String> keys = db.keySet();
    for (String source: keys) {
      buf.append(prefix);
      prefix = ",";
      buf.append(source).append(":").append(db.get(source));
    }
    return ResponseQuery.newBuilder().setCode(CodeType.OK).setValue(
            ByteString.copyFromUtf8((buf.toString())))
    ).setLog(buf.toString()).build();
  }

  if (query.startsWith("Source")) {
    String keyword = query.substring(6).trim();
    if (db.containsKey(keyword)) {
      return ResponseQuery.newBuilder().setCode(CodeType.OK).setValue(
          ByteString.copyFromUtf8(db.get(keyword).toString())
      ).setLog(db.get(keyword).toString()).build();
    }
  }

  return ResponseQuery.newBuilder()
        .setCode(CodeType.BadNonce).setLog("Invalid query").build();
}
```

The blockchain itself stores the validated `source : statement` data submitted by external applications. The ABCI application stores the tallies of facts based on sources, and the tallies are synchronized across all nodes since the ABCI application on all nodes run the same set of transactions that get written into the blockchain.

We use Maven to build an executable binary of the application. You can review the `pom.xml` file in the source code repository to see how to build the executable JAR file.

```
$ mvn clean package
```

You can run the ABCI application from command line and it will automatically connect to a Tendermint Core instance running on the same node.

```
$ java –jar facts-1.0.jar
```

GO Implementation

Tendermint itself is built on the GO programming language. It is not surprising that GO is a well-supported language platform to build ABCI applications. The `main` method in the application listens for ABCI messages on port 46658.

```go
package main

import (
  "flag"
  "os"
  "strings"
  "bytes"
  "strconv"
  "github.com/tendermint/abci/example/code"
  "github.com/tendermint/abci/server"
  "github.com/tendermint/abci/types"
  cmn "github.com/tendermint/tmlibs/common"
  "github.com/tendermint/tmlibs/log"
)

func main() {
  addrPtr := flag.String("addr", "tcp://0.0.0.0:46658", "Listen address")
  abciPtr := flag.String("abci", "socket", "socket | grpc")
  flag.Parse()

  logger := log.NewTMLogger(log.NewSyncWriter(os.Stdout))

  var app types.Application
  app = NewFactsApplication()
  // Start the listener
  srv, err := server.NewServer(*addrPtr, *abciPtr, app)
  if err != nil {
    logger.Error(err.Error())
    os.Exit(1)
  }
  srv.SetLogger(logger.With("module", "abci-server"))
  if err := srv.Start(); err != nil {
    logger.Error(err.Error())
    os.Exit(1)
  }

  // Wait forever
  cmn.TrapSignal(func() {
    // Cleanup
    srv.Stop()
  })
}
```

Similar to the Java application, we will use an in-memory map to store the application state (i.e., the facts tallies) for simplicity.

```
type FactsApplication struct {
  types.BaseApplication

  db map[string]int
  cache map[string]int
}

func NewFactsApplication() *FactsApplication {
  db := make(map[string]int)
  cache := make(map[string]int)
  return &FactsApplication{db: db, cache: cache}
}
```

The CheckTx method handles the CheckTx messages from Tendermint Core. As you probably recall, the CheckTx message is sent when the blockchain node receives a transaction request. The ABCI application simply parses the fact from the message into a source element and a statement element. If the message parses successfully, the ABCI application returns okay, and the transaction is broadcast and synchronized to all nodes on the network.

```
func (app *FactsApplication) CheckTx (tx []byte) types.ResponseCheckTx {
  parts := strings.Split(string(tx), ":")
  source := strings.TrimSpace(parts[0])
  statement := strings.TrimSpace(parts[1])
  if (len(source) == 0) || (len(statement) == 0) {
    return types.ResponseCheckTx{
        Code:code.CodeTypeEncodingError,
        Log:"Empty Input"
    }
  }
  return types.ResponseCheckTx{Code: code.CodeTypeOK}
}
```

> **Note**
>
> The CheckTx message in this example is simplistic. In most applications, the CheckTx message handler method will use the application's current database state to check that the transaction is valid. The application state (i.e., the app hash) is updated by the last block's Commit message. The CheckTx method should never modify the application state.

Next, after the network reaches consensus on the next block, each node will send transactions in this block as a series of DeliverTx messages to the ABCI application. The DeliverTx method handles the DeliverTx messages. It again parses the fact in the message and then tallies by the source in a temporary cache. Since all nodes will see the same set of DeliverTx messages in the same order, they should update the application's database in sequence. That is, a second DeliverTx is working off the database after changes have been made by the first `DeliverTx`. However, the `DeliverTx` itself should update only a temporary (often in-memory) replicate of the database, and the changes are flushed to the permanent (often on-disk) database at `Commit`. This is not only efficient but also ensures the application's database state is always set at the `Commit` state of the last block.

```go
func (app *FactsApplication) DeliverTx (tx []byte) types.ResponseDeliverTx {
  parts := strings.Split(string(tx), ":")
  source := strings.TrimSpace(parts[0])
  statement := strings.TrimSpace(parts[1])
  if (len(source) == 0) || (len(statement) == 0) {
    return types.ResponseDeliverTx{
      Code:code.CodeTypeEncodingError,
      Log:"Empty Input"
    }
  }

  if val, ok := app.cache[source]; ok {
    app.cache[source] = val + 1
  } else {
    app.cache[source] = 1
  }
  return types.ResponseDeliverTx{Code: code.CodeTypeOK}
}
```

When the ABCI application sees the `Commit` message, it saves all the temporary tallies to the map-based data store. It returns the hash of the total count of entries in the data store as the app hash. All nodes have to agree on the app hash after committing this block. If a node returns a different app hash than other nodes, it is deemed corrupt and will not be allowed to participate in the future consensus.

```go
func (app *FactsApplication) Commit() types.ResponseCommit {
  for source, v := range app.cache {
    if val, ok := app.db[source]; ok {
      app.db[source] = val + v
    } else {
      app.db[source] = v
    }
  }
  app.cache = make(map[string]int)

  hash := make([]byte, 8)
  binary.BigEndian.PutUint64(hash, uint64(totalCount))
  return types.ResponseCommit{Data: hash}
}
```

Finally, an external application can query the blockchain for the application state. In this case, a `Query` message will be passed from Tendermint Core to the application. The `Query` method handles this message and returns the tallies for all sources from the data store.

```
func (app *FactsApplication) Query (reqQuery types.RequestQuery)
                                    (resQuery types.ResponseQuery) {
  query := string(reqQuery.Data)

  if (strings.EqualFold(query, "all")) {
    var buffer bytes.Buffer
    var prefix = ""
    for source, v := range app.db {
      buffer.WriteString(prefix)
      prefix = ","
      buffer.WriteString(source)
      buffer.WriteString(":")
      buffer.WriteString(strconv.Itoa(v))
    }
    resQuery.Value = buffer.Bytes()
    resQuery.Log = buffer.String()
  }

  if (strings.HasPrefix(query, "Source")) {
    source := query[6:len(query)]
    if val, ok := app.db[source]; ok {
      resQuery.Value = []byte(strconv.Itoa(val))
      resQuery.Log = string(val)
    }
  }

  return
}
```

The blockchain itself stores the validated `source : statement` data submitted by external applications. The ABCI application stores the tallies of facts based on sources, and the tallies are synchronized across all nodes since the ABCI application on all nodes run the same set of transactions that get written into the blockchain.

We use the default tools to compile and build the GO application.

```
$ go build
```

You can run the application from command line and it will automatically connect to a Tendermint Core instance running on the same node.

```
$ ./facts
```

The Cosmos SDK

Tendermint provides a flexible framework for building business logic on top of its consensus engine. However, as you have seen, we have to write the entire application logic from scratch using ABCI. From Tendermint's point of view, the application data is simply a byte array.

For many blockchain applications, they require the same set of baseline functionalities, such as user accounts/address management, token issuance, and PoS-style staking. It is tedious and error prone for developers to write those components over and over again for all Tendermint-based blockchains. That gives rise to application frameworks on top of the ABCI for common business components. The Cosmos SDK is one such component library for Tendermint. It is written on the GO language. The Cosmos Hub project itself is built on the Cosmos SDK.

The Cosmos SDK is still evolving, and its technical details are beyond the scope of this book. I recommend you visit the Cosmos SDK web site for the latest documentation and tutorials (https://github.com/cosmos/cosmos-sdk). In this section, I will provide a high-level introduction to the design and functions of the SDK. The SDK provides built-in support for basic infrastructure needed for most ABCI applications.

- The SDK allows developers to easily create and maintain any number of key-value data stores known as `KVStore`. Those data stores are used to manage application state data during `CheckTx` and `DeliverTx` operations. For example, `DeliverTx` needs to process all transactions in the block on a cached copy of the blockchain state and commit those changes when the processing is successfully finished.

- The SDK provides a data marshalling and unmarshalling library called go-amino. It allows byte array data in transactions to be easily converted to GO objects back and forth.

- The SDK provides a router object to route all messages from a Remote Procedure Call (RPC) connector to different modules in the SDK for further processing. The router is set up in the way that allows the messages to be processed by multiple modules in any specified order.

In your Cosmos SDK application, you will configure the router for incoming messages. The following is an example from the Cosmos SDK tutorial:

```
app.Router().
    AddRoute(bank.RouterKey, bank.NewHandler(app.bankKeeper)).
    AddRoute(staking.RouterKey, staking.NewHandler(app.stakingKeeper)).
    ... ...
```

Incoming messages in transactions are first processed by the `bank` module and then the `staking` module. `app.bankKeeper` is a callback method implemented by the application developer to process events emitted from the `bank` module. For example, it could respond to events when one user transfers funds to another. The Cosmos SDK provides a library of modules. Currently, most of them are related to handling crypto tokens.

- The `auth` module checks and validates signatures in transactions.

- The `bank` module manages user accounts and addresses for holding crypto tokens.

- The `mint` module manages minting and issues crypto tokens during the operation of the blockchain.

- The `staking` module manages how users could stake their tokens to support network security in a proof-of-stake (PoS) manner.

- The `distribution` module manages how the staking award (interest on staking) is distributed to users.

- The `slashing` module manages how to punish users who staked misbehaving actors in the system.

- The `ibc` module manages the cross-chain asset exchange protocol supported by the Cosmos Hub.

As of April 2019, the Cosmos SDK implements basic functionalities for a generic PoS blockchain. It does not yet support any virtual machine functionalities. To support programmable blockchains, the Cosmos SDK road map calls for incorporating virtual machines as modules to process transactions. The future of Cosmos SDK is bright.

Conclusion

In this chapter, we explored the ABCI protocol and demonstrated how to build blockchain applications. Those ABCI applications allow the blockchain to offload much of the computationally intensive tasks. Developers can now write applications with complex transactional logic in a highly efficient manner. An important space to watch is the development of the Cosmos SDK, which could dramatically simplify the development of Tendermint-based application blockchains.

## 21

Creating a Blockchain Client

In the previous chapter, I discussed how to build Application BlockChain Interface (ABCI) applications to handle the business logic of a blockchain. That allows us to develop complex logic to process, transform, and validate transactions to be recorded in the blockchain. For each transaction, the ABCI application can apply rules, compute its persistent effects (e.g., changes to account balances for a monetary transaction), and save results in an off-chain database. Since the ABCI application can be written in any language and on any software stack and can support arbitrary transactional logic, it allows us to build a variety of different blockchains with specific purposes and optimizations. Each ABCI application is a blockchain.

However, with all its power, the ABCI application is still designed around transactions. In traditional enterprise software terms, the ABCI application is middleware providing business or transactional logic. It does not provide user interface or high-level application logic. Similar to Ethereum, the ABCI applications also require a decentralized dapp (dapp) layer to be accessible to end users. The dapp utilizes data and functions provided by the blockchain (i.e., the ABCI application), and hence the dapp is a client to the blockchain.

Note

The Tendermint dapp is different from the Ethereum dapp covered in earlier chapters of the book. An Ethereum dapp is a client for smart contracts deployed on the blockchain. It is limited to invoking public methods exposed by the contract. A Tendermint dapp, on the other hand, has full access to the transaction records stored in the blockchain, as well as off-chain databases maintained by the ABCI application. It is a "dapp on steroids."

In this chapter, I will demonstrate how to build a dapp on the Tendermint platform, using the facts example from the previous chapter. We will build a web application, but the principle is the same for any type of modern user interface.

Overview of the Approach

The simplest approach to a dapp is to build an external application that interacts with the blockchain application programming interface (API). As described in earlier chapters, the API commands are sent via TCP/IP port 46657 to any node on the blockchain network. The application sends in transactions and queries via the /broadcast_tx_commit and /abci_query API methods, respectively. The dapp exists outside of the blockchain. It is not aware of the inner workings of the ABCI application. This is truly a blockchain as a service setup (Figure 21.1).

However, this type of dapp is just another web site or mobile app. It is typically created and managed by a central entity. It accesses the blockchain through a predefined custom data protocol and lacks in-depth access of the underlying data structure.

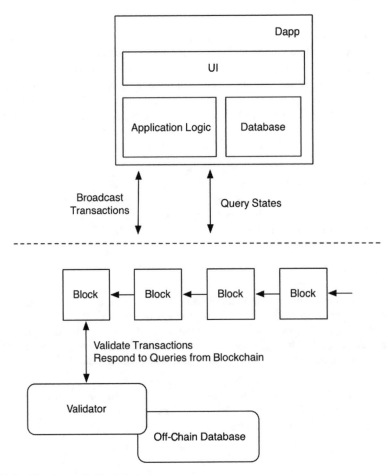

Figure 21.1   The dapp with blockchain as a service

An alternative is to build a distributed application that runs on each node. This application could be deeply integrated with the ABCI application, with local access to databases (Figure 21.2). The advantage of this approach is a higher level of decentralization and a more efficient application architecture. The disadvantages are that it creates a software dependency on the applications at the node level, and it increases the potential security risks for the blockchain, as nodes are serving application services via the Internet. Those disadvantages increase the difficulties of application deployment and management.

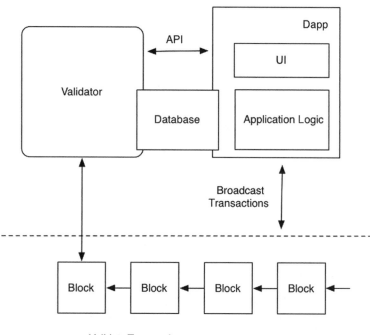

Figure 21.2   A tightly integrated dapp architecture

> **Note**
>
> Even in a decentralized architecture, where the dapp software runs on every node, there still needs to be a centralized entry point. For example, if the dapp is a web app, it still needs a URL. In this case, a lightweight centralized load balancer is needed to direct traffic to the blockchain nodes.

The Sample Application

The sample application shown here is a web app user interface (UI) based on the facts application in Chapter 20. It allows the user to enter facts, with sources and statements, on a web page. And the same page displays the current tally of statements by sources (Figure 21.3).

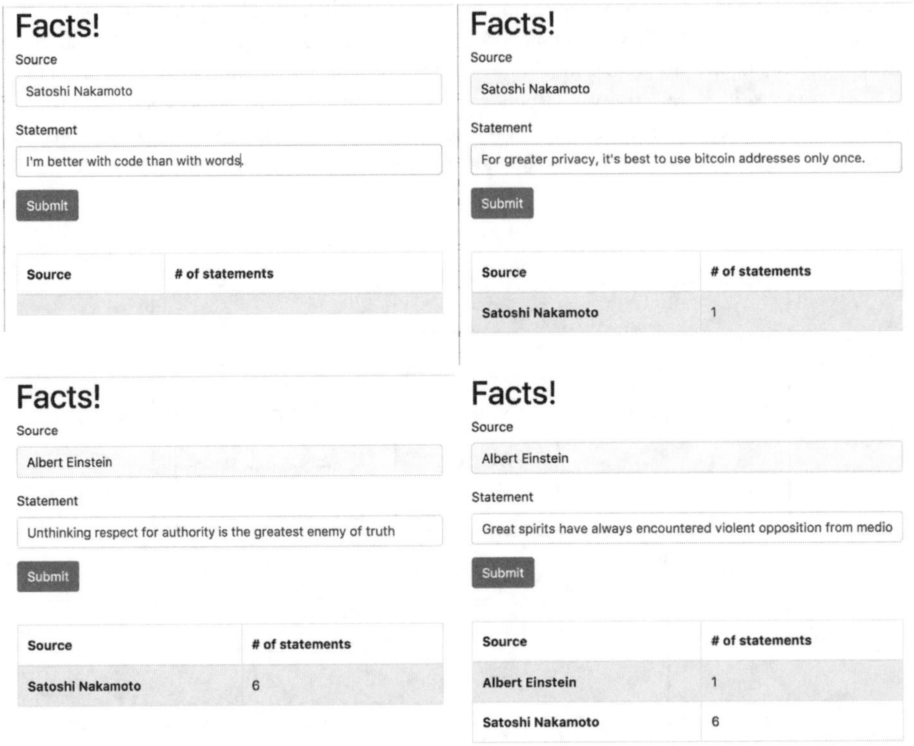

Figure 21.3   The dapp web app for facts

In the next two sections, I will demonstrate how to create this web application in PHP and Java. The PHP application is a simple web application that used the Blockchain API as a back end. The Java application is tightly integrated with the ABCI application.

PHP

We developed a PHP web app to utilize the blockchain API via the TCP socket connection. The blockchain runs Tendermint Core and the facts ABCI application described in Chapter 20.

The PHP code first checks whether this request is a submission of the form, and if it is, the PHP code will send the transaction to the blockchain and wait until it commits.

```
$source = $_REQUEST['source'];
$stmt = $_REQUEST['stmt'];
if (empty($source) or empty($stmt)) {
  // Not valid entry
} else {
  $transaction_req = 'localhost:46657/broadcast_tx_commit?tx="'
      . urlencode($source) . ':'
```

```
      . urlencode($stmt) . '"';
  $ch = curl_init($transaction_req);
  curl_setopt($ch, CURLOPT_RETURNTRANSFER, TRUE);
  curl_exec($ch);
  curl_close($ch);
}
```

Next, the PHP code queries the blockchain via its custom query API to check for the tally of facts based on the source. The query is passed to the ABCI application. As discussed, the ABCI application is responsible for parsing the query, creating a response, and sending the response via the blockchain. The ABCI response is in a structured JavaScript Object Notation (JSON) message. The value field in the response message contains the results encoded in hex characters. The PHP code will parse the hex content and then display the results in a table.

```
<?php
  ... ...
  $query_req = 'localhost:46657/abci_query?data="all"';
  $ch = curl_init($query_req);
  curl_setopt($ch, CURLOPT_RETURNTRANSFER, TRUE);
  $json_str = curl_exec($ch);
  $json = json_decode($json_str, true);
  $result = hex2str($json['result']['response']['value']);
  curl_close($ch);

  $entries = explode(",", $result);
?>
... ...
<table class="table table-bordered table-striped">
  <thead>
    <tr>
      <th>Source</th>
      <th># of statements</th>
    </tr>
  </thead>
  <tbody>
<?php
  foreach ($entries as $entry) {
    list($s, $c) = explode(":", $entry);
?>
    <tr>
      <td><b><?= $s ?></b></td>
      <td><?= $c ?></td>
    </tr>
<?php
  }
?>
  </tbody>
</table>
```

Java

The Java web application accomplishes the same functionalities as the PHP application, but it is directly integrated with the ABCI application's data store. In fact, the ABCI application runs inside the same JVM as the Java web application. Let's look into how this works.

In the Java web application's `web.xml` file, we specify that a servlet will run as soon as the application loads in Tomcat.

```
<servlet>
  <servlet-name>StartupServlet</servlet-name>
  <servlet-class>
    com.ringful.blockchain.facts.servlets.StartupServlet
  </servlet-class>
  <load-on-startup>1</load-on-startup>
</servlet>
```

That servlet loads and runs the ABCI application.

```
public class StartupServlet extends GenericServlet {

    public void init(ServletConfig servletConfig) throws ServletException {
        super.init(servletConfig);
        try {
            // This starts the ABCI listener sockets
            FactsApp app = new FactsApp ();
            getServletContext().setAttribute("app", app);
        } catch (Exception e) {
            e.printStackTrace();
        }
    }
}
```

Next, in the servlet filter in front of the `index.jsp` web page, we first check whether a new fact (source and statement) is submitted in this request. If this is the case, the filter sends the transaction to the blockchain using its regular TCP socket API connection.

```
public class IndexFilter implements Filter {
    private FactsApp app;
    FilterConfig config;

    public void destroy() { }

    public void doFilter (ServletRequest request,
                ServletResponse response, FilterChain chain)
                        throws IOException, ServletException {
        if (app == null) {
            app = (FactsApp) config.getServletContext().getAttribute("app");
        }
```

```java
    String source = request.getParameter("source");
    String stmt = request.getParameter("stmt");
    if (source == null || source.trim().isEmpty() ||
        stmt == null || stmt.trim().isEmpty()) {
      // Do nothing
    } else {
      CloseableHttpClient httpclient = HttpClients.createDefault();
      HttpGet httpGet = new HttpGet(
          "http://localhost:46657/broadcast_tx_commit?tx=%22" +
          URLEncoder.encode(source) + ":" +
          URLEncoder.encode(stmt) + "%22");
      CloseableHttpResponse resp = httpclient.execute(httpGet);

      try {
        HttpEntity entity = resp.getEntity();
        System.out.println(EntityUtils.toString(entity));
      } finally {
        resp.close();
      }
    }

    // Sends the application data store to the web page for JSTL
    // to display in a table.
    request.setAttribute("facts", app.db);

    chain.doFilter(request, response);
  }

  public void init(FilterConfig filterConfig) throws ServletException {
    this.config = filterConfig;
  }
}
```

The filter then queries the ABCI application's data store directly to get a tally of facts by sources. Notice that we do not go through the socket-based blockchain query API for this. While for this simple application the data store query is simple and well supported by the blockchain query API, I can envision application scenarios where the dapp makes heavy use of the off-chain application data store for complex business logic and UI logic.

```html
<table class="table table-bordered table-striped">
  <thead>
    <tr>
      <th>Source</th>
      <th># of statements</th>
    </tr>
  </thead>
  <tbody>
    <c:forEach items="${facts}" var="fact">
      <tr>
```

```
        <td><b>${fact.key}</b></td>
        <td>${fact.value}</td>
      </tr>
    </c:forEach>
  </tbody>
</table>
```

The Java application can be found in the book's GitHub repository. You can build a WAR file ready for Apache Tomcat deployment by running the following Maven build command:

```
$ mvn clean package
```

Conclusion

In this chapter, I showed how to build a complete blockchain application accessible to end users. I showed a web application, but it could easily be a web service to support rich client (i.e., mobile) applications. While it is possible to build completely decentralized dapps, most dapps are created and operated by companies offering services to their users.

Part VI

Cryptoeconomics

Blockchain applications differ from traditional software in one crucial aspect. Through the incorporation of cryptocurrencies, blockchain applications have built-in economic incentives for network security, trust, data exchange, and user behaviors. Besides software architecture, the economic and incentive design is also critical for the success of blockchain ecosystems and applications.

In this part of the book, I will cover incentive designs known as *cryptoeconomics*. We will look into topics such as token classification, token valuation, and crowd-funded token sales and exchanges.

## 22

The Cryptoeconomics of Token Design

While a cryptocurrency is originally invented as part of the blockchain consensus mechanism, subsequent developments have proven that the cryptocurrency is critical for driving blockchains' adoption. A blockchain ecosystem's network effect depends strongly on the cryptocurrency design, which incentivizes how contributors and consumers interact with each other on the network.

In this chapter, I will discuss cryptocurrency (token) designs, known as *cryptoeconomics*. By understanding cryptoeconomics, you will gain a better understanding of exactly what types of applications are suited for blockchains.

There are three broad categories of cryptocurrencies (tokens): network utility tokens, application utility tokens, and security tokens. Some cryptocurrencies can simultaneously belong to multiple categories.

> **Note**
>
> The token classification scheme in this chapter is consistent with the theoretical framework Dr. Catalini and Dr. Gans developed in their pioneering paper "Some Simple Economics of the Blockchain" (https://papers.ssrn.com/sol3/papers.cfm?abstract_id=2874598). They identified two key utilities of blockchain tokens: to pay for the cost of verification and the cost of the network. These correspond to our network utility and application utility tokens, respectively.

Network Utility Tokens

The blockchain establishes collaboration among trustless peers. It can offer "trust as a service," ranging from a secure ledger to enforcement of smart contracts (i.e., guaranteed execution of certain software code) to transparent record keeping. Network utility tokens are used by blockchain users to "pay" for such network services. Users acquire and spend the tokens because they get value and utility from the previously mentioned trust as a service.

A blockchain is a decentralized network, and there is no corporation in the middle to issue orders and give out salaries. The rules and protocols of the blockchain network must be maintained and enforced by the community members (i.e., the contributors) in exchange for tokens. Contributors run computer hardware and software to support blockchain nodes, and they participate in the consensus and governance processes. These contributors are known as *miners* (in proof-of-work [PoW] consensus blockchains) or *validators* (in proof-of-stake [PoS] consensus blockchains). You can read more detailed explanations of PoW and PoS in Chapter 2.

The miners and validators receive tokens for creating new blocks as part of the consensus protocol. They are also "paid" to perform computation to validate the transactions in a block or to execute smart contracts involved in the transactions. This transaction fee is typically paid by parties originating the transactions. As a blockchain matures, the miners and validators should mostly be compensated by fees. This forms a closed loop where people who provide services to maintain the network (miners and validators) receive fees in tokens, they sell those tokens in exchanges, and people who consume network services (users) buy tokens from the exchanges to pay the fees (Figure 22.1).

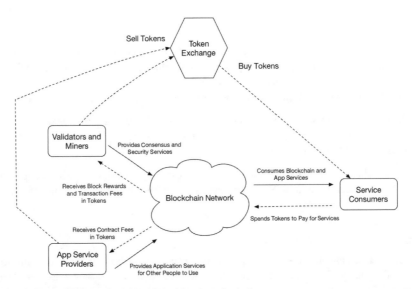

Figure 22.1   The closed loop of a blockchain economic system

Initially, the network utility token has no or little value. As the blockchain network itself becomes useful, more and more people want to use the services the network provides. The fundamental value of a crypto token could therefore be tied to the value of the utility provided by its underlying blockchain network (see the fat protocol theory discussed in Chapter 1). If lots of people are willing to pay to use the network, the crypto tokens will in turn have significant value. Next, let's look at some examples.

Bitcoin (BTC)

Narrowly defined, the Bitcoin network's utility service is to securely and transparently record digital transactions. Broadly defined, however, the utility is to provide a trusted store of value.

Prior to Bitcoin, all publically available digital tokens are infinitely duplicable and hence are useless as a store of value. Today, Bitcoin becomes a store of value (i.e., the Internet gold) because it can be cryptographically stored and moved around. So far, no one has been able to hack the Bitcoin system by recording fraudulent transactions. So, trust is a chief utility provided by the Bitcoin blockchain. It is the same kind of utility that gold or diamond provides for society. Likewise, the valuation of BTC is often compared to the world's gold reserve.

> **Note**
>
> BTC is accepted by a significant portion of the population as "Internet gold" to store value. Its unique characteristics include its first mover advantage (by virtue of being the most widely known cryptocurrency), the security of its ledger (never been hacked), and its limited supply (only 21 million BTC exist). None of these can exist without the work done by the Bitcoin blockchain "miners." People who use BTC today pay to reflect the value of the blockchain network.

As people become interested in using BTC as a secure store of value (i.e., the Internet gold), they pay for the network's bookkeeping services in BTC via transaction fees.

Ethereum (ETH)

The Ethereum network's utility service is to provide a trusted platform that guarantees execution of computer code (known as *smart contracts*). When parties enter into a smart contract on the Ethereum blockchain, both can be assured that the contract will execute as the code is written. This level of integrity is provided by Ethereum community contributors (miners and validators) who run Ethereum nodes. Those community members are paid by the Ethereum crypto token ETH. As more people are interested in using the Ethereum blockchain to enforce their own smart contracts, the demand and value of the ETH go up.

Interestingly, like the BTC, ETH is also increasingly viewed as a store of value but for a different purpose. As decentralized finance (DeFi) applications, such as the Uniswap Exchange, MakerDAO stable coin (SC), and even initial coin offering (ICO) fundraising, take off on the Ethereum network, the ETH is increasingly used as collateral for financial investment. ETH holders are receiving interests, dividends, or "rewards" for their ETHs locked in collateral pools. The ETH has become an investible asset that can generate returns. As we will see later in this chapter, this reduces the velocity of ETH circulation, creating a virtuous cycle for ETH valuation.

There are many efforts to improve the Ethereum blockchain, including the EOS, QTUM, ATOM from Cosmos, and CMT from CyberMiles. Their crypto tokens have similar utility values as the ETH.

ZCash (ZEC)

The ZCash network's utility service is to record anonymous and encrypted transactions so that no one can figure out the parties involved in those transactions. Privacy-concerned users use this utility service to conduct transactions and must pay the network's community of maintainers fees in ZCash for each transaction.

Application Utility Tokens

As discussed in Chapter 1, blockchain networks have the potential to replace corporations as a way to organize production of digital goods and services. Besides trust as a service, a much bigger economic opportunity is for community members to contribute application services to be sold on the blockchain networks. The blockchain aggregates service offerings and conducts buy/sell transactions in crypto tokens. The value of the token can be directly mapped to the value of the aggregated services provided via the blockchain. Let's look at the example of a hypothetical storage sharing coin (SSC) to illustrate how an application utility token might work.

The SSC blockchain provides cloud-based data storage space for users. The storage space is provided by millions of community members who contribute spare hard drive space and Internet bandwidth from their own computers. The blockchain aggregates the fragmented storage space and offers to sell them on-demand on the Internet.

As users demand and use the cloud-based storage provided by the blockchain, they must pay with the SSC token. The blockchain accepts SSC tokens, provides storage space, and distributes SSC tokens to storage space providers. All these are done through protocols and rules codified in software and enforced by blockchain consensus.

The SSC does not necessarily require its own blockchain. It could be implemented as a series of smart contracts on the Ethereum blockchain. The smart contracts specify economic parameters of the system including token supply, fee structure, use of tokens, distribution rules, and so on.

Obviously, the SSC represents just a tip of the iceberg. Besides data storage, community members can provide a variety of useful digital products and services, including intellectual properties, personal data, solar-generated electricity, and medical records.

The common attribute here is that those digital products are valuable in the aggregate. The essential function of the blockchain is to aggregate them from trustless members of the community and fairly distribute the profits. In turn, users are required to pay for the aggregated product and services in the blockchain's native crypto tokens.

Security Tokens

One of most exciting uses of crypto tokens is to represent traditional ownership securities, such as stock shares or even shares in a house or a car. Unlike today's securities, this new form of security is programmable and enforced by smart contracts on blockchains. It opens many compelling use cases in the world of artificial intelligence.

For example, let's consider a self-driving car that acts like a taxi or an Uber car. It makes money and delivers its profits to its owners or stakeholders. With programmable tokens, you can receive the car's profits when certain dynamic conditions are met: when the car is up-to-date on insurance, is traveling in areas and speeds you designate, and is only picking up passengers of a certain profile. In turn, your token will also be responsible for liabilities and losses incurred at those times. A different stakeholder of the same car might want to profit from a riskier business strategy and get paid when the car is taking on more risk. Here are some examples:

- When the car is driving during the day and when the traffic is normal (low risk of collision), owners of token A will receive the profits.

- When the car is driving at rush hour for higher fares and subject to a higher risk of collision, owners of token B will collect the profits and be responsible for the increased risk of loss.

- When the car is driving at night in a high-risk neighborhood to pick up drunken passengers, it will receive the highest fare and has the highest risk of damage. Owners of token C will collect the profits and be responsible for the potential damages.

Today's security regulations are designed for the era of "dumb" shares and bonds. The regulations still need significant updates before the vision of smart programmable securities can be realized. However, there have been many innovative attempts. Here are some examples.

The DAO

The decentralized autonomous organization (DAO) experiment by Ethereum was to raise an investment fund governed by smart contracts in terms of investment decisions and profit distributions. While the effort was unsuccessful because of technical issues, the idea was illuminating. The Securities and Exchanges Commission (SEC) of the United States reviewed the Ethereum DAO and decided it was issuing securities—albeit a programmable, smarter, and much more transparent security than regular shares in a fund.

Token Funds

Multiple traditional venture capital (VC) firms have raised new funds through the ICO mechanism. Examples include the Blockchain Capital fund (http://blockchain.capital/) and the Science Incubator (https://www.science-inc.com/). The stakeholders in those funds are no longer known as limited partners (LPs) but as token holders who have instant liquidity in their shares and will get investment returns through the crypto tokens they hold.

Because of the huge market potential in this nascent market, we recommend you closely follow the developments in this space.

Token Valuation

The use of crypto tokens to consume blockchain services gives valuation to those tokens. In reality, the token price is a major factor in driving adoption and building network effect for a blockchain.

At the time of this writing, a common approach to valuing blockchain networks is to simply multiply the unit token price by the total number of circulating tokens to get a *market cap* (see http://coinmarketcap.com/). This is analogous to valuing a company's market cap by its stock price. However, as we noted in Chapter 1, a blockchain network is very different from a company. For one thing, the blockchain network is not-for-profit and the price-to-earning (P/E) ratio is meaningless. There is no conventional "sales" measure—only transaction volumes on the network (analogous to the gross merchandise value [GMV]).

We believe that a more appropriate approach to value blockchain networks is through their economic output, similar to how national currencies are measured by the economic output (i.e., gross domestic product [GDP]) from nations. On a blockchain network, there are service providers (i.e., miners, validators, application service providers) and consumers. The crypto tokens are designed to facilitate transactions between the parties and, more importantly, to incentivize collaborative interactions in the ecosystem.

> **Note**
>
> For security tokens, the valuation is determined by the performance of the underlying asset- and profit-sharing rules for the token. There are many theories and practical approaches (e.g., the discount cash flow method) to calculate security pricing. I will not discuss them in detail in this book.

Utility Tokens

For network and application utility tokens, macroeconomics theory indicates that the price of each token can be determined by the following factors. The following formula is known as the *value of exchange* equation:

$$Price\ of\ each\ token = \frac{1}{P} = \frac{T}{V \cdot M}$$

- P is the price level, which is the price of services in terms of the token. So, the token price is actually $1/P$.

- T is the total value of services or products the blockchain network community produces in a unit of time (say one year). The long-term value of the token is determined by the value of the underlying services the blockchain provides. In that sense, the token is "backed" by the value of the services.

- M is the total supply of tokens available to exchange for such services and products.

- V is the velocity of money (*monetary velocity*) as measured by the number of times an average token changes hands in the unit of time. It is inverse to the average time token holders hold a token. The higher the speed, the lower the token valuation since each token can be reused to purchase the set number of products and services.

Compared with money supply and velocity in the traditional monetary system, we can estimate V based on how the money supply, M, is utilized in the system.

- M0 refers to cash money in circulation.

- M1 refers to highly liquid and available money, including M0 and checking accounts and traveler's checks. In the United States, M1 USD has a velocity of 5.6 for 2019.

- M2 refers to less liquid money such as savings accounts and money markets. M2 money often carries the purpose of store of value as well as medium of exchange. The USD M2 velocity is around 1.5 in 2019.

As savings accounts dramatically decrease the M2 velocity of USD, the velocity of money is a parameter that can be designed into the blockchain protocol. Here are some examples:

- BTC is often used as a store of value, and hence users tend to hold it for long periods of time. That gives BTC an extremely slow monetary velocity and therefore is very valuable. In other words, people tend to hold BTC for long periods of time, which severely limits the BTC supply on the market, causing its price to go up.

- A utility token for smart contracts (e.g., ETH and CMT) has a natural holding time because of the design of smart contracts. For example, in escrow contracts, the tokens must be held in the contract account for days before the escrowed transaction can settle.

- In an e-commerce blockchain application, buyers often purchase tokens in bulk, and the sellers wait until they accumulate significant amounts of tokens before cashing out. They do that to minimize exchange fees when converting from crypto tokens to fiat currencies (e.g., U.S. dollars).

- In an application utility token like the SSC, the blockchain network could require service consumers to deposit and keep a balance of several days' worth of tokens to ensure uninterrupted services.

Notice that the price computed via the exchange equation represents the current intrinsic value of the token. The actual trade price of the token should reflect people's expectation of the token price in a few years. However, as future money is less valuable than today's money, we will need to apply a discount. Let's assume that the market size is growing at gr percent per year, considering both overall market growth and the blockchain ecosystem's growing penetration of the market; assume the discount rate is dr percent per year. The discount rate, dr percent, is typically between 5 percent and 10 percent depending on the risk of the market. This is the interest rate you incur for borrowing money in this market. After n years, the token price can be discounted to a present value as follows:

$$Present\ token\ price = \frac{T_0 \cdot \left(1 + gr\%\right)^n}{V \cdot M_n \cdot \left(1 + dr\%\right)^n}$$

T_0 is the blockchain network's GDP in the current year (year 0). M_n is the number of floating tokens in year n, which depends on the economic system design. Typically, we use $n = 5$ for computing the present value of the token.

Design Considerations

In general, the more value-add the blockchain network provides, the better it can influence users to hold tokens and decrease the velocity of money. That is why we consider blockchain networks that can aggregate smaller service providers more valuable than ones that simply match buyers and sellers.

A common and rookie design flaw is to build appcoins that act purely as a medium of exchange. That is, the service providers and consumers use the tokens only during a transaction, exchanging the token from and to other currencies immediately before or after the transaction. Since no one holds the token, there is always a glut of such tokens for sale on the market, driving its price down to zero.

Nobel Laureate in Economics Paul Krugman once said, "To be successful, money must be both a medium of exchange and a reasonably stable store of value." As we discussed earlier, an appcoin that is simply used as a medium of exchange is unstable and could crash to zero. The store of value requirement is to give users a reason to hold the currency in between transactions and hence maintain a stable monetary velocity for the system.

However, it is also a chicken-and-egg problem: the currency can become a store of value only if it has a stable monetary velocity. In the case of Bitcoin, the early miners decided to hold it hoping the price would rise in the future. That reduced the monetary velocity and helped to establish Bitcoin's "Internet gold" status as a value store. For most utility tokens, a well-designed protocol could make holding part of the utility (e.g., staking and voting, or a reserve system) and create a value store.

An Alternative Approach

An alternative approach to apply the value of exchange equation is as follows. The benefit of this alternative approach is that it figures out the monetary base of the crypto asset in USD. If the token serves more than one purpose (e.g., both a security token and an application utility token), we can derive the asset base in two ways and then add them together, which we will show here:

$$Monetary\ base\ of\ assets = M = \frac{P \cdot Q}{V}$$

- M is the monetary base of the crypto asset. In other words, it is the total USD value of the tokens. It is the "market cap" of the tokens.

- P is now the price level of the service provided on the network. This price is USD per unit of service.

- Q is the quantity of the service available on the network. Hence, the product of P and Q is the total GDP of the network ecosystem.

- V is the velocity of money in the same period when the GDP is computed.

Similar to the method we used before, we need to discount the future monetary base of the assets back to today's value to take into account the market's future expectation. Let's assume that the blockchain ecosystem is growing at an annual rate of gr percent and the discount rate is dr percent per year (with dr percent being between 5 percent and 10 percent depending on the risk). The present value of the monetary base is as follows. P and Q are both present values.

$$Present\ value\ of\ monetary\ base = M = \frac{P \cdot Q \cdot (1 + gr\%)^{n}}{V \cdot (1 + dr\%)^{n}}$$

To compute the price for each token, you can divide M by the number of free-floating tokens at year n. Again, we typically use $n = 5$ for a reasonable future forecast.

Now, imagine that a token can be used both as a security and as a medium of exchange. The token's market cap value as a dividend-earning security can be computed using the traditional security asset evaluation methods, such as using the discounted cash flow (DCF) methods by discounting and adding all the free cash flow generated from the ecosystem in the future. On the other hand, the token's market cap as a medium of exchange token can be computed from the previous equation. Those two market caps are additive.

> ## Note
>
> The valuation approach discussed in this section was originally proposed by Chris Burniske. You can read more about his investing approaches in his book *Cryptoassets: The Innovative Investor's Guide to Bitcoin and Beyond* (see https://www.bitcoinandbeyond.com/).

We can then divide all tokens in circulation into two categories: earning and payment. If a token is used 30 percent of the time as a payment token and 70 percent of the time as a dividend-earning token, we will put 0.3 token into the payment pool and 0.7 token into the earning pool. The overall token price reaches equilibrium when the price of each use cases matches each other.

$$EP = \frac{M_s}{N_s} = \frac{M_e}{N_e}$$

- EP is the equilibrium price of each token.
- M_s and M_e are the present values of the tokens from dividend-earning security and exchange uses, respectively.
- N_s and N_e are the numbers of tokens primarily used for security or exchange purposes, respectively.

$$\left(M_s + M_e\right) = EP \times \left(N_s + N_e\right)$$

Total token market cap = EP × [total floating tokens]

It is easy to demonstrate that when the token is only a utility token, this alternative method gives the same token price as the formula we used for utility tokens. We simply assigned alternative meanings to components in the value of exchange equation. This new method is easier to apply in situations where there are multiple uses of a token.

Advanced Topics

Now I have covered the basics of token economics. In this section, I will discuss some more complex topics in token design. I will not get into the technical details but aim to provide a glimpse into the world of cryptoeconomics research so that interested readers can explore further on their own.

Nonmonetary Pricing

In the previous section, I discussed the intrinsic value of utility tokens. In the real world, however, we often need to price the token in nonmonetary terms. For example, in a PoW system like

Bitcoin, the miners are awarded for their efforts. If it is too easy for the miners to earn new Bitcoin awards, the market price of Bitcoin will never increase since miners will simply sell their tokens for quick profits as soon as they mine them.

To understand this phenomenon in the medium of exchange framework, it is equivalent to adding token supplies to the system at a faster pace than the growth of the network GDP. It causes the token price to fall due to oversupply.

However, most blockchain networks have mechanisms for future users to earn tokens to balance the increasing network GDP. A primary objective for a public token sale is to jump-start the network effect. Once the token sale is complete, it is often desirable to provide ongoing incentives for new users to earn tokens by contributing to the network effect in other ways. All these lead to increased network GDP and an increased token price for everyone.

For protocol designers, it is therefore important to balance the interests of token purchasers and token earners to make sure everyone receives tokens at a fair cost. To see a well-designed protocol, let's look no further than Bitcoin.

Bitcoin miners do not receive their BTC for free. They need to spend money on electricity, mining machines, data centers, and real estate. If the BTC price goes up in the market, more people will want to join or expand mining operations, hence increasing the computing power (hash rate) on the network. The protocol is designed so that an increased network hash rate will cause the Bitcoin mining algorithm to automatically increase its difficulty, resulting in higher costs for miners. The automatic adjustment of mining difficulty creates a negative feedback cycle that keeps the mining cost always in sync with the current BTC market price. Because of that, there is no free ride in the Bitcoin ecosystem.

In many newer blockchain networks, there are "proof of XYZ" mechanisms for users to earn new tokens from the network. The protocol must have a negative feedback loop similar to the Bitcoin system to ensure that the "cost" of those newly mined or minted tokens is inline with the current market price.

Stable Coins

An important goal of crypto token design is to create a SC that has a stable exchange rate against a fiat currency. There are at least two important use cases for the SC.

- A token must have a stable value to be used as a payment utility. No one will use a wildly fluctuating token to purchase goods since you can never be sure what the price will be in the next hour.

- An SC can act as a hedge or safe harbor for token traders. As we have seen, crypto tokens' prices are all highly correlated. They often go up and down at the same time. For a trader, during a down market, there is no safe token where she can park her money to wait for the market bottom. The only choice seems to be exiting and re-entering the market using fiat currencies, creating problems with taxes, trading speed, or algorithm automations. An SC is in great demand in exchanges.

An SC is a poor candidate for a token sale since no one wants to buy a token that does not appreciate. But algorithmic SCs typically come in pairs, and the token that represents the asset pool does have the potential to go up in price. In the next two sections, I will discuss two common approaches to issue SCs on blockchain networks without central banks.

Fully Collateralized Stable Coins

A collateralized SC can always be redeemed for a stable value at any time. For example, users can purchase SCs for $1 each from the issuer. The issuer could be any centralized entity, and it holds the USD as reserve. The issuer promises to redeem and burn SCs at $1 each at any time. The SCs are then used in transactions in a blockchain network. Each transaction will generate a fee collected by the issuer.

A user can choose to hold and reuse SCs, as opposed to exchanging SCs for USDs immediately before and after use. That is because

- Redeeming SC for USD requires KYC and banking fees.
- Receiving the potential dividend from transaction fees.

The issuer goes through the trouble of holding and exchanging USDs because it could profit from the following:

- Potential fees for SC transactions
- Interest rate on the USDs it holds as collateral

In this scenario, we have a generic SC issuer. In reality, many entities in a blockchain network have additional incentives to issue SCs and more ways to profit from SCs. Here are some examples:

- *Cash flow issuers*: SCs could be issued by a business that has a stable USD cash flow. SCs could be issued from cash income generated by the business and then be rebated to the customers. This allows the business to subsidize and promote certain user behaviors while creating an SC as a side effect.

- *Loan issuers*: SCs can be created from a crypto loan. The issuer could put up Bitcoins as collateral and issue SCs to spend as USDs. When the SC holders redeem their SCs, the issuer would sell Bitcoins to cover USDs. In this case, there must be rules in place to liquidate the Bitcoin collateral into USD when the Bitcoin price drops.

- *Payor issuers*: SCs could be issued by users with high transaction volumes on a trading network. The user deposits USDs required for payments and issues himself SCs. The user then uses the generated SCs for actual payments. The payment recipients can further reuse the SCs for other payments. The issuer holds the USD deposits as liabilities for the outstanding SCs. In this case, the issuer essentially guarantees payments on the entire network, which is arguably the responsibility of heavy users of the network. A key benefit of this approach is that it can be decentralized.

As we can see, there are many reasons for entities to put up collateral assets and issue SCs. We envision a future world with many different SCs for different application scenarios and issuer benefits.

> **Note**
>
> The USDT is the widely used SC. It is backed by the USDs its issuer holds. In theory, USDT holders can exchange USDT to USD at a 1:1 ratio at any time. That gives the USDT a stable price as measured by the USD. However, by relying on the credit and trustworthiness of a central issuer, the USDT is just a small, private, "central bank." This approach is very much against the spirit of the blockchain community. Yet, the popularity of the USDT shows that there is a real need for an SC.

Algorithmic Stable Coins

Another interesting yet unproven class of SCs is called *algorithmic stable coins*. The basic idea is to create an asset pool that buys the token when its price drops and sells it when the price rises. That is to use the market mechanism to create an SC. The key benefit for algorithmic SCs is that they do not require full collateral to remain stable. They have the ability to dynamically attract capital and assets into the system to function as collateral as the market fluctuates.

There have been several attempts to create an algorithmic SC. For example, the Maker protocol creates two interlinked tokens. Both tokens are free-fluctuating. But through the trading of Maker MKR token, the asset-backed DAI token is supposed to reach a stable price. I will not go into the details of the Maker protocol in this book. Interested readers can read its white paper at https://makerdao.com/whitepaper/.

Conclusion

In this chapter, I explained common economic designs of blockchain cryptocurrencies. In the rest of the book, we will explore how to actually build blockchain networks with cryptocurrency support.

## 23

Initial Coin Offerings

By Ash SeungHwan Han

ICO stands for *initial coin offering*, stemming from the common term *initial public offering* (IPO). It has been called a *contribution*, *donation*, or *token generation event* (TGE) according to the project or token's characteristic as well as legal interpretation. In this chapter, I will introduce ICOs and when and how they should be used.

A Brief History

Access to the capital market is a defining characteristic of modern capitalism. For a new business or a project to be developed, a certain amount of capital is typically necessary. Through an ICO, funds are raised, and participants receive blockchain-based tokens issued from the project. If the price of the token goes up, participants earn a profit. If the IPO is the traditional tool of fundraising for a business, the ICO is the new blockchain-based fundraising method.

The first ICO happened in September 2013, involving the ICO of Mastercoin. A total of 4,740 BTC was raised, estimated to be $600,000 based on the BTC price during that period. Run by a foundation, the fund was used to develop Mastercoin and facilitate the ecosystem.

Soon after, other ICOs followed. In 2013, NXT did an ICO, and in 2014, projects such as Ethereum, Counterparty, Digibyte, NEM, Maidsafe, Supernet, Storej, and so on, successfully completed ICOs. In 2015, Augur, Synereo, NEO, and IOTA followed the ICO path. In 2016, the ICO market started to flourish, and more than 70 projects including DAO, Waves, Stratis, Iconomi, Komodo, Golem, and Chronobank did ICOs. In 2017, it is recorded that more than 900 projects raised approximately $6 billion. The ICO market has achieved significant growth.

ICO projects are among the most successful crowd-funding projects in history. The largest ICO was the Filecoin project, which raised $257 million in September 2017. Second largest was Tezos, which raised $232 million in July 2017. At that time, Tezos raised 65,627 BTC and 361,122 ETH, which amounts to $1.4 billion when applying the price as of January 13, 2018.

Ethereum, a project that started in 2014, played a crucial role in promoting ICOs. Ethereum is a blockchain platform where users can directly write code and execute it on the Ethereum Virtual Machine (EVM). On Ethereum, the ERC20 specification provides a standard approach to issuing new tokens, which can then be sold in ICOs.

Thanks to the ERC20 tokens on Ethereum, there is no need to build or maintain one's own blockchain to issue crypto tokens. By using the source code readily available, one can simply use the Ethereum blockchain to issue tokens. Therefore, ICOs become technically much easier, and this lower barrier led to the ICO boom in 2017.

Major platform blockchain projects that have conducted successful ICOs include Ethereum, Cosmos, EOS, Qtum, NEO, Cardano, Waves, NEM, CyberMiles, and so on.

Utility of an ICO

The ICO provides a mechanism to set a market price for a newly invented crypto token. Tradable crypto tokens will eventually have their values determined by the market force of supply and demand. However, at the beginning of a new token, it is hard to predict a market price. The ICO allows early market participants to come to a consensus about a token's worth and offers an opportunity for early adopters to purchase the token at its consensus price.

When Bitcoin was first launched, it did not have a price. Later, when people started to use Bitcoin in transactions and trading, the Bitcoin price fluctuated wildly depending on the time, location, and nature of the transaction. It took years before there was a consensus on the Bitcoin price at any given time. Bitcoin became a real currency for storing and exchanging values after this consensus was reached. By June 2019, it was the ninth most valuable currency in the world in terms of total market cap, after the currency of Japan, China, the European Union, the United States, the United Kingdom, Switzerland, India, and Russia.

As the history of Bitcoin illustrates, it could take years for the market to set a consensus price on a crypto currency. Indeed, for most cryptocurrencies that have not gone through an ICO, they have no price and hence are hard to trade or transact with. Without a tradeable token, the underlying blockchain project cannot provide incentives or build network effects for its community.

Facilitation of the Blockchain Project

As discussed, a key defining characteristic of a blockchain project is its network effect. An ICO contributes to the jump-start of the network effect. A blockchain project expands when more people autonomously participate in and make a contribution to the project. The value of the blockchain project is in the network it creates. If the future value of the network is priced and distributed to the participants from the beginning, then more people will participate and feel ownership in the project. That creates a positive feedback loop to start the network.

From the network effect point of view, it is important to know how many people participate in the ICO and who they are. Generally speaking, it is more advantageous for participants who are diverse and can directly contribute to the project to join the ICO. For instance, if a project is to create a blockchain network for the entertainment business, ICO participations from parties such as singers, actors, record label companies, album distribution companies, and movie production companies will be particularly valuable as they can help grow the network, and hence their own token value, after the ICO.

Network Effect for PoS-Based Projects

As described in Chapter 2, there are two major types of blockchains: proof-of-work (PoW) blockchains and proof-of-stake (PoS) blockchains. While Bitcoin and the original Ethereum are both PoW blockchains, the new generation of scalable and performant blockchains are PoS.

However, when it comes to building network effects, the PoW blockchains have a proven path. The PoW tokens are released gradually to miners who invested real money building the blockchain infrastructure. The miners compete with each other to create a diverse and decentralized network. Yet, the miners have vested interests in seeing the blockchain network succeed and the token price go up as a result.

In the case of PoS blockchains, however, the total number of tokens issued is often fixed (or predetermined at a rate), and it is possible for a single person to own all the tokens. How to create a diverse network with many stakeholders all working to grow the PoS blockchain is therefore a crucial problem. An ICO provides just this mechanism.

A simplistic approach to distribute tokens in a PoS project is to hold a token sale and let people buy the tokens. Yet, this could still result in a monopoly and corrupt the blockchain if someone is willing to purchase a majority of tokens and hold more than 51 percent of the PoS voting power. Such a phenomenon is called a *Byzantine attack* or *51 percent attack*. The solution is to hold a public token sale (i.e., an ICO) and optimize the rules to include as many public participants as possible (i.e., to set individual caps and participation eligibility rules). Therefore, for PoS blockchains, three facts could significantly affect the system stability.

- Possibility of a public ICO
- Number of ICO participants
- ICO fundraising amount

It is imperative to have as many participants as possible, and the total market cap of tokens should be high enough to avoid an attack by one participant or a minority group of participants that tries to dominate the consensus mechanism.

Fundraising

Of course, besides instantly creating a community of real stakeholders to grow the blockchain network, the ICO also helps the project raise money. Most blockchain projects are community projects without a center corporation, making them ill-suited for equity-based investments. Yet, as we have seen repeatedly (e.g., Uber, Amazon, Facebook), building network effect requires a significant amount of capital. The proceeds from the token sale can now be used for such purposes. The ICO can raise funding for technology development, network operations and governance, legal compliance, community incentives, prepayment of future network services, and many other purposes.

Of course, as ICOs become popular, businesses that do not directly utilize the blockchain technology are also raising funding through ICOs. That is an interesting phenomenon that gives rise to the notion of "security tokens"—tokens that represent ownership in an asset rather than a utility payment mechanism on a blockchain. The main rationales for using ICOs primarily as a fundraising mechanism are as follows.

High Demand

The amount of capital is growing explosively in the cryptocurrency market because investors have a high-risk appetite for projects with strong network effects or that can securitize assets in new ways. Compared to traditional venture capital (VC), fundraising through ICOs has a lower difficulty level, and a higher amount of capital can be raised.

Marketing Effect

The ICO marketing effect is analogous to the network effect. Through evangelism of early adopters and buyers, it brings attention to the project from the general public. ICO projects are likely to execute successful global marketing through diverse global channels.

Instant Liquidity

Crypto tokens are instantly tradable, even if they are not listed in exchanges. Also, an exchange listing for crypto tokens is considerably less difficult than stock exchange listings. Through exchanges and trading, projects could earn additional capital and capture more participants.

ICO vs. Traditional Equity Financing

In this section, let's expand on the fundraising aspect of ICO as most people perceive the ICO as a way to raise money. I'll define the characteristics of an ICO compared to the traditional venture capital investment model.

Entry Barrier to Investment

In the traditional venture capital (VC) model, an investor must contribute to a VC fund as a limited partner (LP). A high amount of capital is required to invest, and the general partner (GP), who makes investment decisions on behalf of the LPs in the fund) takes a huge cut in both management fees and carried interests.

However, in the case of an ICO, anyone across the globe can participate regardless of investment capital. The fact that anyone can invest in a startup is what makes ICOs an innovative investment process.

Note

It is important to note that in some countries, including in the United States, there is a risk that some ICOs might be considered security offerings. To comply with security laws, it is highly recommended that ICO issuers check the identity of every investor who participates in the public token sale (known as the *know the customer* [KYC] verification).

Entry Barrier to Fundraising

There are many disadvantages for a startup to receive venture capital equity funding. A venture capital evaluation and due diligence process is often time-consuming and tedious. Since venture capital is a scarce resource, the startup does not have any power in contract negotiation. As a result, the investment contract often heavily favors the investor putting the projects and its founders in potential jeopardy. In addition, the venture investors often have excessive control over the business decision-making process.

ICOs allow for a public and worldwide participation of the investment process from the beginning. Whereas a VC deal may be dead after several unsuccessful meetings with venture capitalists, ICOs can target certain investors from a much larger pool. In 2017 and 2018, many ICO projects have raised more capital in a shorter period of time compared to venture capital-funded projects.

Regulation/Paperwork

A typical venture capital investment deal requires regulatory approvals as well as a lot of administrative work. Even after a venture capital deal is finalized, it may take a long time (even months) for the funding to be in place and for the team to begin working on the project. Currently, ICOs require a minimum amount of regulatory oversight, they require little paperwork (it is often enforced by smart contracts on Ethereum), and the funding is immediate. However, all these might change in the future as more and more countries decide to regulate this. For example, most ICO projects have already volunteered to exclude Chinese and U.S. residents from their public sales. Of course, that also means the project has to register and conduct KYC for all potential participants before they can invest. That is something that cannot be done with blockchain smart contracts alone.

Looking toward the future, there are a few regulations in the United States that can serve as legal frameworks for fully regulated and compliant ICOs.

- *Regulation D 506(c)*: This is to offer the token sale to accredited investors only. There is no investment or fundraising limit. While this sounds like a straightforward path, it also severely limits the token's liquidity and its network effect. The token will have to be traded on a security exchange after their issuance.

- *Regulation crowdfunding*: This allows anyone to invest, but the project is limited to raising less than $1.07 million per year. This is a great approach for smaller projects, such as software development, but not a viable option for projects aiming to build large networks. The fundraising limit is simply too low for network projects.

- *Regulation A+*: This allows anyone to invest, but the project is limited to raising $50 million per year after a qualification process with the SEC.

It is possible that Regulation A+ will become the framework for future ICOs. This type of ICO is also known as security token offerings (STOs). As of the first half of 2018, projects and the U.S. SEC are both exploring how to best move forward.

Liquidity after Fundraiser

Liquidity is the key reason ICOs have seen such unprecedented growth. In a traditional venture capital investment deal, liquefying (or "cashing out") the investor's asset required the investors waiting until the next round of investment or the IPO to take place. That takes time and runs the risk of the next investment round not taking place at all.

Meanwhile, because an ICO takes place on the blockchain, the investment transactions can be executed without a middleman. Furthermore, if the crypto asset is listed on a cryptocurrency exchange, this in turn creates added liquidity. The abundance of liquidity encourages more people to enter the market.

Community Participation

For a blockchain project, community participation is often crucial for the network effect and the success of the entire project. However, a venture capitalist's role in a project extends only as far as raising capital, not building a community.

Meanwhile, an ICO, in itself, is a process of building a community. The community the ICO builds in its investment stage could later become a foundation that the project grows upon.

Risk

Equity-based venture capital investments and ICO investments carry different types of risks.

A typical ICO project tends to be in an earlier stage than a typical project seeking a venture capital investment. Most ICO projects receive funding with only its technology vision and network building road map. In terms of project maturity, ICOs can be considered high risk.

However, since ICO projects can achieve liquidity much faster than VC deals, the risk for an investment loss is much reduced since investors do not tie up their capital in the project until the very end. In terms of liquidity risk, ICO should be considered to have lower risk than equity investments.

Market Size

The traditional venture capital market is massive. According to an industry database Crunchbase, approximately 22,700 startups have received in total $213 billion of investment.

According to data gathered by Coindesk, ICOs received about $3.5 billion in funding from January 2017 to November 2017. ICOs were an exponential capital influx in 2017.

Evaluating an ICO Project

In this section, I will discuss how to evaluate an ICO project by looking into its key components. A typical ICO consists of the following components: project, team, capital, community, and legal framework.

Project

The project is the objective of the ICO. The nature of the project dictates how much capital should be raised during an ICO and how the tokens should be allocated for various purposes. A clear goal, road map, and timeline should be defined. The project should be realistic in terms of its goals as well as its timeframe.

Team

Like any entrepreneur effort, the team determines the ultimate success of the project. The team should consist of entrepreneurs, managers, and domain experts in all the specialty areas required by the project. Each member's roles should be clearly designated. In evaluating the project, we should consider each team member's level of dedication to the project, such as the full-time employment status.

Fundraising Structure

The ICO raises funding by selling tokens. The token sale structure can vary a lot from project to project. For example, all tokens can be released for sale at once. Oftentimes, however, part of the available tokens can be designated for a pre-ICO round for a specific group of investors (i.e., a private sale), and the rest will be sold to the public at a later date.

Token Distribution Table

The distribution of the tokens created by an ICO plays a crucial role in forming the project's ecosystem. Typically, portions of the tokens are set aside for the team, ICO participants, and/or development of the ecosystem. The distribution plan should be set according to the project's goals.

Community

As we mentioned, creating and growing a community plays a crucial role for an ICO blockchain project. The public blockchain is decentralized, and therefore its utility increases relative to its participants and its network. While the ICO helps jump-start the growth, the community must generate its own growth and create positive network effects after the ICO. There must be a clear mechanism for the ICO participants to keep involved in the project. The community may answer questions, host events, or contribute to the technical development of the project.

Most projects look to grow a global community. For example, Bitcoin and Ethereum communities host various events across the globe and share a great sense of togetherness.

Legal Framework

Since the purpose of an ICO is to build a blockchain network, it is typically conducted by a nonprofit organization (i.e., foundation) that provides governance and custodianship of the network. Because of various legal risks in countries around the world, many ICOs select Singapore or Switzerland as the legal location for their foundations. However, the work is often done in junction with a for-profit company that provides services to the foundation through contracts. It is a complicated structure that has to be set up under sound legal guidance. ICO investors are encouraged to review the legal setup and investor protection provided by the foundation that raises funding.

During the ICO, the foundation also needs to be in tune with changing legal landscapes around the world. For instance, it must exclude citizens or residents from certain countries to avoid policy bans or potential security law violations.

ICO Participation Risk

As a largely unregulated form of fund raising, current ICOs carry significant risks to novice investors. In this section, we will discuss some common risk factors associated with ICO projects.

Hacking Risk

ICOs are highly technical, involving cryptocurrency accounts, smart contracts, KYC procedures, etc., and have a lot of money at stake. Because of that, they are subject to extensive hacking.

The ICO projects themselves can be hacked. High-profile projects, such as the DAO, Polkadot, and Coindash, have all fallen victim to hacking incidents and resulted in the loss of hundreds of millions of dollars. In such cases, while the investors may still receive the tokens as promised, the loss of investment funds will adversely affect the development of the project.

The process of participating in an ICO in itself can also be risky. Some participants have fallen victim to phishing attacks, sending investment funds or receiving tokens at wrong addresses.

Project Development Risk

Like every startup, the ICO project itself might fail even after raising funding, which ultimately renders the tokens sold in the ICO worthless.

- The whole ICO might be a scam. For instance, the purpose of the ICO was not the project, rather the ICO itself.
- The technology to achieve the project goal doesn't exist or cannot be developed.
- The project cannot develop network effect and find enough users to participate.
- Better solutions already exist in the market.
- There is no market need for the solution provided.

All those issues can be mitigated by conducting due diligence on the project. However, regular retail investors often lack the resources and expertise to do due diligence. This could give rise to professional and independent ICO rating agencies.

Team Risk

Ultimately, the success of any project depends on the team. Humans in the team are also often the most uncertain and risky part of the project. ICO project teams have disbanded and disappeared with the fund in the past. The sizable amount of capital may cause conflict within the team. Some projects fail as team members cannot agree on how to fairly compensate each other. Yet some teams are found out to be technically incapable of carrying out the project.

Conclusion

In this chapter, I discussed what an ICO is and why it is so important to blockchain projects beyond simple fundraising. There are many risks associated with this form of unregulated fundraising, but when done right, it can also bring huge rewards both financially and in the form of a community of collaborative users.

An ICO is simply an event of raising capital and jump-starting the community, and it is the beginning of a long journey. To be successful and create value for its tokens, each project must focus on its goals. Let the marathon begin!

## 24

Cryptocurrency Exchanges

By Ash SeungHwan Han

A key component in the cryptocurrency ecosystem is the exchange. When I say that the Bitcoin in my account is worth $10,000 U.S. dollar (USD), it means that I can exchange it for $10,000 USD right now and take the USD to a bank. Cryptocurrencies (tokens) can have values and liquidity only when they are actively traded. As discussed in previous chapters, crypto tokens can only be part of the blockchain incentive design to facilitate network effects when they have established and well-accepted value among the community members. In this chapter, we explore the services offered by today's cryptocurrency exchanges. I will discuss different types of exchanges and their roles in the ecosystem.

Exchange Types

Exchanges allow people to trade cryptocurrencies against other cryptocurrencies, as well as against fiat currencies such as the USD. In general, there are three types of exchanges.

Fiat Currency Exchanges

A fiat currency exchange allows conversion between cryptocurrencies and fiat currencies. They must be licensed by governments to do business with banks so that you can send and receive fiat currencies through your bank accounts or bank-issued credit cards. Those exchanges are subject to strict government regulations and typically allow only a handful of well-known cryptocurrencies (such as BTC and ETH) to be exchanged directly into fiat currencies.

The fiat currency exchanges are typically the most reputable and reliable exchanges as they are regulated by the government as semi-financial institutions. However, they are also the most restrictive and centralized. For example, they need to verify and record every user's detailed personal information for anti-money-laundry and tax purposes. While convenient, their existence does not fit the decentralized world view of blockchain cryptocurrencies, and because of that, many consider those fiat currency exchanges only an immediate step toward a truly decentralized financial system.

Representative fiat crypto exchanges that handle U.S. dollars include Kraken and GDax (from Coinbase).

Tokens-Only Exchanges

A token-token exchange only allows trading pairs between crypto tokens. Since there is no fiat currency involved in trading, those exchanges are much less regulated and hence can grow much faster. This type of exchange represents by far the largest trading volumes in the crypto currency world at the time of this writing. However, as regulations tighten around those exchanges, their future growth is in question. Specifically, maybe those exchanges do need to be regulated and all participants must use real names and pay taxes on their earnings.

Most tokens-only exchanges also provide trading pairs against some kind of asset-backed "stable coin" as a way for people to temporarily park their assets during market fluctuation without actually converting to fiat currencies. Such asset-backed tokens include the USDT, which is supposed to be backed by USD deposits in traditional banks at a 1:1 ratio. The legal status of those asset-backed tokens is also murky.

Representative token-only exchanges include Binance, OKEX, and HuoBi. The current generation of token-only changes is also highly centralized with a single for-profit company operating the exchange. The exchanges sometimes issue their own crypto tokens (e.g., BNB from Binance) that facilitate marketing and shifts profits from the company's equity holders to token holders via discounts and buybacks.

> ### Note
> In countries where crypto token trading is outright banned, there is another type of exchanges called over-the-counter (OTC) exchanges. These exchanges only list orders and let parties find each other and trade off the platform. There is often a mechanism for parties to report the completion of the trade and release the order. It is like Craigslist for crypto trading!

Security Token Exchanges

A security token exchange is an emerging trend in the world of crypto currencies. It is for trading tokens that are classified as securities. Like regular stock exchanges, such exchanges will be subject to security laws. Many classes of securities can be traded only by accredited investors under strict regulations. This type of exchange is highly centralized, but it also represents the greatest opportunities for mainstream adoption of crypto tokens. Tokenized security offerings are also known as *security token offerings* (STOs).

There are many current efforts to build exchanges for security tokens. Notable projects include the following:

- The OpenFinance Network (http://OpenFinance.io) is one of the first fully compliant exchanges for security tokens in the United States. It creates an open technical standard called S3 (Smart Securities Standard; see https://github.com/OpenFinanceIO/smart-securities-standard), which connects ERC20 token contracts to know your customer (KYC) and anti-money laundry (AML) services on the OpenFinance network. That allows ERC20 tokens to determine which trades are compliant with securities laws and act accordingly.

- The tZero project has already raised $100 million from an ICO to build a regulatory-compliant exchange for trading tokenized security.

- The Templum project is building a securities platform for ICOs and secondary trading.

- Circle, a crypto P2P payment company, has recently acquired U.S.-based crypto exchange Poloniex to build a regulation compliance security token exchange.

- The Harbor project is building a decentralized compliance protocol for STOs and security token exchanges.

- The Polymath project aims to build a blockchain system that captures all investors' personal profile to determine who can trade what kind of securities with whom. This is an ambitious project that can serve as the technology backbone for security exchanges.

As you can see, there have been many attempts to build security tokens. If those efforts are successful, the crypto asset landscape will be drastically reshaped.

Decentralization

As discussed, one of the greatest problems of today's crypto token exchanges is centralization. For an ecosystem that is built on the idea of decentralization, it is ironic that the critical infrastructure is dominated by centralized corporations. There are a few reasons for this.

- For fiat currency exchanges, the legal requirements from banking regulators (i.e., real identifies of traders and liability for wrongdoing) make it necessary to have centralized operating entities.

- However, most crypto trading volume is not on fiat exchanges. Most trading happens on token-only exchanges. For token-only exchanges, a centralized model makes it more efficient to match trade orders and hence can create more trading depth, which is crucial for the exchange's utility value.

- Centralized exchanges can incentivize participation and active trading and hence create more depth.

Decentralization would not require trading parties to send tokens and assets to an exchange's accounts and trade within the exchange system. A decentralized exchange could match trading parties anywhere in the world and then exchange tokens directly from the parties' private wallets. A decentralized exchange is not an operating entity, but a network protocol, probably existing as a smart contract on a blockchain.

Besides ideological reasons, there are also compelling practical reasons to create and use decentralized exchanges. For example, decentralized exchanges are much safer. Crypto exchanges are magnets for hackers. Almost all exchanges have been hacked in the past. So, the process to send and store crypto assets on the exchange's account is not always safe. It is, of course, much safer to trade directly from your own private crypto wallets, as the case with decentralized exchanges.

There are many great, yet experimental, ideas for decentralized exchanges.

- EtherDelta and BTS are the original decentralized exchanges on Ethereum and BitShare blockchains. They are smart contracts that allows traders to place orders and execute trades from private accounts.

- Newer protocols such as the Kyber Network attempts to do more than just exchanges. They offer varied financial services such as complex contracts and payments.

- DAEX is a protocol for decentralized settlement. The idea is that centralized exchanges are great for match making, but the settlement of accounts (i.e., actual transfer of token assets) should be done from traders' private accounts to be safe. So, DAEX could provide decentralized security to centralized exchanges.

- 0x is a protocol that takes apart all modules of a trading network, from wallets to order booth to trade protocol and interfaces. It allows you to build a new exchange from scratch and adopt any level of decentralization in each module.

- The Bancor protocol aims to create a new smart contract-powered token that can act as intermediary to provide trading counterparty to any token in the world. The exchange rate is computed by the protocol rather than by trade orders, and hence there is always liquidity. While the Bancor system suffers from implementation problems (the current system is demonstrated to have significant risk for "front running"), it is an idea worth exploring.

- Uniswap is an algorithmic liquidity protocol similar to Bancor but without the ICO token. It simply allows market makers to contribute to liquidity pools, and the users can trade against the pools based on prices determined by the algorithm. It is becoming one of the most popular decentralized exchanges on Ethereum.

- All these systems work on single blockchain networks. The smart contract for decentralized exchange must exist on some blockchain, and it can only handle assets on this blockchain. The Polkadot and Cosmos IBC protocols provide asset exchange mechanisms across blockchains. They can ensure the token destruction on the sender's blockchain and creation on the receiver's blockchain. They provide a basis for cross-chain decentralized exchanges.

There are many active research and experimentations on decentralized exchanges. In the next few years, we will see which ideas will be accepted by the market!

Products and Services

The products and services from all exchanges, regardless of whether they are decentralized, are similar.

- All exchanges offer spot trading, where you can immediately trade tokens and assets you already own. These are assets already in your wallet or in your account with the exchange.

- Many exchanges provide futures trading. This is a method in which there is a transaction based on the future price of an already existing token. Generally, futures exist in 1 day, 7 days, 30 days, etc., and when a certain date arrives, the current price is compared to the futures price, and the change is derived.

- For tokens that do not already exist, some exchanges let you trade IOUs. While the actual token has not been issued, it is a type of futures trading with a premise that it is swapped to the future token. For example, in the days leading up to the Bitcoin SegWit hard fork, regular Bitcoin and SegWit Bitcoin were both traded in the market before SegWit actually happened.

- Some exchanges support margin trading. In this scenario, the amount that can be traded can be larger than what one actually has. If there is margin trading with ten times leverage, it has an effect of trading 10 Bitcoins with 1 Bitcoin. Therefore, if there is a 10 percent price increase, you can earn 100 percent profit. Of course, the opposite case happens during a loss.

One of the more interesting "products" many exchanges offer is the exchange's own crypto tokens, known as *platform coins*. Examples include BNB from Binance, and HT from Huobi. These tokens are used to incentivize users on the exchange to trade more and refer more users to the exchange. They typically provide discounts on trading fees, referral bonuses, and even profit sharing from the exchange. Many people in the community, including regulators, consider those tokens similar to stocks issued by the exchanges, as opposed to utility tokens.

Besides trading services, some exchanges attempt to provide more traditional financial services in the crypto world. For example, exchanges could provide custodial services to help funds manage and account for their tokens. Coinbase is one of the first legally compliant crypto custodial services in the United States. The exchange could act as a "bank" to lend its users tokens and charge an interest. The exchange could also offer a portfolio of tokens as a "mutual fund" or even "index fund" for sale to investors.

Conclusion

Exchanges are critical parts of the crypto token ecosystem. And they are often extremely profitable for its operators because unlike exchanges in traditional finance, crypto exchanges are unregulated and can engage in wide ranges of activities including trading against its own clients. The great challenge today is to make exchanges safe through the right amount of decentralization and to figure out the legal frameworks the exchanges should operate under.

Getting Started with CyberMiles

CyberMiles is an Ethereum-compatible public blockchain with delegated proof-of-stake (DPoS) consensus. While it brings many feature enhancements to the Ethereum ecosystem, it can also serve as a much faster, much cheaper, and more reliable alternative to the Ethereum blockchain. All Ethereum smart contracts can run without modification on the CyberMiles blockchain. Furthermore, the CyberMiles ecosystem has easy-to-use developer tools that are improved versions of their Ethereum counterparts. Therefore, CyberMiles is a good choice for you to learn the Ethereum protocol and get started with application development.

While there are many tools that can get you quickly started with Lity, smart contracts, and dapp development on the CyberMiles public blockchain, to really learn how the blockchain works, you should start a node and synchronize it with the blockchain network. The node can run on a server or even on your own laptop if needed. In this appendix, I will describe how to run a CyberMiles node using Docker and how to interact with the node using command-line tools.

Deploy a Node

The quickest way to deploy a CyberMiles node is to use Docker for the latest node software and to use a snapshot for the up-to-date blockchain data. The following instructions show you how to build a CyberMiles testnet node. First, you have to install the Docker software: https://docs.docker.com/install/.

A Docker image for Travis is stored on Docker Hub. The testnet environment uses the vTestnet release, which can be pulled automatically from Travis.

```
docker pull cybermiles/travis:vTestnet
```

Next, let's download the blockchain configuration and data into a local directory, $HOME/.travis, which we can then make accessible to the Docker container. The configuration files are here:

```
$ rm -rf $HOME/.travis && mkdir -p $HOME/.travis/config
$ curl https://raw.githubusercontent.com/CyberMiles/testnet/
```

```
master/travis/init/config/config.toml > $HOME/.travis/config/config.toml
$ curl https://raw.githubusercontent.com/CyberMiles/testnet/
master/travis/init/config/genesis.json > $HOME/.travis/config/genesis.json
```

You should edit the `config.toml` file to change the node's name to your own.

```
$ vim ~/.travis/config/config.toml
# here you can change your name
moniker = "<your_custom_name>"
```

Then, download the latest block data snapshot here:

```
$ wget $(curl -s http://s3-us-west-2.amazonaws.com/travis-ss-testnet/
latest.html)
```

Extract the tar file and copy the `data` and `vm` subdirectories from the uncompressed directory to `$HOME/.travis`. Finally, start the Docker container by mapping the local computer's `$HOME/.travis` directory to the Docker container's `/travis` directory.

```
$ docker run --name travis -v $HOME/.travis:/
travis -t -p 26657:26657 cybermiles/travis:vTestnet node start --home
/travis
```

You can start a CyberMiles mainnet node using a similar process. The only difference is that the configuration and blockchain data download URLs. You can learn more at https://travis.readthedocs.io/en/latest/connect-mainnet.html.

Interactive Console on the Node

Once a CyberMiles node is synchronized to the blockchain, you can use the Travis program to connect to it and send commands and interactions to the network. All you need to do is to attach the `travis` command to the node. The following command should be run on the same computer as Docker:

```
$ docker exec -it travis bash
> ./travis attach http://localhost:8545
```

> **Note**
> Never expose port 8545 outside the firewall when you have the `personal` module enabled. Hackers will be able to steal all your cryptocurrencies stored on the node if you do so.

Travis opens an interactive console in the new terminal, and you can use the `web3-cmt` JavaScript API to access the blockchain. For instance, the following commands will create a new account to hold virtual currency on this network. Just repeat the `newAccount()` command a few times, and you will see a few accounts in the `cmt.accounts` list. As mentioned earlier, each account consists of a pair of private and public keys. Only the public key is recorded on the blockchain in each transaction that involves this account.

```
> personal.newAccount()
Passphrase:
Repeat passphrase:
"0x7631a9f5b7af9705eb7ce0679022d8174ae51ce0"
> cmt.accounts
["0x7631a9f5b7af9705eb7ce0679022d8174ae51ce0", ...]
```

When you create or unlock accounts from the Travis console, the private key of the account is stored in the keystore file on the attached node's file system. Next, you can send some of your CMT from one account to another. Or, if your node is on the testnet, you can get some testnet CMT from the faucet at https://travis-faucet.cybermiles.io/.

```
> personal.unlockAccount("0x7631a9f5b7af9705eb7ce0679022d8174ae51ce0")
Unlock account 0x7631a9f5b7af9705eb7ce0679022d8174ae51ce0
Passphrase:
true
> cmt.sendTransaction({from:"0x7631a9f5b7af9705eb7ce0679022d8174ae51ce0",
to:"0xfa9ee3557ba7572eb9ee2b96b12baa65f4d2ed8b", value: web3.toWei(0.05,
"cmt")})
"0xf63cae7598583491f0c9074c8e1415673f6a7382b1c57cc9b06cc77032f80ed3"
```

The last line is the transaction ID for the transaction to send 0.05 CMT between the two accounts. In the next example, let's see how to build and deploy a smart contract and then call its function.

To build a smart contract from source, you can use the Europa integrated development environment (IDE). Or, you can use the command-line lityc compiler, which provides more advanced features than Europa, such as security and compliance checks (see Chapter 15). The goal is the same: to generate application binary interface (ABI) and bytecode from the Lity/Solidity source code so that they can be deployed on the blockchain. Let's see how to use lityc for this purpose. You can install lityc following the instructions at https://lity.readthedocs.io/. The following commands generate the bytecode and ABI definition from the HelloWorld.lity source code:

```
$ lityc --bin HelloWorld.lity
======= ./HelloWorld.lity:HelloWorld =======
Binary:
608060405234...

$ lityc --abi HelloWorld.lity
======= ./HelloWorld.lity:HelloWorld =======
Contract JSON ABI
[ { "constant": false, "inputs": [], "name": "kill",
"outputs": [], "payable": false, "stateMutability": "nonpayable",
"type": "function" }, { "constant": false, "inputs": [ {
"name": "_new_msg", "type": "string" } ], "name": "updateMessage",
```

```
"outputs": [], "payable": false, "stateMutability": "nonpayable",
"type": "function" }, { "inputs": [], "payable": false, "stateMutability":
"nonpayable", "type": "constructor" }, { "constant": true, "inputs": [],
"name": "owner", "outputs": [ { "name": "", "type": "address" } ],
"payable": false, "stateMutability": "view", "type": "function" }, {
"constant": true, "inputs": [], "name": "sayHello", "outputs": [ {
"name": "", "type": "string" } ], "payable": false, "stateMutability":
"view", "type": "function" } ]
```

On the Travis console, you can now deploy the contract bytecode and ABI to the CyberMiles blockchain.

```
> personal.unlockAccount(cmt.accounts[0],'1234');
> bytecode="0x608060..."
> abi = ... the ABI output ...
> contract = web3.cmt.contract(abi);
> contractInstance = contract.new(
   {
     from: web3.cmt.accounts[0],
     data: bytecode,
     gas: "4700000"
   },
   function(e, contract) {
     console.log("contract address: " + contract.address);
     console.log("transactionHash: " + contract.transactionHash);
   }
 );
```

Once the contract is deployed with a confirmation from the blockchain, you will see its contract address printed on the console. You can now call its functions.

```
> contractInstance.sayHello.call({from: cmt.accounts[0]})
Hello World
> contractInstance.updateMessage.call("Hi", {from: cmt.accounts[0]})
```

Alternatively, you can get the contract instance from its deployed address and then call its functions.

```
> contractInstance = web3.cmt.contract(abi).at("0x1234ABCD...");
```

The Travis console provides reliable and interactive access to the CyberMiles blockchain. We highly recommend you get familiar with it and use it to explore the blockchain.

Conclusion

The CyberMiles blockchain is optimized for e-commerce applications. It is fully compatible with the Ethereum blockchain yet is much faster, cheaper, and safer. It has a full suite of development and deployment tools to facilitate smart contract and dapp development. Hence, the CyberMiles blockchain is an excellent alternative to get started with Ethereum application development and beyond.

Index

A

T

Z